Ageing and Social Policy in Ireland

Other social policy titles published by UCD Press

Contemporary Irish Social Policy
2nd edition edited by
SUZANNE QUIN, PATRICIA KENNEDY,
GABRIEL KIELY and ANNE MATTHEWS

Care and Social Change in the Irish Welfare Economy
edited by BRYAN FANNING and MICHAEL RUSH

Irish Social Policy in Context
edited by GABRIEL KIELY, ANNE O'DONNELL,
PATRICIA KENNEDY and SUZANNE QUIN

Disability and Social Policy in Ireland
edited by SUZANNE QUIN and BAIRBRE REDMOND

Theorising Irish Social Policy
edited by BRYAN FANNING, PATRICIA KENNEDY,
GABRIEL KIELY and SUZANNE QUIN

Mental Health and Social Policy in Ireland
edited by SUZANNE QUIN and BAIRBRE REDMOND

Ageing and Social Policy in Ireland

edited by
Patricia Kennedy
Suzanne Quin

University College Dublin Press
Preas Choláiste Ollscoile
Bhaile Átha Cliath

First published 2008
by University College Dublin Press
Newman House
86 St Stephen's Green
Dublin 2
Ireland
www.ucdpress.ie

ISBN 978-1-904558-95-8

Cataloguing in Publication data
available from the British Library

Typeset in Ireland in
Adobe Garamond and Trade Gothic
by Elaine Burberry, Bantry, Co. Cork
Index by Jane Rogers
Text design by Lyn Davies
Printed in England on acid-free
paper by CPI Antony Rowe

Contents

Contributors to this volume

JOHN BRENNAN is Principal Social Worker, Peamount Hospital. He is Chairperson of the Irish Association of Social Workers' Special Interest Group on Ageing. He is a member of the Health Information and Quality Authority's Working Group on the National Quality Standards for Residential Care Settings for Older People. He has a background in hospital social work and since 1998 has specialised in social work with older people.

TONY FAHEY is Professor of Social Policy in the UCD School of Applied Social Science. He was formerly Research Professor in the Economic and Social Research Institute (ESRI). He was a lecturer in Sociology in NUI Maynooth from 1987 to 1992 when he joined the staff of the ESRI. He has carried out research on a range of topics connected with the family in Ireland and on older people, housing, demography and religion.

PATRICIA KENNEDY is a Senior Lecturer in Social Policy in the UCD School of Applied Social Science. Her most recent publications include *Motherhood in Ireland, Creation and Context* (2004) and *Maternity in Ireland a Woman-Centred Perspective* (2002). She is co-editor of *Theorising Irish Social Policy* (2004), *Contemporary Irish Social Policy* (1999 and 2005) and *Irish Social Policy in Context* (1999). She co-founded the Irish Social Policy Association in 1997. She is a founder member of the European Research Network for the Promotion of Sexual and Reproductive Health Rights of Refugees and Asylum Seekers.

JOE MORAN worked with refugees and asylum seekers in the public and voluntary sector for almost ten years. He currently teaches Social Policy at the Waterford Institute of Technology and at the Institute of Technology, Carlow/Wexford Campus. He studied at University College Cork, Trinity College Dublin, University of Liverpool and the Institute of Public Administration.

MICHELLE NORRIS joined the staff of the UCD School of Applied Social Science in 2005. Prior to that she was Director of the Housing Unit, an agency funded by the Department of the Environment, Heritage and Local Government and the City and County Managers' Association. In addition, she was a lecturer at the Department of Applied Social Studies, University College Cork and a Community Development Officer in the Housing Department of Cork City Council.

ANNE O'CONNOR is Disability Officer in Dublin City University. She has undertaken research in areas such as advocacy, quality of life indicators for persons with severe and profound disabilities and Daphne, a European project which explores initiatives to combat violence against people with disabilities. She has also been the Irish co-ordinator for the project: Advancing Inclusionary Practice in Post-Secondary Education in Canada and the European Union 2002–4. Anne was awarded one of the Ireland Canada University Foundation scholarships in 2004.

ORLA O'DONOVAN is based in the Department of Applied Social Studies in University College Cork. Her teaching and research are centrally concerned with the politics of health and medicine. Much of her recent research has been focused on patients' organisations and health activism, together with work on the politics of pharmaceutical policy.

JOAN O'FLYNN is a Programme Manager with the Combat Poverty Agency and previously worked there as Head of Information and Public Education and as Editor of *Poverty Today*, 1994–2005. Prior to this she worked with the Action Group for Irish Youth (AGIY), a London-based charity working to promote the needs and interests of Irish people in Britain.

ANNE O'LOUGHLIN is Senior Social Worker in St Mary's Hospital, Phoenix Park, Dublin. Her social work career has been in the geriatric medicine service of North Dublin City and County. She was formerly President of the Irish Association of Social Workers.

MARIA PIERCE is a PhD student affiliated to the Social Policy and Ageing Research Programme, School of Social Work and Social Policy, Trinity College Dublin. Her doctoral thesis is examining the social construction of ageing in Ireland. She was previously on the teaching staff of the School of Applied Social Science, UCD. She has completed research for the Equality Authority on the intersection between ethnicity and disability, and on European and Irish gender equality, lone parents and social and information services at local level.

MARTINA PRUNTY is a graduate of NUI Maynooth and Trinity College Dublin. She completed a postgraduate internship with the Combat Poverty Agency in 2005 and returned to the Agency in 2006 to work as a research intern.

SUZANNE QUIN is an Associate Professor in the School of Applied Social Science, UCD. She has worked in St Vincent's Hospital, the Eastern Health

Board and as Head of the Social Work Department in the National Rehabilitation Hospital. She has also lectured in Social Policy in Trinity College Dublin and in the Institute of Public Administration. She has co-edited a number of books for UCD Press.

NESSA WINSTON lectures in Social Policy at UCD. Her main areas of research are social policy, housing and sustainable development. She currently holds a Government of Ireland Fellowship for comparative research on sustainable urban regeneration. She has recently published in this area in the international journals *Social Policy and Administration*, *Local Environment* and *Social Indicators Research*. She has conducted a major review of Irish housing policy for the Irish Department of the Environment, Heritage and Local Government. She is an active member of European Network of Housing Researchers (ENHR) working group on housing and sustainability in urban contexts.

Abbreviations

A & E	Accident and Emergency
AD	Alzheimer's Disease
AGIY	Action Group for Irish Youth
BUPA	British United Provident Association
BURDIS	Burden of Disease in Old Age Network Project
CEO	Chief Executive Officer
CHD	Coronary Heart Disease
CoE	Council of Europe
CPA	Combat Poverty Agency
CSO	Central Statistics Office
DoEHLG	Department of the Environment, Housing and Local Government
DoSFA	Department of Social and Family Affairs
EANIG	Elder Abuse National Implementation Group
EEC	European Economic Community
EMEA	European Medicine Agency
ENHR	European Network for Housing Research
ESFEU	European Social Fund Evaluation Unit
ESRI	Economic and Social Research Institute
EU	European Union
FÁS	Foras Áiseanna Saothair (Irish National Training and Employment Agency)
GAIE	Gross Average Industrial Earnings
GHQ	General Health Questionnaire
HEN	Home Education Network
HeSSOP	Health and Social Services for Older People
HIQA	Health Information and Quality Authority
HRB	Health Research Board
HSE	Health Service Executive
IADL	Instrumental Activities of Daily Living
IAG	Independent Advisory Group
IAU	Irish Abroad Unit
ICCR	Interdisciplinary Centre for Comparative Research in the Social Sciences
ICSH	Irish Council for Social Housing
ILO	International Labour Organisation
IMF	International Monetary Fund
INO	Irish Nurses Organisation

INSHQ	Irish National Survey of Housing Quality
INPEA	International Network for the Prevention of Elder Abuse
IPA	Institute of Public Administration
ISSDA	Irish Social Sciences Data Archive
LAA	Living Alone Allowance
LIS	Living in Ireland Survey
LRC	Labour Relations Commission
MCI	Mild Cognitive Impairment
MHSOP	Mental Health Services for Older People
MMSE	Mini Mental State Examination
NACPC	National Advisory Committee on Palliative Care
NAPS	National Anti-Poverty Strategy
NCAOP	National Council on Ageing and Older People
NCD	Non-Communicable Disease
NCO	National Children's Office
NDA	National Disability Authority
NESC	National Economic and Social Council
NESF	National Economic and Social Forum
NGO	Non-Government Organisation
NHS	National Health Service
NICE	National Institute for Health and Clinical Excellence
OACP	Old Age Contributory Pension
ODPM	Office of Deputy Prime Minister (UK)
OECD	Organisation for Economic Co-operation and Development
ORAC	Office of the Refugee Applications Commissioner
PADL	Physical Activities of Daily Living
PES	Principal Economic Status
PHN	Public Health Nurse
PRIAE	Policy Research Institute on Ageing and Ethnicity
PRSI	Pay Related Social Insurance
QNHS	Quarterly National Household Survey
RIA	Royal Irish Academy
RP	Retirement Pension
SILC/EU SILC	Survey on Income and Living Conditions
SLAN	Survey of Lifestyle, Attitudes and Nutrition
SONAS	Healthcare and Childcare across Ireland
TCD	Trinity College, Dublin
UCD	University College Dublin
UN	United Nations
UNECE	United Nations Economic Commission for Europe
UNHCHR	United Nations High Commissioner for Human Rights

VHI	Voluntary Health Insurance
WGEA	Working Group on Elder Abuse
WHO	World Health Organisation

Chapter 1

Introduction

Suzanne Quin
Patricia Kennedy

Ageing and Social Policy in Ireland brings together the writings of specialists in a range of areas relevant to the situation of older people in Ireland. The overall subject of ageing and social policy is of current relevance and will remain so in the coming decades. This is because Ireland, like other European countries, is facing demographic changes and parallel policy challenges. The average life expectancy has increased quite dramatically in recent decades. The average life expectancy for a man in Ireland at age 66 is now 80.6 years while, on average, a woman at the same age will have a further 17.9 years to live. *Social Inclusion: Building an Inclusive Society*, the National Plan for Social Inclusion (Government of Ireland, 2002), outlines a vision for older people in which they are enabled to maintain their health and well-being, live active and full lives, independently and in their own homes and communities for as long as possible. It envisions older people participating in social and civic life, having sufficient income to support an acceptable standard of living, and having access to good quality services in the community, including: health, education, transport, housing and security.

As Pierce reminds us in chapter 2, there is a longstanding history and a close connection between ageing and social policy. She outlines how the origins of social policy towards older people in Ireland may date back to the Poor Relief (Ireland) Act of 1838, which was the first statutory provision for the poor in Ireland. This formed the foundation stones of Ireland's social welfare system. Pierce argues that, as recipients of social security benefits and users of health and social care services, issues relating to older people and the problems of ageing and old age have moved on to the front line of policy debates in Ireland as in many other countries. Yet social policy as it relates to older people is not simply a response to the issues and problems of ageing and old age. The idea that the lives of older people and the problems of ageing and old age have been and continue to be constructed and reconstructed through social policies has been developed from a political economy of ageing which suggests that the experience of ageing is determined to a large extent by

socio-economic structures and policies. It has, however, been criticised for excluding the role of older people themselves, a theme which Pierce explores in detail. She suggests that older people are agentic – always actively constructing their social world.

In modern societies, Ireland being no exception, agency is often, though not exclusively, viewed in terms of participation in the labour market. Fahey, in chapter 3, utilises data from a nationally based research study to examine labour market participation of older people in Ireland and how this might be influenced by public policy. He concludes that older people are now being encouraged to remain in the workforce. This policy requires greater flexibility in pension arrangements and the development of options such as a phased approach to retirement, an approach favoured by the majority of older people in employment.

Labour market participation is very closely related to income security, a theme taken up by Prunty, in chapter 4 on poverty and ageing. Drawing on data from the EU Survey on Income and Living Conditions, she emphasises the importance for older people of the role of social transfers in preventing poverty. She presents data on poverty levels for older people compared to younger age groups in four areas – income and income poverty, deprivation, housing conditions and consistent poverty. She focuses on some particularly vulnerable groups of older people before presenting a short section on the relationship between living conditions and health. Some of these issues are taken up in later chapters.

In chapter 5 Norris and Winston focus on housing and accommodation for older people, poignantly indicating that: 'Housing is not simply a "roof over the head" but it is also a location in which the person can foster social networks, family bonds and access services. So housing can have an immense impact on the well-being of older people.'

Brennan, in chapter 11, highlights the needs of older people who require help with activities of daily living. Today, the vast majority of older people in Ireland live independent lives at home. However, for the minority who require care, the reality of service delivery is such that funding for care services is below the European average (NESF, 2005: 5). As a consequence, personal social services in the community remain patchy, inconsistent and inequitable. There has been little attempt to underpin service provision with legislation. Brennan suggests that policy appears to be developed in a reactionary way and this ad hoc approach can be seen in the current Health Service Executive (HSE) moves to engage with the private sector via the new home care packages in providing community-based care services. The traditional mix of public, private and voluntary provision is thus further complicated because the roles and responsibilities of these sectoral providers, as well as entitlement issues, have not been fully clarified.

In chapter 9 Quin argues that good health is of crucial importance in old age as it is at any other stage of the life span, but for older people it is 'the key determinant of their ability to remain independent and autonomous' (Feldman, 1999: 272). She points out that many can now expect to spend between one fifth and one quarter of their lifespan within the category of 'older person'. She highlights ageism in health care and the particular challenges of providing for the mental health needs of the older population. The fact that personal social services are subsumed under the health budget means that the provision of these services (of critical importance to many of the older old population) may lose out in the multiple demands made on health care provision. There are many issues which need to be addressed by policy makers in this sphere.

Orla O'Donovan addresses the important role of the pharmaceutical industry in healthcare for the elderly in chapter 8. She focuses on the importance of advocacy groups, using the treatment of Alzheimer's Disease as a case study. The particular needs of other specific groups are addressed by several contributors to this volume. In chapter 12 O'Loughlin, for example, focuses on the emergence of elder abuse policy in Ireland. Looking at Ireland in an international context, she examines significant events and developments that have had an impact on the emergence of elder abuse as a social issue. She discusses the adequacy of responses to it as well as the challenges of developing preventative strategies in this area. Anne O'Connor draws our attention to the needs of another particularly vulnerable group of older people in chapter 10. With increased life expectancy, people are at risk of acquiring disabilities as they age. O'Connor examines the issue of older people who experience the late onset of disability, specifically people who acquire a disability owing to the ageing process. She also examines the needs of people who have had a disability since childhood, a group now experiencing longevity in much greater numbers. As with the general population, people with a lifelong disability are benefiting from improvements in medical and social advances, resulting in increased life expectancy (WHO, 2000). For some living with a lifelong disability, the onset of the ageing process can happen prematurely and bring with it the possibility of additional complications.

Older people are not a homogeneous group. Many of the issues addressed in this book are intensified for older people from ethnic minorities and new communities, a theme taken up by Moran in chapter 7. He highlights the invisibility of older immigrants in terms of public perceptions, policy and service provision. Older immigrants, he argues, face problems in common with all older people in the population in relation to health and personal social services, poverty and housing, but their situation can be further complicated by language and cultural differences, lack of understanding and fear. He finds a lack of basic statistical data on older people among immigrant populations in Ireland. Moreover, in his review of policy documents on older people, only one (NESF, 2005) refers to the needs of ethnic minority groups.

In a similar vein, in chapter 6 Joan O'Flynn focuses on the particular needs of returned emigrants, who though constituting a small number require specific supports and services. O'Flynn indicates that return elder migration has attracted less 'scholarly attention' than elder migration and there is limited research and policy focus on the nature, extent and experiences of older Irish return migrants. To address this lacuna, O'Flynn presents a short overview of the current data trends relating to inward migration and older return migrants. This is followed by an exploration of some theoretical explanations for return migration before outlining key legislative and policy contexts and an overview of the range of supports available to potential older return migrants.

This book explores many factors affecting ageing in Ireland today. It serves as an appraisal of policy developments to date and as a point of departure for future challenges. It is ideal for undergraduate and postgraduate students eager to familiarise themselves with the challenges for older people, their families, service providers, and policy makers. It introduces conceptual and theoretical writings on ageing, thus will serve as a good resource for those approaching gerontology for the first time. The book will be pertinent to a range of training courses for social workers, psychologists, doctors, nurses, care workers and any other groups employed in working with older people. It will also be relevant to the vast array of agencies engaged in policy creation and implementation in this area. Each chapter addresses a specific area of social policy, forming a complete unit in itself. Taken together, the chapters provide the reader with a readily accessible and wide-ranging overview of ageing and social policy in Ireland.

The active participation and integration of older people in society are important goals in contemporary Ireland. This book conveys the key role that policy planning and service provision play in this area. The chapter contents indicate that there are many issues in the areas of income support, housing, health, and personal social services related to ageing in Ireland that must be addressed in order to ensure that the aim of maximising opportunities for older people to actively engage in civic and social life is achieved.

Chapter 2

Constructions of ageing in Irish social policy

Maria Pierce

Introduction

Ageing and social policy share a longstanding history and close connections. The origins of social policy towards older people in Ireland might be dated to the Poor Relief (Ireland) Act of 1838, which was the first statutory provision for the poor in Ireland. The workhouse system, otherwise known as 'indoor' relief, formed a central feature of the Irish Poor Law. Relief was initially granted only in the workhouse and preference was given to the 'aged' and others such as the sick and children who fell into the category of 'deserving poor' (Burke, 1987). The workhouse system provided an institutional solution to the problem of providing relief for destitute older people in the nineteenth century. It was out of the workhouse system that much of the existing pattern of long-term institutional care for older people gradually emerged and the break-up of the workhouses laid a tradition of providing care to older people in institutions that are distinct from hospitals. With the passing of the Poor Relief Extension Act of 1847, a meagre and restricted form of 'outdoor' relief was introduced, where money or food was granted to recipients who remained at home or in the community (Burke, 1999). These formed the foundation stones of Ireland's social welfare system. One might even go so far as to say that they were the precursor to Ireland's community care system.

Older people have always been one of the main subject groups of health and social care policies. This has also been the case with respect to social welfare policies. For example, the national means-tested supplementary welfare allowance scheme, which replaced 'outdoor' relief in 1975, was generally directed to older people (O'Loughlin, 2005). The Non-Contributory Old Age Pension introduced in 1909 preceded other social security payments. Today, older people are major recipients of social security benefits and schemes, with old age accounting for over a quarter of social security expenditure (McCashin, 2004).

As recipients of social security benefits and users of health and social care services, older people and the problems of ageing and old age have moved on to the front line of policy debates in Ireland as in many other countries. Yet social policy as it relates to older people is not simply a response to the problems of ageing and old age. The idea that the lives of older people and the problems of ageing and old age have been and continue to be constructed and reconstructed through social policies has been developed from a political economy of ageing perspective (Estes at al., 2003; Estes and Associates, 2001; Quadagno and Reid, 1999; Walker, 1999). Estes, one of the earliest proponents of this perspective in the USA, suggests that:

> The major problems faced by the elderly in the United States are, in large measure, ones that are socially constructed as a result of our conceptions of aging and the aged. What is done for and about the elderly, as well as what we know about them, including knowledge gained from research, are products of our conceptions of aging. In an important sense, the major problems faced by the elderly are the ones we create for them (Estes, 1979: 1).

The political economy of ageing perspective, which takes up aspects of Marxism, emphasises macro level influences of the state and the economy on the experience of ageing and the conditions of old age (Estes et al., 2003; Walker, 1999). A key assumption of the political economy of ageing perspective, as highlighted by Estes et al. (2003: 21), is that ageing and old age 'cannot be considered or analysed in isolation from other societal forces and phenomena'. They are 'directly related to the nature of the larger society' (Estes et al. 2003: 20). This chapter adopts this approach to examine social, economic and political aspects of Irish social policy towards older people as it has evolved over the last four decades.

The political economy of ageing perspective would suggest that the experience of ageing is determined to a large extent by socio-economic structures and policies. It has, however, been criticised for excluding the role of agency (Blaikie, 1999; Katz, 1996). The experience of ageing and old age by older people is inextricably bound up with social policy. However, little attention has been paid to 'deciphering the world of older people as subjects' (Hazan, 1994). O'Loughlin (2005: 228) identifies this as one of the key challenges facing policy makers in Ireland. A second focus of this chapter is to briefly consider the ways in which social constructionist perspectives focusing at the micro (and meso) level(s) can make it possible to think about older people as being agentic, always actively constructing their social world.

Constructions of ageing in Irish social policy: through the lens of political economy

The institutionalisation of age-related retirement

A significant feature of the post Second World War evolution of social policy with regard to older people across Europe was the establishment and/or consolidation of national pension systems with universal coverage (Walker, 1999). This typically spanned the period from the 1940s to the early 1970s. Ireland lagged behind the European experience with regard to this post-war welfare settlement. As Fanning (2003: 6) writes: 'Ireland, by contrast [to Britain], did not experience a "big bang" welfare resettlement after the Second World War. Change was characterised by a gradual expansion in the provision of welfare in some areas.'

Although the origins of pension policy in Ireland date from the beginning of the twentieth century with the introduction of the Old Age Non-Contributory Pension in 1909, Ireland was slow to establish a national pension system. The Social Welfare Act of 1952 could be regarded as the establishment in Irish social policy of an overall national system of social security, albeit a limited one. However, it excluded social insurance pensions, which marked a major departure from the more comprehensive Beveridgean system in the UK. With a stagnant economy in the 1950s, it was not until 1961 that the Old Age Contributory Pension (OACP) was introduced in Ireland. Even so, social insurance pensions in Ireland were limited as the self-employed, public servants and people above a certain income threshold for social insurance contributions were excluded under the provisions of the 1960 Social Welfare Act. With the introduction of Retirement Pension (RP), the reduction of the age of eligibility to 66 for OACP and 65 for RP and the abolition of the pension ceiling for contributors to social insurance, public pension coverage was extended to a greater proportion of the population during the 1970s, contributing to the spread of fixed age retirement. Thus, the consolidation of a national pension system and the 'institutionalisation of age-related retirement' (Walker, 1999: 369) could be dated in Ireland to as late as the early to mid-1970s.

The consolidation of retirement as a social and economic institution became an important determinant of the meaning of ageing and old age (Walker, 1999). The reforms extended rights and entitlements to old age pensions. Associated with this was the image of retirement as a gateway to a new lifestyle, with leisure activities and creative hobbies (Phillipson, 1982). However, it also led to widespread economic dependency of older people and encouraged a view that past a certain age an individual's social worth was diminished, which in turn contributed to age discrimination. This was reinforced by the view that older people needed less income than those of the 'economically active' so that public pensions were set at rates considerably below average earnings

(Walker, 1999). Also a strict adherence in Ireland to a wide range of policies up to the 1970s that institutionalised and reinforced women's exclusion from social security and work rendered older women especially vulnerable and dependent (Conroy Jackson, 1993; Kennedy, 1999).

The 'enormous problem' of ageing-related care

A second feature of social policy across Europe during the period stretching from the 1940s to the 1970s was an expansion of health and social care services for older people (Walker, 1999). In Ireland, proposals to reform the system of care for older people emerged with the publication in 1968 of the *Care of the Aged Report* (Government of Ireland, 1968), which continued to dominate Irish government policy towards older people until the late 1980s. The report encouraged the view that older people in need of care represented 'an enormous problem' for society:

> the total number [of persons aged 65 years and over] is so great that the provision of services for the proportion in need of help still presents the community with an enormous and a growing problem to which there is no ready or simple solution (1968: 13).

Despite concerns about the dignity of older people and its interests in changing public attitudes towards older people, the report emphasised the most vulnerable and needy older people (Gallagher, 2006) and inadvertently highlighted the problems that old age was believed to inevitably bring, such as physical, sensory and cognitive decline, chronic ill health, isolation and loneliness. There was little sense in the report of older people in need of care being able to fulfil valuable social roles and engage in social activities. Furthermore, older people were particularly notable for their absence from care debates.

Ironically, the largely negative stereotypes portrayed in the *Care of the Aged Report* afforded legitimacy to policy developments for older people. The report stressed a need for improvement in the standards of services, both at institutional and community level, as well as a need for an expansion of services over time and across place. Besides, the report revealed much about the very nature of the Irish welfare economy at the time. The expansion of community care services, albeit from an extremely low level, was cast as being integral to meeting the care needs of older people and achieving the primary objective 'to enable the aged who can do so to continue to live in their own homes' (Government of Ireland, 1968: 49). The community care reforms recommended were based on a commitment to the principle of a mixed economy of welfare with 'a host of bodies . . . involved in the provision of services for the aged' (Government of Ireland, 1968: 49). A key role was envisaged for the voluntary sector in the provision of domiciliary social care services with health authorities contributing towards the costs involved. The role envisaged for the state *vis-à-vis* the family was a residual one and one in which 'the public authority should endeavour to help the family' but 'not take over from it' (Government of Ireland, 1968: 45). The community care reforms introduced by the *Care of the Aged Report*, however, marked a departure from a strict interpretation of the principle of subsidiarity (Timonen and Doyle, 2006: 42) and were resonant of a wider shift in the mid-1960s from the 'tradition of viewing all state social intervention as an outsider's intrusion into the family and the voluntary sector' (Conroy, 1999: 37). In the two decades following the publication of the *Care of the Aged Report*, the expansion of health and social care services in Ireland led to some enhancement of the welfare of older people, although progress was somewhat limited due to shortcomings in services and the many gaps in service provision (Department of Health, 1988).

Retirement and the problem of unemployment

Throughout the 1970s and early 1980s, interrelated changes in retirement and labour market polices precipitated the reconstruction of ageing in the UK and other Western European countries (Walker, 1999). Many of these changes similarly impacted upon Ireland. During this period, the trend towards complete cessation of work after the age of 65 accelerated so that the withdrawal of older people from the labour market became one of the distinctive features of old age in most advanced industrialised countries (Phillipson, 1998). Although Ireland traditionally had a pattern of very late retirement for men, the consolidation of the national pension system contributed to the decline from the 1970s in the labour market participation of those aged 65 years and over, which was particularly marked for men (NESF, 2003).

Alongside this, a real sense of economic crisis across the European Union in the 1980s led to a 'blurring of the boundaries between economic activity and retirement' (Walker, 1999: 362). Many older workers, especially men, found themselves on the margins of the labour market a number of years before they reached state retirement age (Phillipson, 1998). In Ireland 'emigration was constructed as a "useful safety valve" . . . for unemployment' (Fanning, 2003: 11). Nevertheless, unemployment had risen sharply to 17.4 per cent by 1986 with almost two thirds of the unemployed classified as long-term unemployed. Many of the workers made redundant during the recession in the early 1980s became long-term unemployed and/or discouraged from seeking employment. More than half of the retirees surveyed as part of a major Irish study on retirement had retired before 65 years, triggered in part by redundancies and job losses resulting from the economic downturn and a sharp decline in economic activity at the time (Whelan and Whelan, 1988).

The proliferation of employment and policy measures designed to encourage early retirement was also a key feature of this period (Walker, 1999). As a means of reducing the recorded unemployment figures in the late 1980s, a pre-retirement allowance was introduced in Ireland, which allowed unemployed people who were in receipt of unemployment assistance and approaching retirement age to 'pre-retire'. The pre-retirement allowance gave the same rate of payment as the unemployment assistance, but with the pre-retirement allowance the obligation to be available and seeking employment was removed (Cousins, 1995). With few programmes such as training or job matching to assist older workers, Irish labour market policies tended to reinforce the trend towards early retirement. In addition, both the retention and re-entry of older workers was affected by age discrimination by employers, identified as one of the key barriers to employment among older workers. Age discrimination in recruitment, promotion and training was believed to exist by a large majority of the general public of all ages, as indicated by an EU wide survey conducted in 1992 (Walker, 1993). This view was consistent with the findings of a more recent survey of the unemployed carried out in County Galway in 2000 which found that 'age' was regarded as the biggest impediment to obtaining work among the over 55s (Public and Corporate Economic Consultants, 2001).

Alongside emigration, then, retirement during this period was constructed as a solution to the problem of mass unemployment in Ireland. While the position of older women in Ireland is harder to disentangle, the growth in early retirement led to a transformation in the social meaning of ageing particularly for men. It changed from one marked by age-related retirement to a much broader construction of ageing built around labour market criteria (Walker, 1999).

The ageing 'crisis' – consensus or conflict

The 1980s and 1990s have been identified as a significant and historic turning point in discussions about the nature of old age, the point at which the focus shifted to the so-called 'ageing crisis' and ageing came to be seen as an economic problem in its own right (Phillipson, 1998). The main concern was that with rapid population ageing there would be fewer people in employment to shoulder the burden of paying to support the large population of older people. Population ageing was reconstructed in terms of a threat to economic growth and to the affordability of existing social welfare regimes. International organisations such as the World Bank and the OECD tended to paint a bleak picture. For example, the highly influential report of the World Bank (1994: 7) entitled *Averting the Old Age Crisis* warned that 'If trends continue, public spending on pensions will soar over the next fifty years'. Typically, the market and privatisation were proposed as the main alternative to state services and supports.

Likewise, there was mounting concern by national governments about the economic consequences of population ageing. In Ireland, despite having a relatively favourable demographic situation, the 1990s was a time of warnings that in years to come there would not be the resources to pay for older people in need (Cousins, 1995: 25). The following comes from a report of the National Pensions Board (1993: 47):

> The Board notes that demographic patterns indicate a considerable increase in the proportion of elderly people in the population over the first half of the next century. This will have a significant impact on the future costs of social welfare pensions, which are set to increase by 90%. At the same time the ratio of persons in the economically active age group to those over 65 is projected to fall from 5.4 to 1 currently to 3 to 1 by the year 2035. This would result, in the absence of any change, in an increasing [*burden*] of the cost of pensions falling on future generations of PRSI contributors and taxpayers. This is an important factor in any consideration of the development of future pension development and raises serious questions about the capacity of the present financing arrangements to meet those emerging costs.

There was, however, no general consensus as to the future impact of population ageing in Ireland as illustrated by *The Years Ahead* Report (Department of Health, 1988). The report, which devoted an entire chapter to 'Demographic Change and the Elderly', adopted the view that the favourable age dependency ratio in Ireland made it 'easier to support services for the growing number of elderly persons' and argued that 'the decline in births presents an opportunity to redeploy the resources saved in social welfare, health and education to services for the elderly' (1988: 32). Incidentally, an underlying assumption of the report was that 'increases in the number of people living into old age would be matched by a *pro rata* increase in the numbers who are ill or dependent' (Ruddle, Donoghue and Mulvihill, 1997: 43).

Pessimistic predictions about the pressures on the economy and state expenditure as a result of ageing populations were contested abroad by many leading authorities including Ermisch (1983: 287). In Ireland, the Combat Poverty Agency (CPA) and analysts at the Economic and Social Research Institute (ESRI) were at the forefront in broadening the debate and examining the assumption that an increase in the population of older people would automatically give rise to unsustainable increases in the level of state services and supports and therefore threaten the affordability of the Irish welfare system (Fahey and FitzGerald, 1997; Fahey, 1998). For example, Fahey (1998) argued that Irish health services offered a powerful case to support the view that population trends had little impact on the evolution of health services and that the impact of population ageing on health services had been exaggerated and would not in reality be so dramatic. Following an examination of the likely impact of future demographic trends on welfare and income support requirements in Ireland, Fahey and FitzGerald (1997: 116) concluded that:

> it is paradoxical that fears should be raised in Ireland today about an impending 'demographic crisis' or 'population time-bomb'. If ever in the last two hundred years of Irish history there was a time *not* to speak of demographic crisis, it is now. For the first time in the modern era, it is possible for Ireland to look forward with some confidence to a period of well-balanced performance combined with economic progress.

The new millennium: opportunity or burden

The current phase, dating from the 1990s, offers both optimistic and pessimistic constructions of ageing (Walker, 1999), both of which find expression in policy terms in the Irish context. On the one hand, there are indications that ageing may be reconstructed in more positive terms. Several developments and initiatives are notable in this regard. The emergence of organisations such as Age and Opportunity have encouraged the spread of positive images of ageing, have promoted old age as a period of opportunity, and endorsed new norms of age-related behaviour. Initiatives such as the Positive Ageing Week aim to dispel any negativity around ageing and to emphasis the positive aspects that ageing holds for older people. More recently, the Older and Bolder campaign, a joint initiative between several non-governmental organisations aimed at mobilising support for the development of a National Strategy for Older People, has been launched. Such initiatives might suggest that organisations representing older people in Ireland are 'actively involved in demonstrating the potential for a new meaning to be applied to ageing' (Walker, 1999: 374). Besides, there have been notable improvements in the overall well-being of older people. Generally, they are healthier, more able and active and are living longer than ever before.

Positive ageing constructs and improvements in the overall well-being of older people have generated new policy debates in Ireland. One of these is centred on older people's ability to work. A growing number of older workers would prefer to have the choice of whether and when to retire rather than be forced to retire from the labour market through illness or unemployment, or as a consequence of obligatory or mandatory retirement age. Legislative approaches go some way towards increasing the prospects for older people to participate in the labour market. The Employment Equality Act, 1998, introduced to address discrimination in relation to employment on nine grounds including the grounds of age, offered protection against certain types of workplace discrimination for workers up to the age of 65 years. The upper age limit was removed with the passing of the Equality Act, 2004,[1] although certain exemptions apply in relation to the age ground. Provisions for a rise in the retirement age may offer new work-related opportunities and incentives. For instance, the Public Service Superannuation (Miscellaneous Provisions) Act, signed into law in 2004, gave effect to increases in the pension age for new entrants to the public service. Under the terms of the Act, the minimum pension age was raised to 65 for most new entrants to the public service.

A focus on the rich supply of valuable experiences, wisdom and skills that many older people possess may provide an opportunity for older people to be constructed as productive members of society. This is important as it acknowledges the contemporary reality that not all older people wish to cease working and that not all older people are beyond employment. However, the reconstruction of ageing in terms of economic activity in the form of paid employment must be seen in the context of the considerable social change and unprecedented economic growth that Ireland has experienced since the middle of 1990s in the era of the so-called Celtic Tiger. The current policy of encouraging greater labour market participation of older workers, a reversal of policies in the 1970s and 1980s that supported the early exit of older workers from the labour market, arose in the context of this economic growth, labour market shortages in Ireland in the 1990s and amid concerns at international and European level about the ageing workforce. Cousins (2005: 111) maintains that, in the Celtic Tiger era,

> Policy developments have been almost entirely shaped by economic and labour market developments and that, partially because of the suddenness of the economic turn-around, there has been no clear long-term vision as to the role of social policy other than as a basic support for economic development.

It might therefore be argued that the identification of older people as a potential pool of workers fits in nicely with policy concerned with the pursuit of economic growth.

The reconstruction of ageing in terms of economic activity raises important issues for older people. This is particularly so, in the context of pressure on employees to be more adaptable, pressures of travel time, increasing workplace stress, and increased pressure to continue lifelong learning (NESF, 2003). The reality may be that with few opportunities to move to lighter work or part-time work, older workers are confronted with the choice of continuing working at the same pace or taking retirement. In addition, older workers may be caring for older relatives in an informal capacity and combining work and caring can be extremely difficult. Added to this can be the responsibilities

1 Employment Equality Act, 1998 and the Equality Act, 2004 are known together as the Employment Equality Acts, 1998 and 2004.

and demands of partners, dependant children and sometimes grandchildren as older women especially in Ireland appear to be increasingly caring for grandchildren due to the lack of adequate childcare (NESF, 2003). As such it implies a different organisation of work and care, and as a consequence, a different organisation of the relationship between paid and unpaid work.

The development of constructs such as 'positive ageing' and 'productive ageing' mark a move away from 'the traditional monolithic view of the old as poor, frail, and unemployable' (Hudson, 2005: 10). Yet, positive images of ageing can at times be overly exaggerated and may not adequately reflect the reality of the day-to-day lives of many older people. The positive ageing discourse has led the differentiation of older people into the 'young-old' and 'old-old' (Featherstone and Hepworth, 1995). However, as Vincent (2003: 167) points out, this differentiation does not overcome the problem of old age; 'it merely postpones it'. Positive ageing promotes the image of old age as a period of activity but fear and anxiety of and hostility towards 'deep old age', which is associated with decline, dependency and death, remains (Featherstone and Hepworth, 1995). Vincent (2003: 167) is of the view that focusing on biological failure in the 'very old' leads to a construction of ageing that 'generates and prolongs its low esteem'. In addition, there is also the possibility that people will be blamed for failing to age properly and not continuing to lead fit and active lifestyles (Vincent, 2003).

Another area of contemporary debate surrounds public responsibility in relation to the financing of services and supports for older people. A neo-liberalism approach has been deployed by many governments in developing social policies and as a basis for curtailing the role of the state in welfare provision. At an international level, an obvious example comes from the area of pensions policy, where 'the World Bank and the IMF have been at the forefront of attempts to foster a political climate conducive to the residualisation of state welfare and the promotion of private and voluntary initiatives' (Yeates, 2001: 122). In the US neo-liberalism has played a significant role in efforts to privatise the social security programme (Estes and Associates, 2001).

Ireland has favourable demographic circumstances with a relatively low proportion of older people in the population and a broadly benign economic climate. Notwithstanding this, in the field of pension policy, Ireland has drawn heavily on policy at an international level and adopted a view that supports the expansion of private provision (underpinned by regulation and tax relief) rather than state pension provision (McCashin, 2004). This is, however, an area of controversy. State pensions have traditionally been linked with ideas about social rights and social citizenship and the theme of intergenerational solidarity where the risks associated with growing old are shared across generations and among social groups. Older people are central to this. However, the promotion and funding of private pensions by the state places a greater responsibility on individuals to provide for their own future. The reconstruction of ageing as an individual risk rather than a collective right thus poses a major challenge to the position of older people (Estes et al., 2003).

Neo-liberalism has also played a role in the transformation of long-term care policy towards older people. In the US, for example, the ultimate failure of President Clinton's Health Care Reform Plan in the 1990s, which included a major proposal on long-term care for older people, paved the way for a reform of care that was driven by the private sector. With the election of President Bush, privatisation was further accelerated (Estes and Associates, 2001). In the UK, 'neoliberal ideologies of New Labour's "Third Way" are in full swing' with respect to long-term care, which are predicated on publicly unaccountable private provision, according to Player and Pollock (2001: 252).

In Ireland there has been a major shift in long-term care policy over the past decade towards encouraging private sector involvement in the care of older people. Public subsidisation of private nursing home care is a striking feature of Irish long-term care policy towards older people. This takes the form of tax incentives to nursing home providers, a nursing home subvention scheme that covers part of the cost of private nursing home care to individuals and the contract funding of beds in private nursing homes. Part of the thinking behind this is driven by the perception that private sector nursing home care offers certain advantages. These include savings to the Exchequer for not having to provide public long-term care facilities and more choice for older people (O'Shea, 2002). The emergence of private sector agencies is also becoming a more significant feature of the mix of home-based care of older people in Ireland. One of the factors driving the fast pace of expansion of this sector is the introduction of publicly financed home care packages to provide financial support towards the care needs of older people in community settings (Doyle, 2006).

The privatisation of long-term care has serious implications for the health and well-being of older people currently receiving long-term care in Ireland as well as future generations of older people. Player and Pollock (2001: 149) describe the way in which long-term care has been made into a market sector in the UK and argue that the implications of subjecting long-term care to the logics of profitability is that 'recipients of care within the private sector increasingly become vectors of market forces, the bearers (or sufferers) of this interplay of demand and supply for a commodified set of services'.

In the private nursing home and private home care sector in Ireland, the question of increased standards and regulation is at the centre of debates surrounding the care of older people. Unsurprisingly, this in turn raises concerns about the impact that changes such as mandatory training and supervision would have on the costs of private care provision. In the private home care sector, at least in Dublin, there is optimism about the future growth and expansion of the sector and many providers would welcome increased regulation (Doyle, 2006). Nevertheless, there is always the possibility that in the face of increased costs and falling profitability (and in the absence of government subsidies and interventions), some private companies may choose to leave the long-term care sector with older people bearing the consequences. As such the plight of older people in need of long-term care has become more rather than less pronounced in Ireland.

Deciphering the world of older people

Care and older people's voices

In the field of care, older people who receive care and use social services are often constructed as dependent (Shakespeare, 2000). A consideration of the experience of care by older people is necessary in order to challenge this conceptualisation (Morris, 1991) and, according to Williams, F. (2000), must be a central principle in the organisation and delivery of social services. Yet, the voice of older people receiving care is rarely heard (Shakespeare, 2000). Research incorporating the views of older people using social services in Ireland has been carried out. Most notable are studies assessing health and social services from the perspective of older people living in the community (Garavan et al., 2001; McGee et al., 2005; O'Hanlon et al., 2005). These largely quantitative studies shed some light on the expectations of older people for care, and their preferences regarding family or professional care, amongst others. The subject matter of these studies might also be approached from a social constructionist perspective.

A micro-level approach

Hearing what older people have to say about care is one of the leading concerns of writers for whom a central focus is the social construction of ageing at a micro level. The emphasis on the subjective experience of ageing is particularly prominent in the work of Gubrium (1993). The central thrust of this approach is qualitative, which can take a number of directions (Gubrium and Holstein, 2000), including qualitative open-ended interviews, ethnography, and narrative analysis (Gubrium and Holdstein, 1999). This approach seeks to interpret the process of ageing in terms of interactions between older people and others in society as well as among older people themselves. It underlines that ageing may be socially constructed within interpersonal relations such as between a daughter and mother in a caring relationship; a social care worker and a care recipient; a doctor and patient (Walker, 1999). For example, Hockey and James (1993) have noted that 'infantilisation' of very elderly people is common to everyday familial caring practices. Very elderly people can experience the process of infantilisation as deeply humiliating. It has consequences too for the wider community of older people. Child-like images may percolate out and be used to describe older people in the wider community, including those who lead active and independent lives, leading to a subtle form of age-based discrimination (Hockey and James, 1993; Bytheway, 1995).

The centrality of context

For Gubrium (1993: 50) 'taking account of how the elderly give voice to experience requires that context be given its due'. In other words, while all things are meaningful, the particular meaning varies according to the context. Gubrium (1993: 50) uses the concept of 'local culture' to provide a way of conceptualising how context fills ageing with particular meaning. Local cultures such as familial and friendship networks, residential care settings and support groups can each provide a context, albeit changing, for attributing meaning to topics like quality of life and care-giving. This brings us to the meso level, with social constructionists focusing on the 'social worlds' or the settings in which constructions of personal meanings emerge and evolve. Here, the emphasis is on the influence of organisational and institutional structures and processes on the experience of ageing and the way in which individuals construct personal meanings in their daily lives through these organisations (Estes et al., 2003). For example, Gubrium (1975), using the concept of 'social worlds' in an ethnographic study, showed that administrators, care staff and residents in a single nursing home had remarkably different perspectives on the meaning of care and care-giving.

Care recipients as 'active agents'

The question of 'who can be, or are, defined as subjects with agency' is an important issue in social policy debates (Lewis, 2000: 4). A central premise of social constructionism is that human beings are agents (Sarbin and Kitsuse, 1994). In his seminal work, *Asylums,* sociologist Erving Goffman (1961) argued that a major problem of long-term institutional care is that it homogenises individual identities into institutional identities. A predominant image is that of long-term care institutions where older people live passively without any autonomy or independence. However, research on the social construction of identity paints a more complex picture. For example, Paterniti (2003) shows that although the daily practices of 'bed-and-body' work in nursing home facilities require residents to be passive recipients of care, the personal narratives of residents reveal that they can also be active agents in establishing their own personal identities and fending off unwanted labels.

A critical perspective

Social constructionists bring a critical perspective to discourses on ageing such as the image of ageing as an illness, which serves as a dominant narrative of human ageing in western societies (Hepworth, 2003: 89). In western society, the understanding of illness and disability is predominantly shaped by biomedical concerns. Approaches to the care of older people are often based on this model. For example, viewing dementia in biomedical terms legitimises medical control over people living with dementia such as using physical restraints and medication to control 'wandering' older people in long-term care facilities (Lyman, 2000). A social constructionist approach would consider the impact of the biomedical model on caregivers and families as well as the older person. From this perspective it might be appropriate to look at how the stresses of living in a care environment exacerbate the physical and mental problems experienced by older people, result in increased control and dependency of older people, and determine decisions about institutionalising older people (Lyman, 2000).

Conclusion

This chapter has examined the relationship between constructions of ageing and Irish social policies towards older people over the last four decades. It does not, however, claim to be an exhaustive account of the ways in which ageing has been constructed and reconstructed through Irish social policy. A significant feature in the 1970s of Irish social policy as it relates to older people was the consolidation of the national pension system. With the rise of age-related retirement, older workers became excluded from the labour market and old age became associated with retirement age. While social welfare policy played a major role in constructing the meaning of ageing, it also contributed to the quality of life of older people. In the early 1970s older people in Ireland had a higher risk of low income than any other major group. However, by 1980 the position of older people had improved significantly, reflecting increases in state old age pensions over that period (Cousins, 2005). In a similar way, in the field of care, ageing was predominantly regarded as a social problem. At the same time, the need to reform the system of care for older people was a noteworthy aspect of social policy.

In the 1980s, as retirement was constructed (alongside emigration) as a solution to an economic crisis and rising unemployment, labour market criteria became an important determinant of ageing and old age, at least for men. At the same time, the focus of policy shifted from regarding ageing as a social problem towards a view of ageing as an economic problem, with population ageing reconstructed in terms of an economic threat both to economic growth and to existing welfare supports. The lack of consensus regarding the implications for Irish society of population ageing reminds us that the 'ageing crisis' is itself socially constructed. Given the range of factors involved, it would be inaccurate to portray population ageing as a crisis or threat just because the numbers in a particular age group are increasing and 'by the simple mistaken translation of demographic projections into social realities' (Phillipson and Walker, 1986: 11).

According to Walker (1999: 375), 'the legacy of the past is very influential'. In particular, he argues that the tendency to regard population ageing as an economic burden is likely to be an enduring one. Such a view of ageing together with others emphasising ageing as a time of retirement, decline and burden may coexist in the new millennium with more positive constructs of ageing. For example, a more positive picture of ageing may be emerging with the traditional view of older people as inactive and unemployable giving way to a construction of older people as active and productive members of society. However, this may be limited by a preoccupation with activity and production in the workplace and policy concerned with the pursuit of economic growth. In other words, the reasoning behind positive ageing and productive ageing policies may be closely linked to concerns about the fiscal implications of population ageing.

Chapter 3

Ageing, the labour market and retirement

Tony Fahey

Introduction

Old age is often associated with retirement, so much so that entry into old age is often thought to occur at that age in the mid-60s when most people become entitled to old age or retirement pensions and exit the world of paid work. Retirement, it might be said, is one of the great social inventions of the modern world. It came into being in the late nineteenth century when pensions systems were first created and it extended into a major phase of life during the twentieth century as greater prosperity gave rise to more generous and widespread pensions and as people both retired earlier and lived longer, thus lengthening the span of years people spent in retirement. Retirement has thus now come to be seen as a characteristic part of the process of growing old.

However, the linkage of ageing with withdrawal from the world of paid work and entry into the world of retirement, while valid in many respects, is easy to oversimplify. Many people follow the stereotype in that they work up to age 65 or 66 and then retire, but many others follow a different route, for example, by retiring early or by exiting work in ways other than through retirement. Gender is a particularly obvious complicating factor – some women are likely to be *entering* paid work at the same age many men are retiring, while the still large number of older women who define themselves as in home duties are neither in paid work nor in retirement. It is useful therefore to get a more rounded view of the link between ageing and labour market processes and how retirement fits into that picture. The chapter first outlines some of the reasons why these issues are important, and indeed why their importance has ratcheted up in recent years as people have become more aware of population ageing and its social and financial implications. Then, focusing on Ireland, it examines the transitions between the worlds of paid work and retirement and how these have changed over recent years, particularly in view of the boom in employment that has occurred in this country since the early

1990s. The third main topic is the consequences of exit from work for older people – how it affects their well-being and how that impact is shaped by the nature of the exit and the circumstances that flow from it.

General issues

Although increased human longevity could be regarded as a major achievement of modern civilisation and a great boost to human well-being, it has ramifications for the economy and the public finances that are not always comforting. The most serious pressures are mediated through pensions systems, and some alarm about trends in old age and retirement has arisen as a result (an influential statement of the general worries caused by population ageing, including its implications for pensions, was contained in a World Bank report published in 1994 under the title *Averting the Old Age Crisis* (World Bank, 1994; for a recent assessment relating to the EU, see Carone et al., 2005; for a forecast of the impact of ageing on public finances in Ireland, see Barrett and Bergin, 2006). There are three separate elements to the population trends that give rise to concerns about pensions in developed countries generally, though as we will see, not all of these are present in Ireland to the same degree as elsewhere. The first element is that older people are living longer, the second is that they are retiring earlier and the third is that they have fewer adult children, reflecting the smaller families they had during their family formation years.

The first two of these trends taken together mean that the years spent in retirement have greatly increased. In Ireland in the early 1970s, for example, people qualified for the state's old age pension at 70 years of age, and men could expect to live for a further 9.7 years after that age (for women at age 70, life expectancy was higher at 11.9 years). Beginning in 1973, the qualifying age for the old age pension was stepped down year by year until it reached 66 years in 1977, where it still remains. Today, the average 66-year-old man can expect to live a further 14.6 years (the corresponding life expectancy for women is higher at 17.9 years). Thus, to look just at men, the average number of years spent in receipt of the old age pension rose from 9.7 years in the early 1970s to 14.6 years today, an increase of 51 per cent. This a large extra load for the pensions system to carry.

The biggest contributor to this extra load since the early 1970s was the lowering of the qualifying age for the pension rather than increased longevity. In addition, over much of this period workers increasingly exited the labour force before reaching retirement age, so that the years of economic inactivity were greater even than what the 'official' retirement age would lead one to expect. In a sample of retirees in Ireland surveyed in 2001, for example, the average age of retirement was 61.6 years and only 30 per cent had worked up to age 65 (Fahey and Russell, 2001: 29). The trend towards younger retirement ages has slowed down or reversed in recent years, partly because policy makers and pension authorities have become opposed to it for financial reasons. In the future, public policy may strive to *raise* the qualifying age for pensions, though, in view of the high incidence of early exit from work at present, a more urgent requirement from a policy point of view would be to encourage more workers to stay in the labour force up to existing retirement age (OECD, 2006b). The employment boom that has occurred in Ireland since the mid-1990s has also tended to raise age of exit from the labour force among older people in recent years, though, as we shall see below, that effect is not straightforward. Against this background, increased longevity rather than lower age of retirement is likely to take over as the main driver of the rising pension's burden in the future.

The third trend mentioned above – falling numbers of children – adds to concerns about the pensions and population ageing because it means that eventually there will be fewer people in the prime adult ages and thus fewer workers and tax-payers available to generate the economic activity and the state revenues needed to fund pensions. The consequences of this trend are already hitting in many developed countries. For example, in Italy in 1960, there were 7.1 prime-age adults (those aged 15–64) for every elderly person (aged 65 or over), but by 2000, there were only 3.7 prime-age adults per elderly person and it is possible that by the year 2040 there will only be 1.6 (UN, 2002a). Ireland has so far escaped this trend: in 1960, there were 5.1 prime-age adults in Ireland for every elderly person, which was not a high level compared to other countries at the time. Remarkably, however, by 2002 that ratio had *risen* to 6.1. Ireland is the only country in the developed world which has more prime-age adults per elderly person now than it had in the middle of the twentieth century. For the time being at least, therefore, the growing imbalance between older and younger people found in many national populations in the developed world is not a concern in Ireland.

A number of aspects of Ireland's demographic development account for this situation. One is the relatively high birth rates by rich country standards found in Ireland. This keeps the youth population at a relatively large size. In particular, a baby boom occurred in Ireland between the late 1960s and early 1980s, and the bulge generation that it created is still aged only 25-40 years. That age-cohort provides a strong platform for the support of the older population for some time to come. A second factor is high emigration of young adults in the 1950s, which meant that the cohorts entering old age in the 1990s and early part of this decade were smaller than they otherwise would have been. A third reason is the slow rate of improvement in older-age longevity in Ireland in the second half of the twentieth century, especially among men: in 1986, life expectancy among men at age 60 (15.9 years) was virtually the same as it had been in 1926 (15.8 years). It is only since the late 1980s that improvements in older men's longevity have emerged in Ireland, though these improvements have been quite substantial in recent years. Of course, Ireland's present advantageous age-structure will not last forever, since the large numbers of 25–40 year-olds in Ireland today will eventually become large numbers of pensioners and will tilt age ratios towards the elderly. This shift is likely to become pronounced from around the mid-2030s onwards (OECD, 2006b; Barrett and Bergin, 2006). In the meantime, however, Ireland is reaping a 'demographic dividend' from its favourable age-structure. This is important to the evolving relationship between ageing, the labour market and retirement among older people in Ireland.

A focus on the cost of pensions and the worrying economic consequences of population ageing could be criticised as excessively gloomy and as encouraging a view of older people as a social problem (less alarmist views on the economic significance of population ageing are possible – see, for example, Disney, 1996). An alternative approach is to consider the issues from the point of view of older people, focus on their rights and entitlements, and see how these might best be met in changing circumstances. The recent development of equality legislation in Ireland is an important instance of what that can involve, and is particularly relevant to the place of older people in the labour market. It has introduced age as a ground on which direct and indirect discrimination and harassment are prohibited in employment, vocational training, access to employment and conditions of employment, as well as in a number of areas not connected with employment. Here the focus is on the well-being of older people and how the job market might serve their rightful needs, rather than the other way around. This approach, taken in conjunction with the 'problem' view of population ageing outlined earlier, raises questions about the fit that arises between what older people might want and what is good for the economy and the wider society. These are questions we will return to later in this chapter.

Older workers

The peak years of people's involvement in the world of paid work run from around their mid-20s to their late 40s. Labour force participation drops quite sharply after age 50 and is already well below the peak when we get to those aged in their early 60s (figure 3.1). Women at all ages are less involved in the labour force than men and show a fall in participation in the peak years of family formation (late 30s and early 40s), but as in the case of men, a steady decline among those aged in the their 50s and early 60s is also evident.

Figure 3.1 **Labour force participation rates by age group and sex, 2006**

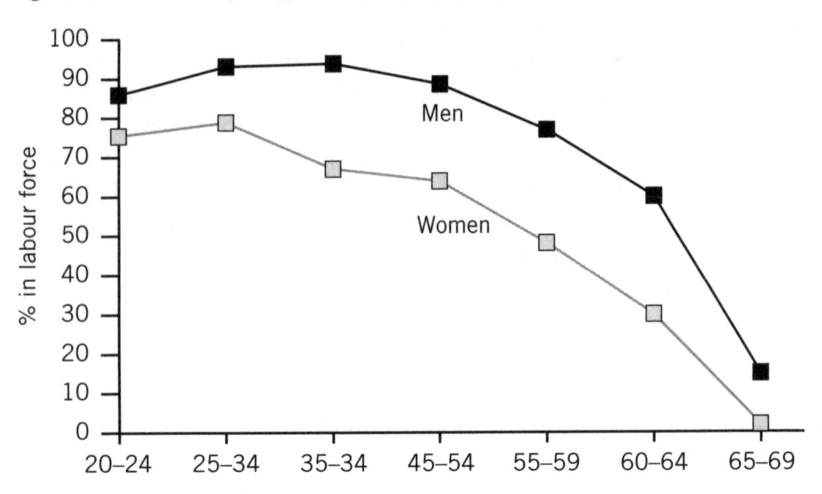

Source: CSO Database Direct (Quarterly National Household Survey, Q3 2006)

Figure 3.1 tells only of the situation across age groups at a single point in time (2006). In order to appreciate the present situation fully, it is necessary to look at developments over time. This is done in the first instance in figure 3.2, which shows the percentage at work among selected older age groups over the period 1983 to 2005. The striking feature here is the sharp rise since the mid-1990s in the level of employment among women aged in their late 50s and early 60s (increases occurred also among younger women but they are not our concern here). Among women aged 55–59 years, employment doubled between 1994 and 2005, rising from 23 per cent to over 46 per cent, while a smaller but still notable increase occurred among women aged 60–64 years (from 15 per cent to almost 29 per cent in the same period). The trends for men in these age bands show less movement and also change direction in the middle of the period we are looking at. Up to the mid-1990s, employment rates among men aged in their late 50s and early 60s were falling slightly, reflecting a broad international trend towards earlier exit from the labour force (OECD, 2006b). Since then the rates have turned upwards. By 2005, older male employment rates had risen almost though not quite to the levels last seen in the early 1980s. We also see from figure 3.2 that some men and women continue to work after the normal retirement age, with small though significant percentages at work in the age band 65–69 years. More men than women are at work at this age, though in both cases, it is mainly the self-employed, many of whom are farmers, who account for those at work (Russell and Fahey, 2004: 21; OECD, 2006b: 106). The data do not tell us how many of the self-employed at older ages are fully active in their work and how many are in fact only nominally involved, though it is likely that this category of workers is best thought of as in gradual transition from the world of paid to that of retirement.

Figure 3.2 **Percentages at work (ILO basis*) among older Irish people, 1983–2005**

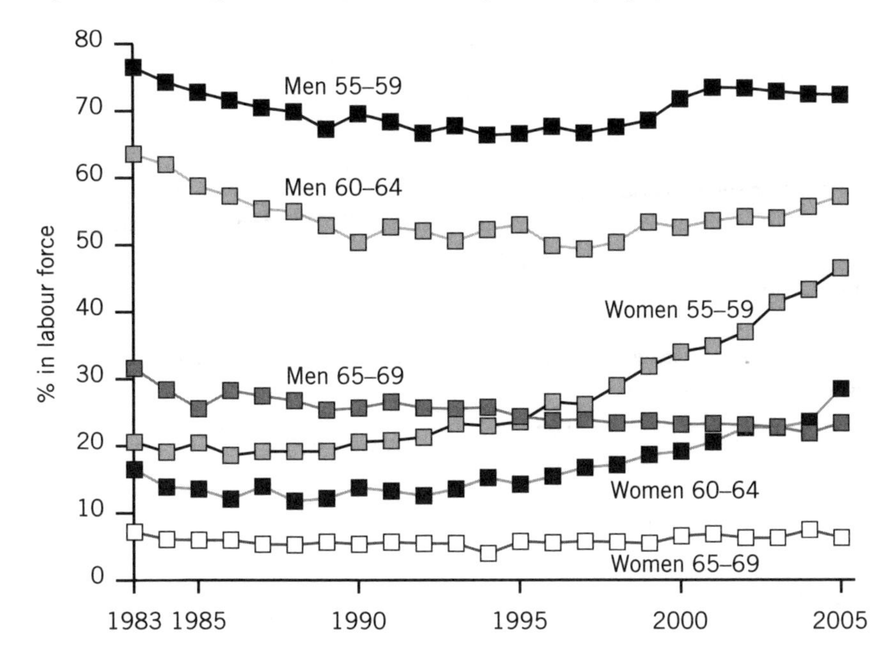

Source: Eurostat New Cronos database (Labour Force Survey Quarterly Series) at http://europa.eu.int/estatref/navigation.htm (accessed February 2007)

* The International Labour Organisation definition of 'work' refers to at least one hour's activity in the week before survey date, carried out for pay or profit or as an unpaid assistant in a family farm or business.

The trends in the numbers of older people at work over recent years do not reveal the full complexity of how their relationship to the labour market has changed in this period. We can get a better sense of this complexity by looking at the changing proportions of older men and women in a number of economic status categories, as set out in table 3.1. Among women aged 55–59, the shifting distribution across economic status categories in 1994, 1997 and 2002 indicates that the rising numbers at work over the period were drawn mainly from home duties, though in the latter part of the period (1997 to 2002) there was also a small decline in the proportion who were retired. Among women in the next age group (60–64), the rising proportions at work over the period were accompanied by a small increase in the proportion who were retired. This would suggest that exits from work to retirement in this age group increased over the period but were more than counter-balanced by entries into work from other categories, with home duties providing the main reservoir for new workers. For women, therefore, labour market conditions over the past decade have been such that both the employment rate and the retirement rate could rise at the same time, with a decline in the numbers defining themselves as economically inactive (mainly 'in home duties') being the main driver of both developments.

A comparison of the shaded cells for women in table 3.1 indicates how those who were 55–59 in 1997 changed their economic status profile by the time they were 60–64 in 2002. The percentage who were retired more than doubled as they made this age-transition (going from 4.1 per cent to 9.6 per cent) while the percentage who were at work declined only by a small amount. Again, this illustrates how the impact of increases in retirement on the size of the workforce in this age group was offset by inflows to work from home duties, unemployment and the 'others' category.

Table 3.1 **Economic status (PES* basis) among females and males, age groups 55–59 and 60–64 in 1994, 1997 and 2002**

	Females					
	Age group 55–59			*Age group 60–64*		
	1994	*1997*	*2002*	*1994*	*1997*	*2002*
At work	20.1	23.4	35.4	13.4	15.3	21.8
Unemployed	1.2	1.3	1.8	1.1	0.5	0.6
Student	0.1	—	0.5	—	0.0	0.2
Home duties	71.9	68.1	56.2	75.9	72.7	65.3
Retired	4.2	4.1	2.8	7.4	8.9	9.6
Others	2.5	3.1	3.2	2.2	2.6	2.5
Total	100	100	100	100	100	100

	Males					
	Age group 55–59			*Age group 60–64*		
	1994	*1997*	*2002*	*1994*	*1997*	*2002*
At work	64.8	64.5	72.6	51.7	48.5	52.8
Unemployed	11.7	9.6	5.6	8.7	6.4	4.4
Student	—					
Home duties	1.0	0.8	0.5	1.4	1.3	0.3
Retired	12.5	13.1	11.5	26.9	32.3	31.1
Others	9.9	12.0	9.6	11.3	11.6	11.3
Total	100.0	100.0	0.1	100.0	100	100

Sources: Labour Force Survey 1994, 1997 (CSO 1994, 1997); Quarterly National Household Survey Quarter 2 2002 microdata (available from Irish Social Science Data Archive – http://www.ucd.ie/issda).
Note: The shaded cells in this table connect the same age-cohort in 1997 and 2002.
* Principal economic status, which refers to what people define as their 'normal' situation.

Among men also, table 3.1 shows that the proportions at work increased between 1994 and 2002, though the increases were smaller than among women. The unemployed were the main source of these extra workers in this period. The percentage of men who were unemployed more than halved between 1994 and 2002, dropping from 11.7 per cent to 5.6 per cent among 55–59 year olds and from 8.7 to 4.4 per cent among 60–64 year olds. These declines are significant because in the past older workers have had greater difficulty in exiting unemployment than other groups and therefore have been particularly prone to long term unemployment. Here we see that that the phenomenal economic growth experienced in the late 1990s had strong positive effects for the older unemployed. The retired and 'others' (which consists mainly of those on long-term sickness and disability) also made some contribution to the increased numbers at work in the 55–59 year old group but did so only after 1997: prior to 1997, the percentage of 55–59 year old men classified as retired and 'other' increased but it declined slightly thereafter. Among 60–64 year old men, by contrast, the percentage who were retired rose between 1994 and 2002, while the percentage classified as 'other' remained stable. This indicates that all of the slight increases in the percentage of men at work in this age group between 1994 and 2002 were due to the fall in unemployment.

Comparison of the shaded cells for men in 1997 and 2002 shows the extent of the move from both work and unemployment into retirement as 55–59 year olds made the transition into their early 60s. The percentage who were retired tripled during this transition (going from 13.1 to 31.1 per cent) while the percentages at work and unemployed declined accordingly. It is notable, however, that there was no change in the proportions classified as 'other'. This category consists mainly of those with sickness or disability and appears to be a quasi-retirement category which makes the transition into full retirement only after age 65. It reminds us that declining physical capacity can be a cause of exit from work for a substantial minority of older workers. It thus highlights the significance of health as well as pensions and retirement as a factor in the overall pattern of transition out of the labour market for older people.

A further part of the overall picture concerns the destination of those who exit employment in the later years of their working life. Data from the Living in Ireland Survey (LIS), carried out in Ireland between 1994 and 2002, enable us to track older workers who left their jobs in this period and to see where they exited to (the LIS was a 'panel survey', which involves repeated interviews with the same sample of respondents over a period of time – in this instance, with interviews taking place once per year over an eight-year period). An analysis of these data by Russell and Fahey (2004: 34–43) found the pattern of exits from work among 50–69 year olds shown in figure 3.3. Among men, almost seven out of ten (69 per cent) exited to retirement, but even in this period of falling unemployment, one in five exited to unemployment – a quite large role for unemployment in the circumstances. A further one-in-ten exited to illness or disability. Thus despite the dominance of retirement, almost one in three older men who left their jobs in this period exited to destinations other than retirement.

Figure 3.3 **Destination of exits from employment among 50–69 year olds, 1994–2000 (%)**

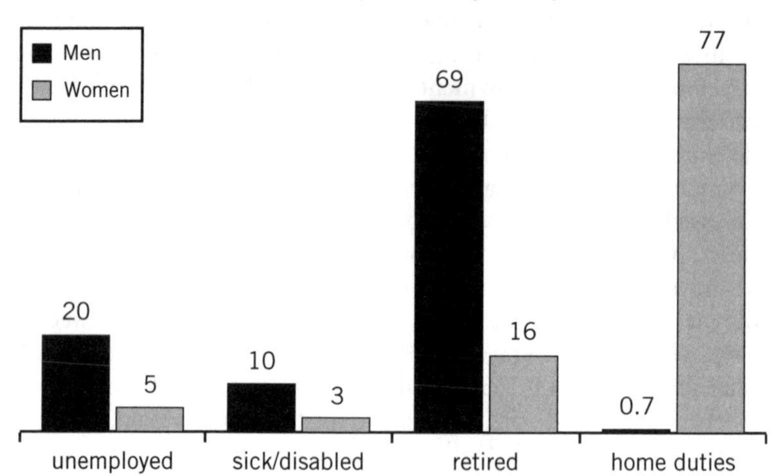

Source: Russell and Fahey, 2004: 36 (data from LIS, 1994–2000)

The situation of older women who left their jobs was quite different, with only a minority – 16 per cent – exiting to retirement and the majority – 77 per cent – exiting to home duties. Neither unemployment nor illness or disability was important in their case, though those exit destinations did occur to a small degree. It is difficult to tell from these data whether women's identification of themselves as having exited to home duties rather than retirement reflects actual characteristics of the nature of the transition they made (perhaps having to do with pension entitlements – or the lack of them) or subjective perceptions of their main role in life. Since the mid-1990s, the large number of women aged in their 50s and even early 60s who made the transition from home duties to paid work, coupled with what we see here is the tendency among older women workers to exit their jobs for what they define as home duties rather than retirement, suggests that housewife role, rather than the paid work element of their later working careers, continues to be central to their self-identification. This is likely to change in the future as the cohorts of women with longer and more continuous attachment to the world of paid work approach retirement age. The 'new woman' that is then likely to emerge is not so much the working wife with her own career and income, since she is already well established on the social landscape, as the retired woman with her own pension and a self-identity based on her former career rather than on an ongoing role as a housewife.

Consequences of exit

The final general issue we wish to consider is the consequences of exit from work for older workers. Leaving behind the work habits and routines of a lifetime and entering a non-working role is a major life transition and can be expected to have large social, psychological and financial consequences. The key question is how well older people cope with these consequences and whether their net effect is good or bad. Here we have space to look only at a couple of pieces of evidence on this complex question.

The panel data from the Living in Ireland Survey mentioned earlier is a good source of information for this purpose, since it allows us to make 'before and after' comparisons among older workers who exited from work over a period of years. It also contains a wide range of measures not only of people's material circumstances (such as incomes, living standards and housing conditions) but also of their physical and psychological health and well-being. Focusing again on the sample aged 50–69 in the LIS and picking out those who made a transition out of work into any of the exit destinations referred to earlier, we can compare their situation before they made that transition to that after they made the transition and thus identify the effect of the transition itself on any indicators we choose.

One common concern about the consequences of leaving the workforce as ageing proceeds is the psychological impact. Figure 3.4 uses an indicator of psychological distress from the LIS data to examine this issue (the GHQ Psychological Distress scale – see Russell and Fahey, 2004: 30 and 64 for details and further references). The concern here is not just that exit from the labour force can have an effect on older workers' psychological well-being but also that the nature of the exit, as defined by the destination it leads to, can shape that effect. The results in figure 3.4 confirm that the effect does vary by destination. It is negative among those who exited to unemployment, with their average distress score post-exit being 1.54 points higher than pre-exit (on a 12-point scale). Exit to illness or disability was also negative but interestingly not to the same degree as exit to unemployment. Exit to retirement, by contrast, was marginally positive and exit to home duties marginally negative, though in both cases the effect was so small that it would be safer on statistical grounds to count it as no effect at all. Thus, as far as this indicator is concerned, for older workers to be made unemployed or to have to leave their jobs because of illness or disability was likely to be distressing, but to leave for retirement or home duties was not at all distressing and, in the case of retirement, may even have tended to reduce psychological stress.

Figure 3.4 **Impact of exit from work on psychological distress among 50–69 year olds in Ireland, 1994–2000**

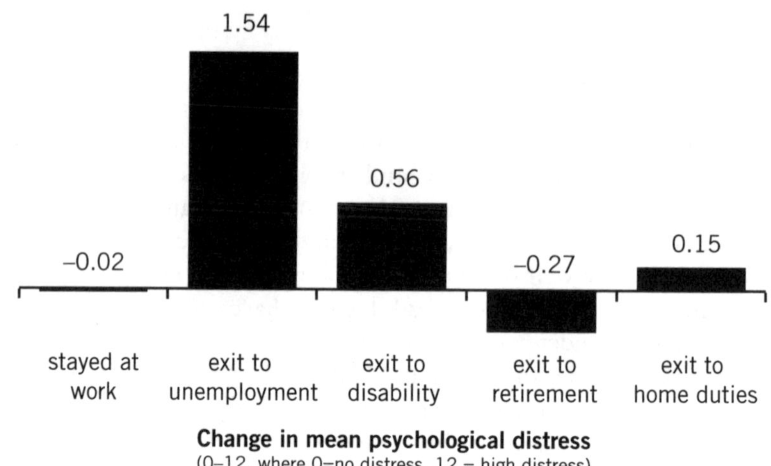

Source: Russell and Fahey, 2004: 38 (data from LIS, 1994–2000)

When we look at the *material* circumstances of older workers, we find that the effect of exit from the labour force is negative in some important respects, mainly in that income falls and the risk of income poverty increases. In the LIS panel data, for example, about one in five of older workers who exited work fell below the poverty line on making the transition (with the poverty line defined as 60 per cent of median income – Russell and Fahey, 2004: 38). The proportion falling into poverty was particularly high among those who exited to illness/disability (31 per cent) and unemployment (28 per cent), while among retirees it was 18 per cent (Russell and Fahey, 2004: 38). However, the significance of this effect is difficult to determine, even from the point of view of material living conditions. Older people in Ireland have long shown a distinctively weak connection between income and living standards: though their incomes are low, they seem to have better living standards and a lower risk of experiencing material hardship than those low incomes would lead one to expect (Layte et al., 1999). It is not entirely clear why this should be so, though it is most likely to be explained by the low outgoings of older people – they no longer have dependent children, they may already have acquired the large household durables they need, and their mortgages are paid off (for an assessment of the impact of home ownerships and low or absent mortgage obligations on poverty risk among older people see Fahey, 2003).

In any event, retirees own evaluation of their situation is generally quite positive, as figure 3.5 shows in connection with a sample of retirees interviewed in 2001. Just over 70 per cent said they enjoyed life more since they stopped working, while 77 per cent agreed that not working gives them the opportunity to do what they really want to do. The only negative note was that over half missed the social contact that came from being at work and that they lost on retirement.

Figure 3.5 **Satisfaction with life after retirement**

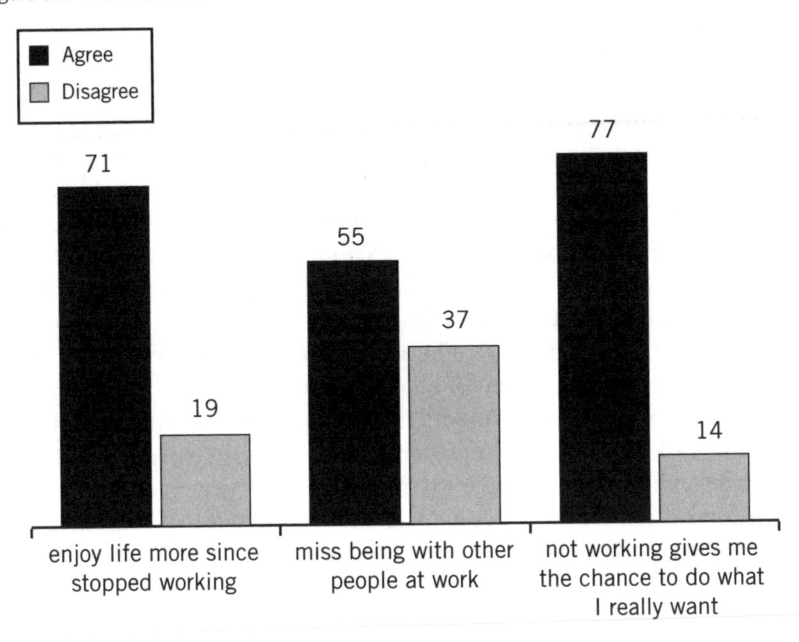

Source: Fahey and Russell, 2001: 43 (data from survey of 55–69 year olds, 2001)

Conclusions

This brief account of the links between ageing, the labour market and retirement has shown that entry into old age is not always simply a matter of endings one's working life in the paid labour force and entering retirement. For one thing, these patterns do not arise at all for many women, since their main life's work has been in home duties and the question of retirement does not arise for them in the way it does for paid workers. Furthermore, in the booming labour market conditions found in Ireland over the past decade, older women have moved out of housework and flooded *into* paid jobs in large numbers, leading to a doubling of the older women's labour force participation rate since the mid-1990s. For these women, ageing has entailed a period of entry into rather than exit from paid work.

Even among men, only a minority follow the standard path of working up to their mid-60s and then retiring. Many men retire early, and many others leave work either because of unemployment or disability. The economic boom has also had its effects on these patterns among men, mainly in that it has reduced the threat of unemployment among older workers. The reduction in unemployment among older workers has enabled their employment rate to rise but without any reduction in the incidence of early retirement, thus leading to the paradoxical outcome that employment rates and retirements could rise at the same time.

The impact of retirement on older workers seems to be generally positive, or at worst neutral. Their incomes may drop but that does not seem to have as bad an effect on their living standards as one might expect. They seem generally to feel less stressed – or at least no more stressed – than when they were at work and to enjoy the freedom that retirement brings. The picture is quite different for those who exit work to become unemployed or because of illness or disability: they are the only category who generally seem to suffer from their exit from paid jobs. The reduction in unemployment in recent years is thus an important gain for older workers, though it continues to be a real problem for a minority. A reduction in illness or disability as a cause of exit from work would be an important benefit to be pursued in the future. Otherwise, exit from work and entry into retirement generally seems to be a positive transition for most people and adds to the sense of retirement as a highly valued aspect of the ageing process.

Chapter 4

Poverty and ageing

Martina Prunty

Introduction

This chapter explores the issue of older people in poverty in Ireland. It is based on original research undertaken as part of a research internship at the Combat Poverty Agency (CPA). The research took the form of a secondary data analysis of the 2004 round of Survey on Income and Living Conditions (EU–SILC), a European Union-wide survey which is conducted in Ireland by the Central Statistics Office (CSO) and overseen at an EU level by Eurostat. The dataset was made available by the Irish Social Sciences Data Archive (ISSDA). The chapter begins by defining two concepts of poverty – income poverty and consistent poverty. It then presents data on older people in poverty in the EU context. It presents empirical evidence on older people in poverty on which policy recommendations can be made. The role of social transfers, an aspect of social policy particularly important in preventing poverty (Layte et al., 1999) is explored. This leads to an assessment of the impact of old age pensions in relation to poverty. Data is presented on poverty levels for older people compared to younger age groups in four areas – income and income poverty, deprivation, housing conditions and consistent poverty. The chapter then presents data on some particularly vulnerable groups of older people before presenting a short section on the relationship between living conditions and health. Finally, the chapter concludes with some recommendations.

Measures of poverty

For over a century attempts have been made to define and measure poverty. Absolute definitions are no longer utilised in Western societies. Relative definitions are more commonly used. Relative income poverty is the official

This chapter is based on a Combat Poverty Agency funded research working paper entitled 'Older people in poverty in Ireland: an analysis of EU-SILC 2004 (available at www.combatpoverty.ie).

EU measure and is also referred to as the risk of poverty rate. People who have an income which is less than a particular threshold are said to be income poor. A threshold for poverty assessment is usually set at 60 per cent of the median income but 70 per cent and 50 per cent are also sometimes used. The median value is preferable to the mean value as it is less sensitive to extreme values (in this case, extremely low or high incomes) and so gives a more accurate representation. However, this income-only definition of poverty does not measure other factors which may be associated with low income and so another measure is also used – consistent poverty. This is the official Irish government definition. Consistent poverty measures income but also recognises deprivation which is the enforced lack of material items that are seen by the majority of the population as attainable, and the associated exclusion. There are eight non-monetary indicators used in EU-SILC. These items are seen as forming elements of basic deprivation (Whelan et al., 2003). The term 'consistent poverty' therefore, refers to having less than 60 per cent of the median income but also lacking one or more of these basic items. When this measure is used in surveys, the respondent is asked if they found themselves in one or more of the following scenarios owing to lack of money:

- Having had no substantial meal on at least one day in the previous two weeks
- Being without heating at some stage in the previous year
- Experienced debt problems arising from ordinary living expenses
- Unable to afford two pairs of strong shoes
- Unable to afford a roast once a week
- Unable to afford a meal with meat, chicken or fish every second day
- Unable to afford new (not second-hand) clothes
- Unable to afford a warm, waterproof coat

These eight indicators have been reviewed by the ESRI (for further details on the new deprivation scale see Maitre et al., 2006). The new basic deprivation set will in future ask if the respondent is or was unable to afford:

- To keep the house adequately warm
- To buy presents for friends and family once a year
- To replace worn-out furniture
- To have family or friends for a meal or a drink once a month
- To have an afternoon/evening out for entertainment in the previous two weeks

Having introduced the basic poverty concepts, let us now turn attention to poverty levels in Ireland.

Poverty levels in Ireland

Relative poverty persists in Ireland despite recent unprecedented economic growth. According to the Living in Ireland Surveys (LIS) of the 1990s, relative income poverty increased from 15.6 per cent in 1994 to 21.9 per cent of the general population in 2001 (ESRI, 2003). In 2004, 19.4 per cent of the total population were income poor (ESRI, 2003). The rate of poverty differed according to age groups. Of particular concern are the trends in poverty rates for older people throughout the 1990s. In 1994, the income poverty rate was 5.9 per cent for those aged over 65 years but by 2001 it had increased to 44.1 per cent (ESRI, 2003). In comparison, the 18–64 age group saw a decrease from 21.1 per cent in 1994 to 17.1 per cent in 2001 (ESRI, 2003).

The Living in Ireland surveys were the main source of data on poverty from 1994 to 2001 until 2003 when it was replaced by EU-SILC. Income poverty is the official EU indicator of poverty. There are eighteen official EU indicators, known as the Laeken indicators, of which this is one. The income poverty indicator is used by Eurostat to compare EU states and their performance on social inclusion issues. Ireland has been found to have a high-income poverty rate when the general populations are analysed. A 2005 analysis of income data for 22 industrialised countries found that Ireland had a high rate of income poverty along with Australia, The United States, Israel and Russia (Wiepking and Maas, 2005). In a European context, Ireland's income poverty rate is among the highest, along with Slovakia and Greece according to 2003 data (Guio, 2005).

The average poverty rate for the EU25 countries for people aged over 65 years in 2003 was 18 per cent. The figure for Ireland was higher at 40 per cent (Zaidi, 2006). This is considerably higher than the rate arrived at by the Central Statistics Office (CSO) in Ireland. This disparity is due to the fact that Eurostat use a different definition of income. Eurostat do not include income from private pensions when measuring income while our national calculations do. Secondly, contributions to non-private pensions are deducted from gross income when calculating the EU definition of disposable income. In fact, the poverty rate in Ireland according to Eurostat of 40 per cent was second only to Cyprus at 52 per cent. Thus it is clear that while the poverty rate for older people in Ireland has decreased since the 1990s, the population of Cyprus has a higher income poverty rate than the Irish population in general but also a higher rate than people of the same age who live in other EU states. The most recent data shows that Ireland has the second highest rate of income poverty for those aged over 65 years. According to the Eurostat figures, older people living in Ireland, Cyprus and Slovenia are twice as likely as younger people to be income poor (Zaidi, 2006). Ireland's population is growing older due to increased life expectancy and lower birth rates. The numbers of people aged over 65 years of age are projected to increase from the 2001 level of 430,000 to over 1.1 million by 2036 (CSO, 2006b). If trends in poverty rates continue to rise as they did in the 1990s there will clearly be an even larger number of older people living in poverty in the future. The issue of older people in poverty is therefore a crucial issue for Ireland in the twenty-first century.

The policy context

The National Anti-Poverty Strategy (NAPS) 2003–5 identified older people as a group requiring a special focus, particularly those living alone:

> The overall objective is to eliminate consistent poverty for older people and to improve their access to appropriate health, care and housing supports, and to support older people to live independent and fulfilling lives (Department of Social, Community and Family Affairs, 2002: 15).

Specifically, the strategy aims to reduce the consistent poverty rate for older people to less than 2 per cent by 2007 and to ensure adequate heating systems are in place in all local authority rented dwellings for older people by the end of 2007. The new social partnership agreement, *Towards 2016*, has adopted a lifecycle policy framework. This lifecycle framework recognises key life stages – children, people of a working age, older people and people with disabilities. The framework aims to view policy from the perspective of the individual, thereby encompassing all of their policy needs. A number of priority areas have been identified for older people, particularly health and social care services; educational and employment opportunities. In relation to income, the agreement commits to the ideal that all older people should have an income which allows them to maintain an acceptable standard of living.

Research context

The key study regarding older people in poverty in Ireland is by Layte, Fahey and Whelan (1999). The study, entitled *Income, Deprivation and Well-Being Among Older Irish People*, was published by the Economic and Social Research Institute (ESRI) in conjunction with the National Council on Ageing and Older People (NCAOP). It used the 1994 and 1997 waves of the LIS and also the 1987 Survey of Poverty, Income Distribution and Usage of State Services as a data source. The main findings of this study were that older people had higher income poverty rates than younger groups but had lower rates of deprivation and consequently, lower consistent poverty rates. They found that some sub-groups of older people such as women who lived in rural areas were more vulnerable to poverty. They also found housing deprivation to be high in terms of problems such as living in damp conditions (see chapter 5 below).

In 2003 Whelan et al. updated some of the findings of Layte et al. They found that the percentage of older people in income poverty increased from 5.9 per cent in 1994 to 44.1 per cent in 2001. These rates were considerably higher than for those in the 18–64 age group who experienced an increase from 12.1 per cent in 1994 to 17.1 per cent in 2001. The LIS data showed that gender influenced whether or not an individual was likely to be income poor. According to the 2001 data, women aged 65 and over had a poverty rate of 22.2 per cent compared to 12.9 per cent of men aged over 65 years. In summary, Whelan et al. found that income poverty rates for those aged over 65 years increased from 1994 to 2001 with women having considerably higher income poverty rates than men. This chapter updates these findings with 2004 data.

Social transfers

Social transfers are particularly important to older people as the vast majority are not in paid employment. The average equivalised pre-social transfers income of older people in Ireland in 2004 was €3,303 per year. As previously mentioned, the median can be more representative than the mean and in this case the median was €00.00 which means that the norm was for older people to have no income without social transfers. As the median is less sensitive to extreme values this suggests that most of the sample clustered around lower end of values and that the average may be skewed by relatively few high incomes. People who have a total income which is less than 60 per cent of the median are said to be below the poverty line. In real terms, the 60 per cent poverty line was €185 per week or €9,680 per year in 2004. In the same year, the non-contributory pension rate for those aged under 80 years of age was €154 which means that anyone who relied on this pension as their sole source of income would automatically fall below the poverty line; they would automatically be income poor. Measuring the risk of income poverty at this level of income measurement (before social transfers) showed the rate was 87.4 per cent which means that without social transfers the poverty rate would be 87.4 per cent among older people. Including social transfers in the calculation of income showed the average income for older people was €13,934 (again the median was lower at €10,856 which suggests the average was skewed by relatively few high incomes) as shown in table 4.1 below. The difference, therefore, in average income pre and post social transfers was €10,630. In other words, social transfers made up on average, €10,630 of the annual income of an older person in Ireland. In fact, this means that 76.2 per cent of average income of those aged over 65 was made up of social transfers. At this level of income measurement the income poverty rate for older people was 27.1 per cent or 122,860 people. This is the official figure of income poverty in Ireland for those aged over 65 years. In this case social transfers have a poverty reduction effect of 68.9 per cent for those aged over 65 years as shown in table 4.1.

In contrast, the data show that social transfers were worth an average of €3,468 to those aged 15–64 years with a poverty reduction effect of 46 per cent. Table 4.1 shows that average pre social transfer income for those aged 15–64 years was €16,391 and €19,860 post social transfers.

Table 4.1 **Comparing poverty reduction effect of social transfers by age group**

	Mean pre social transfers income	*Mean post social transfers income*	*Value of social transfers*	*Poverty reduction effect*	*Income poverty rate*
	€	€	€	%	%
0–14 years	14,382.17	17,814.03	3,431.86	44	21.2 (€179,315)
15–64 years	16,391.89	19,860.93	3,468.46	46	17.6 (€485,951)
65 + years	3,303.72	13,934.58	11,063.36	68.9	27.1 (€122,860)

In 2004, people aged over 65 years had a higher income poverty rate than the two younger age groups (0–14 years and 15–64 years) as is illustrated in figure 4.1. The lowest income poverty rate is for those aged between 15 and 64 years (17.6 per cent of people in this age group were income poor in 2004). This means that 485,900 people in this age group had a weekly income which was less than €185 per week. The next highest rate is for children aged between 0 and 14 years with a poverty rate of 21.2 per cent or 179,315 children. Finally older people had the highest rate at 27.1 per cent or 122,860 people.

This clearly shows the importance of social transfers to the incomes of those aged over 65 years. The role of social policy is to re-distribute resources. Old age pensions are a way of redistributing income across life cycles rather than across individuals (Dennis and Guio, 2003). The important role played by social transfers, and in particular, old age pensions, are clear from the results of the current study. The next section examines levels of deprivation.

Figure 4.1 **Income poverty rates according to age groups**

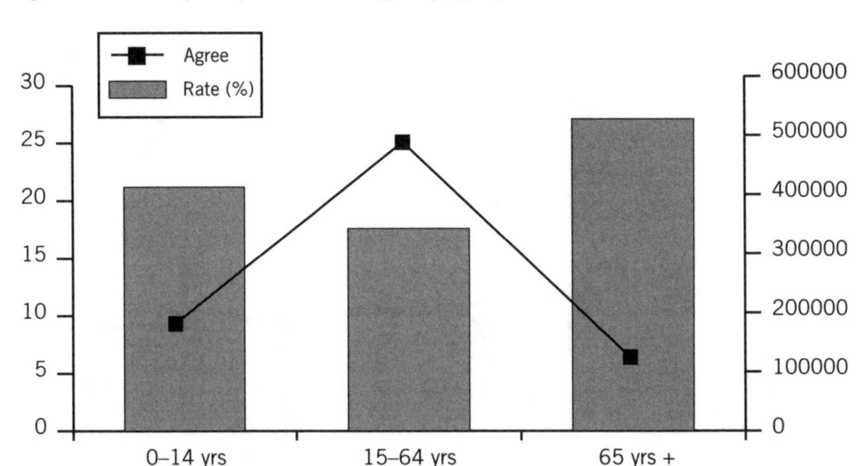

Deprivation

When levels of deprivation on the original eight items were compared between older people and the other two age groups, the results showed that older people had the lowest levels of deprivation on all eight items as shown in figure 4.2. Table 4.2 displays the exact rates of deprivation for the eight items. Among the age groups, children had the highest levels of deprivation. For example, 7.3 per cent of children lived in a household that had to go without heating at some stage in the previous 12 months due to lack of money; 7.5 per cent of children lived in a household which could not afford to buy new, rather than second-hand clothes. In contrast, the deprivation rates for older people on these items were 3 per cent and 3.6 per cent respectively. While income poverty rates are higher for older people, their deprivation rates tend to be lower in general. Possible explanations for this lower level of deprivation than would be expected, are that non-cash transfers play an important role in reducing the amount of necessary expenditure for an older person. Patterns of consumptions and levels of expectation have also been suggested as possible contributors to this result (Layte et al., 1999).

New deprivation items

The results for the five new deprivation items reveal a similar pattern to the original eight items. However, it is clear that deprivation rates are higher on these items for all groups. This suggests that these new items are better at capturing the experience of deprivation than the original items. Again, older

Figure 4.2 **Basic deprivation indicators by age groups**

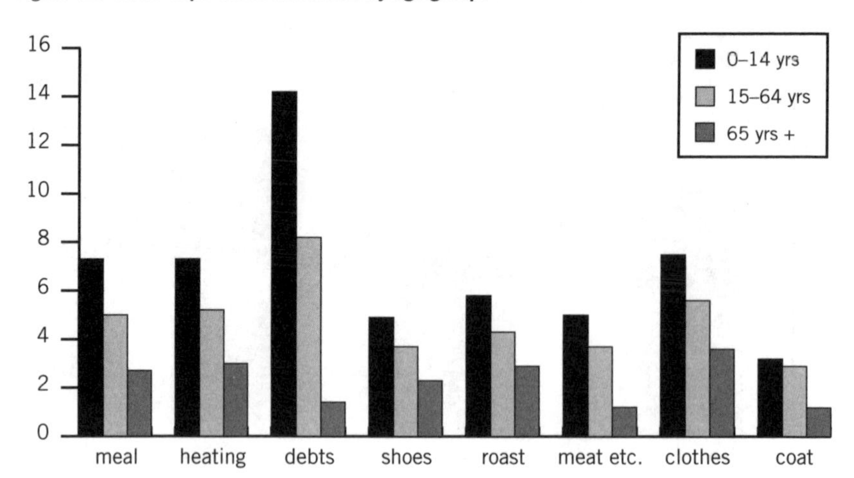

Table 4.2 **Original eight deprivation items comparing age groups**

	Substantial meal	*Without heating*	*Debts*	*Two pairs of shoes*	*Roast once a week*	*Meat etc.*	*New clothes*	*Coat*
	%	%	%	%	%	%	%	%
0–14 years	7.3	7.3	14.2	4.9	5.8	5	7.5	3.2
15–64 years	5	5.2	8.2	3.7	4.3	3.7	5.6	2.9
65+	2.7	3	1.4	2.3	2.9	1.2	3.6	1.2

people have lower rates of deprivation on these indicators than younger people. For example, 17.9 per cent of children live in households which cannot afford to replace worn out furniture while the rate for older people is 7.9 per cent (see figure 4.3).

Other deprivation indicators

These items, while not in the official set of indicators can offer an insight into what Whelan et al. called the 'potentially poor' i.e. people who are deprived of these items (2003: 56). This means that while certain individuals may not be deprived of any of the basic set of items, they may be suffering a form of secondary deprivation of items that are just outside the definition of basic items. The age pattern is repeated for these other deprivation items with older people again having lower levels of deprivation except for the variable about the ability to save some income regularly. For this item, older people had a

Figure 4.3 **New deprivation indicators by age groups**

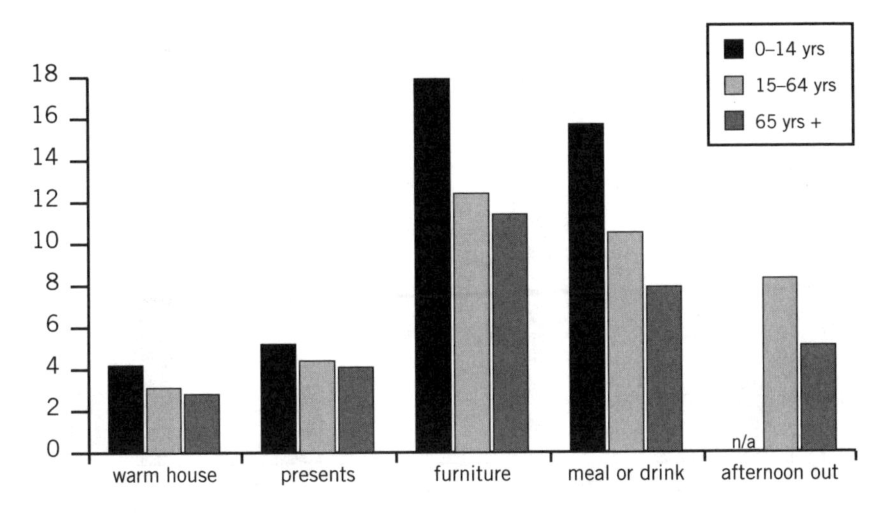

Table 4.3 **New 8 deprivation items comparing age groups**

	Warm House	*Presents*	*Furniture*	*Meal or drink*	*Afternoon out*
	%	%	%	%	%
0–14 years	4.2	5.2	17.9	15.7	n/a*
15–64 years	3.1	4.4	12.4	10.5	8.3
65+	2.8	4.1	11.4	7.9	5.1

*data for children not available.

very similar rate to those aged 15 to 64 years. The high rate of deprivation for both age groups is worrying. This suggests that almost 58.9 per cent of people aged 15–64 years cannot save some income regularly with older people reporting almost the same at 59 per cent. This means that if many people of a working age cannot save income regularly, they will not have savings or a pension plan to support themselves upon retirement from the formal economy. They are then likely to be dependent on the state pension and as we have seen, will consequently have a high chance of experiencing poverty. This inability to save some income regularly during the working phase of life, therefore creates a form of persistent poverty from which it is difficult to escape and so the working people of today who cannot save are likely to be the poor older people of tomorrow.

Figure 4.4 **Other deprivation items**

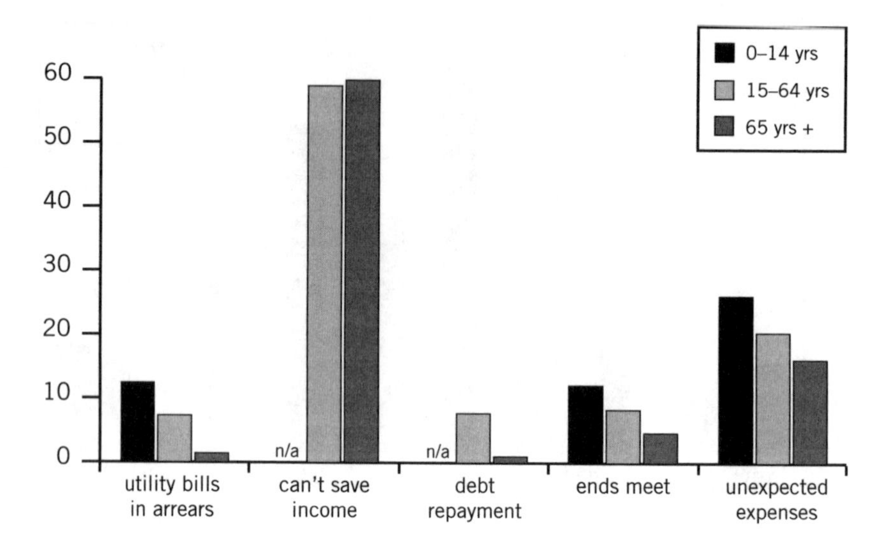

Table 4.4 **Other deprivation indicators comparing age groups**

	Utility bills in arrears	*Can't save some income regularly*	*Debt repayment is a heavy burden*	*Great difficulty in making ends meet*	*Can't pay unexpected expenses*
	%	%	%	%	%
0–14 years	12.4	n/a*	n/a*	12.1	26.1
15–64 years	7.3	58.9	7.7	8.3	20.4
65+	1.4	59.8	1	4.7	16.2

*data for children not available.

Standards of housing conditions

The data suggest that older people have the highest rates of deprivation of housing related items when compared to other age groups (see figure 4.5). Analysis of single item housing indicators showed that older people were less likely to have central heating, a bath/shower, hot water, running water and a toilet in their homes than younger people as shown in table 4.5. They were also more likely to have damp walls/leaking roof/rotting doors and windows. This supports previous research which found that older people are less likely than younger age groups to experience basic deprivation but more likely to experience housing deprivation (Fahey and Murray, 1994; Layte et al., 1999). This may be explained by the fact that older people tend to live in older houses and so after a certain time period these buildings need maintenance or improvements. Layte et al. also point out that older people tend to be less likely to engage in having home improvements carried out and that because the housing stock in which they live tends to be older and in worse condition: the cost of the necessary work tends to be high. The current policy position is to support older people who wish to remain living in the community for as long as they wish as opposed to entering full-time residential care. Based on these results, the schemes which have been put in place to improve living conditions appear to be inadequate. Despite home improvement schemes aimed specifically at this age group, many older people still do not have basic housing amenities. Previous studies have shown reluctance on the part of older people to leave their homes in favour of other accommodation, even when their home is sub-standard in some way. Fahey and Murray found that even among those older people who lived in defective housing only 20 per cent would consider moving to more suitable accommodation (1994: 170). According to the results of the current study, the highest rates of deprivation on housing-related items were a lack of central heating, having damp walls, leaking roof, rotting windows or doors.

Figure 4.5 **Percentage of people experiencing housing deprivation according to age group**

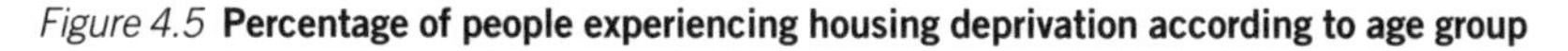

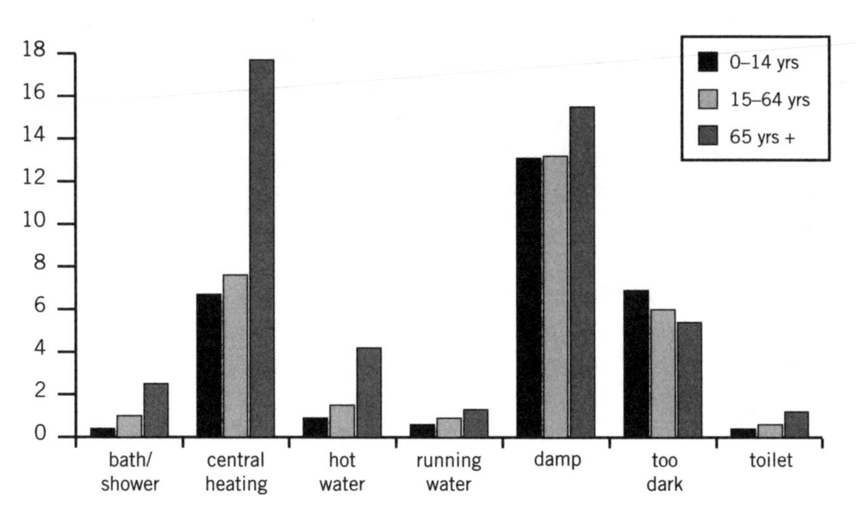

Consistent poverty

Consistent poverty is the official Irish government poverty measure. For the total population, just under seven per cent (6.8 per cent: 275,661 people) of the sample were in consistent poverty in 2004. There was little gender difference in consistent poverty rates in the general population – for women the rate was 7.4 per cent (150,781) and for men it was 6.2 per cent (124,880). The reason for this may be because while income is very much on an individual basis, some items measured on the deprivation scale, such as lack of heating, would apply to all members of a household. However, there are significant age group differences. While income poverty rates increased with older age groups, the opposite is true in relation to consistent poverty. Children have a much higher rate of consistent poverty (9.5 per cent: 80,616 children), according to the 2004 data, than those in the 15 to 64 years group (6.5 per cent: 179,875) or the 65 years and over age group (3.3 per cent: 15,170) as shown in figure 4.6. An explanation for this may be that older people have lower consistent poverty rates because of their accumulation of assets which younger people may not have. The relatively low rates of consistent poverty may be related also to services and non-cash benefits received by older people. Younger people who do not receive such benefits and must pay for fuel out of their income may be forced to go without it if they are experiencing financial difficulties. The National Economic and Social Council (NESC) report *The Developmental Welfare State* states that for older people, access to services may be more important than cash payments in terms of reaching good living standards and social inclusion (2005). This point has also been made by Layte et al. (1999) who stated the importance of the quality and availability of social care and health services for the quality of life of an older person. Consequently, poor quality or expensive services can mean that older people who need them but cannot access these services can be in a position of enforced deprivation.

Table 4.5 **Consistent poverty rates according to age groups**

Age group	*Consistent poverty rate*
0–14 years	9.5% (80,616)
15–64 years	6.5% (179,875)
65+ years	3.3% (15,170)

Figure 4.6 **Consistent poverty rates of age groups**

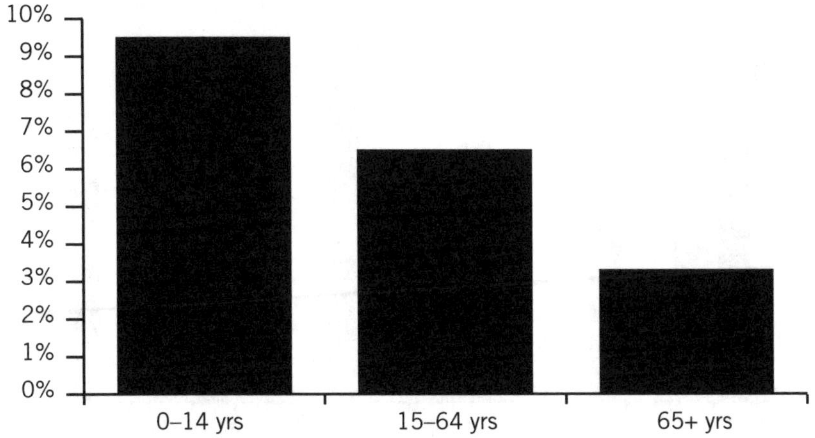

Vulnerable sub-groups of older people

The data suggested that some sub-groups of older people were more vulnerable to poverty than others, in particular those living alone and those living in rural areas. Looking at income poverty rates (figure 4.7) shows that rural-dwellers were more likely to be income poor, as were those who lived alone; those living in the Border, Midland and Western regions; and those who had lower levels of education. It is interesting to note that the income poverty gap between older women and older men has decreased. In 2003, 32.3 per cent of women were income poor, compared to 26.4 per cent of men. However, in 2004 the gap had narrowed to 28.2 per cent for women and 25.8 per cent for men. Women tend to have higher poverty rates at all stages of their lives, not just in old age. This may be explained by the fact that women are more likely than men to spend time out of the formal economy. This means that in old age they are less likely to have an adequate pension and so tend to be reliant on the state pension for their income.

Older people living alone had particularly high levels of housing deprivation. Over one quarter did not have central heating while almost eight per cent did not have hot water. Almost six per cent did not have a bath or shower and three per cent did not have an indoor toilet. These findings support conclusions of Layte et al. (1999) that elderly people living alone are more likely to experience housing deprivation. Table 4.6 demonstrates that those living alone have higher rates of housing deprivation than those who lived with someone.

Figure 4.7 **Income poverty rates according to sub-group of people aged over 65 years**

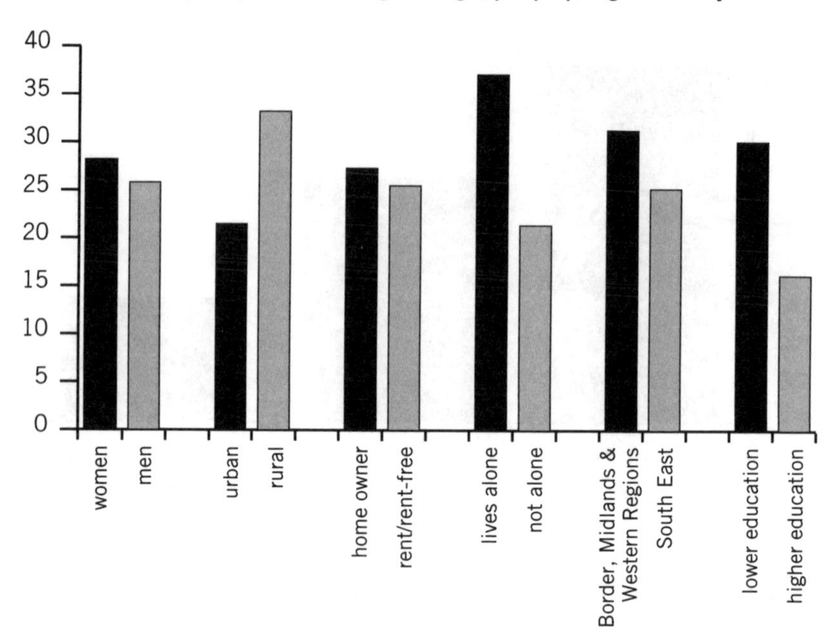

Table 4.6 **Rates of deprivation on housing deprivation items according to household composition**

	Bath/ shower	Central heating	Hot water	Running water	Damp walls etc.	Too dark	Toilet
	%	%	%	%	%	%	%
Lives alone	5.5	26.1	7.6	1.6	19.2	6.9	2.4
Lives with someone	0.9	13	2.2	1.1	13.4	4.5	0.6

Living conditions and health

Analysing some health variables according to whether the person lives in a house with damp problems or not suggests that damp can contribute to negative health outcomes. Figure 4.9 shows that people who lived in damp accommodation were less likely to report that their health was good, that they were more likely to have a chronic illness and also more likely to say that their activities were limited by a health problem.

Figure 4.8 **Housing deprivation according to household composition**

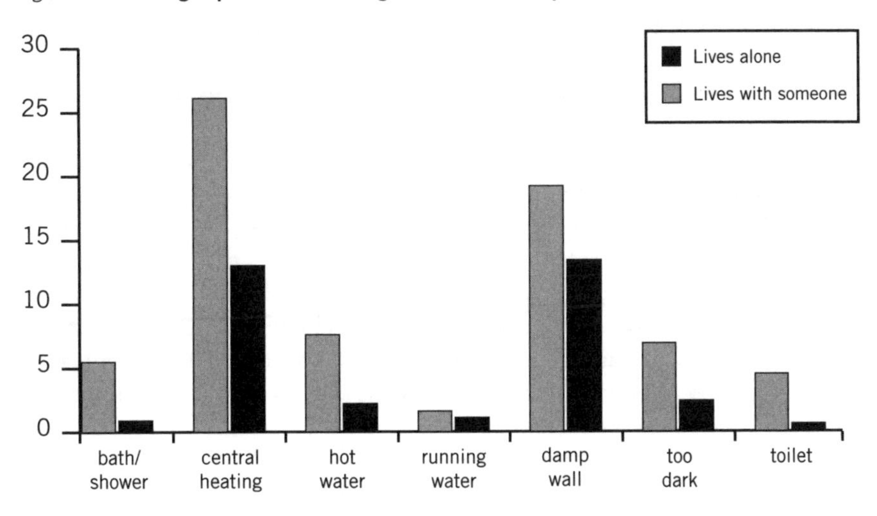

Figure 4.9 **Relationship between damp living conditions and health**

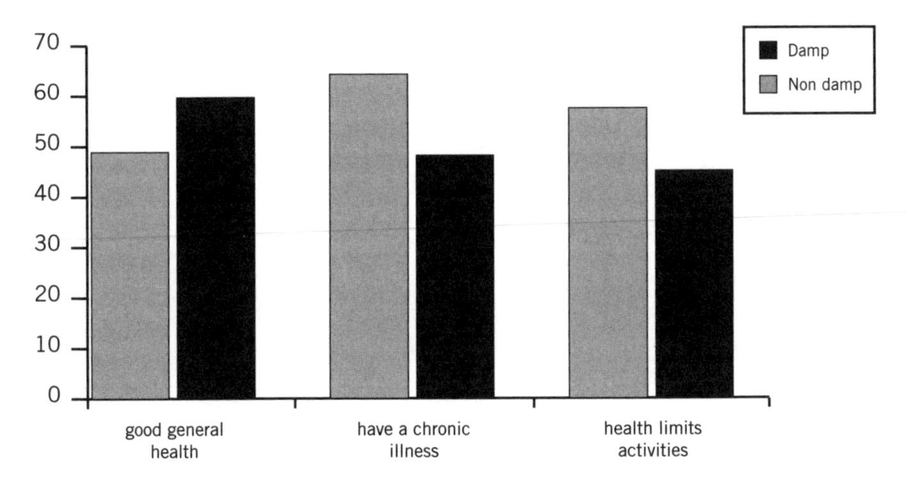

Conclusion

This chapter illustrates the important poverty reduction effect of social transfers for older people. In order to reduce the higher poverty risk for older people it is necessary to link pension rates to wages. The new social partnership agreement, *Towards 2016* has made some progress on increasing the value of state pensions relative to Gross Average Industrial Earnings (GAIE) but targets have not been made clear. This analysis of the 2004 data has shown that older people who live alone are particularly vulnerable to poverty and deprivation. It would thus be beneficial to increase the Living Alone Allowance. This allowance has a current value of €7.70 per week for those aged between 66 and 79 (for those aged 80 and over it is €10 per week). However this allowance has not increased since 1995. With numbers of older people expected to increase in the future, the numbers of income poor people among that demographic group will increase unless the issue of income inadequacy is tackled. In 2004, 58.9 per cent of people aged between 15 and 64 years said they could not afford to save some income regularly. This suggests that a large group of people are unlikely to have any savings/pension for when they leave the formal economy. Some form of compulsory pension scheme is necessary to ensure greater pension coverage. Equally analysis has shown that many older people are living in sub-standard accommodation thus existing home improvement schemes need to also be reviewed.

Chapter 5

Housing and accommodation for older people

Michelle Norris
Nessa Winston

Introduction

Housing is not simply a 'roof over the head' but it is also a location in which the person can foster social networks, family bonds and access services. So housing can have an immense impact on the well being of older people. Older people in Ireland live in a variety of housing situations – what Silke refers to as 'the continuum of housing status' (Silke, 1994: 16). While some older people live in institutional settings or in the homes of relatives, the latest Irish National Survey of Housing Quality (INSHQ) 2001–2 reveals that the vast majority of people aged 65 years and older live in dwellings which they own – 84 per cent own these dwellings outright and 5 per cent have a mortgage (Watson and Williams, 2003). Others rent from a private landlord (2.5 per cent), while 6.5 per cent live in local authority provided 'social housing' – housing provided at a reduced or subsidised rent to low income or vulnerable groups. The voluntary and co-operative housing sector is also a significant provider of social housing for older people. Although no disaggregated data are available from official sources on this form of accommodation, research by the Irish Council for Social Housing (2005) indicates that there are 79 voluntary and co-operative housing associations providing a total of 3,165 dwellings for older people. Indeed the number of older people housed by this sector is likely to be significantly larger than this because it does not include older people living in mainstream estates.

The evidence available suggests that most older people would prefer to remain living in their own homes as their health and mobility declines. For example, two recent surveys of the views of this population found that the vast majority would prefer their long-term care to be in their own homes with family members caring for them rather than Health Boards (now Health Service Executive) (Garavan et al., 2001; O'Hanlon et al., 2005). When asked about long-term care in a residence other than their own home, sheltered or group housing was relatively unpopular, acceptable to 24 per cent of respondents living in the Health Service Executive Eastern Region and 18 per cent in the Western Region (2005). The least favoured option was moving to a nursing home (O'Hanlon et al., 2005). Another study of the views of older people revealed that many saw moving to a nursing home as their only option when their health deteriorated and this was a cause of concern to the respondents (Stratton, 2004).

As health and mobility declines, housing suitability becomes an issue for older people. Some older people may need to move because their existing home is isolated from required services and social supports or they may wish to relocate to somewhere where they feel more secure. They may need to make structural repairs or adaptations to their existing home to ensure it continues to meet their needs or move to alternative accommodation the design of which is more suitable for a person with limited mobility. There is evidence to suggest that some older people are in institutions because their homes are no longer suitable rather than because they actually require high levels of care. For example, a national review of acute hospital bed capacity showed that 70 percent of the bed days lost in one major hospital were accounted for by patients over 65 who could not be discharged to return home due to inadequate social and community supports (Department of Health and Children, 2002a).

This chapter examines non-institutional housing and accommodation for older people. The opening section of the chapter focuses on the housing conditions of this population using data taken from the aforementioned INSHQ. It examines the housing tenure and conditions of older people in Ireland as well as their housing costs and the housing wealth they possess compared to other age groups. This is followed by an examination of the supports available to enable older people to continue living in their own homes and the main types of accommodation in which they live: owner occupied housing, social housing and supported and sheltered housing. In the case of each of these housing options, the policies and statutory supports relevant to older people are critically examined in view of the available research evidence on the challenges which they face living in these settings. The conclusions to the chapter then identify the key challenges related to the housing and accommodation of older people in Ireland, suggest how they could be addressed and speculate on the approach which government is most likely to adopt to this issue.

Housing tenure, conditions and costs among older people in Ireland

Housing tenure

Figure 5.1 below, which employs INSHQ data, sets out the housing tenure of households which contain a single person aged 65 years or households which include multiple adults (but no children) of whom at least one is aged

65 years or over. It reveals that the housing conditions of older people are quite distinctive from the rest of the Irish population. For instance, the levels of home ownership, particularly of outright ownership without a mortgage, are significantly higher among the older age group than is the case among all households – 87 per cent of all adult households of which one member is aged 65 years or over owned their home outright in 2001–2 compared with 45 per cent of all households surveyed. Older people are also less likely to live in private rented accommodation than is the population at large.

Figure 5.1 **Housing tenure of older people and all households, by household type, 2001–2**

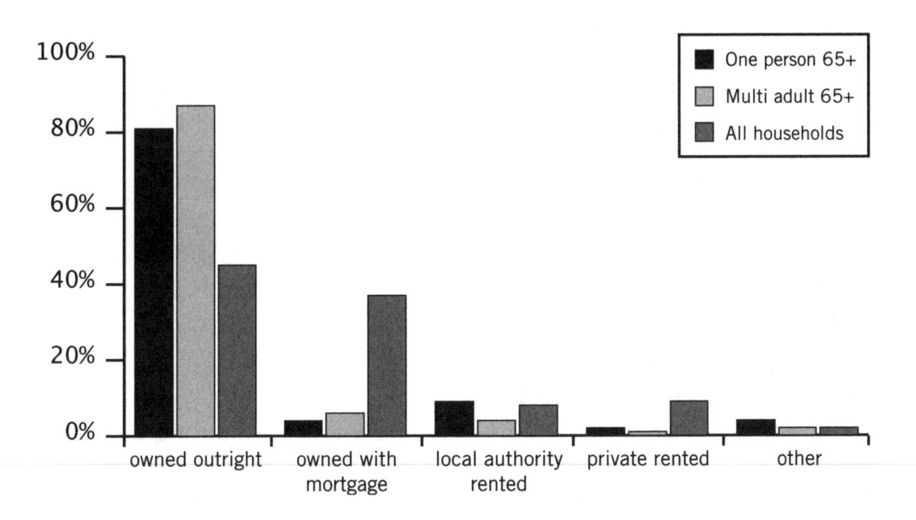

Source: Watson and Williams (2003)

Housing conditions

Table 5.1 summarises the available evidence regarding the housing conditions of older people compared with all households. In this regard, it reveals a mixed picture. On the one hand, the quality of dwellings and the extent of reported problems in dwellings inhabited by older people, particularly those aged 65 years and older living alone, is poorer than the housing stock in general. For instance, older people living alone are less likely to have hot water and central heating and more likely to suffer problems related to dampness and sanitary facilities in their dwellings than is the case for the population in general. On the other hand, compared with other households, older people tend to live in relatively 'good' neighbourhoods so have fewer problems in relation to graffiti, neighbouring homes in poor condition, vandalism and public drunkenness.

Table 5.1 **Housing conditions of older people and all households by household type, 2001–2**

Housing Conditions		*One person 65+*	*Multi-adult 65+*	*All households*
Dwelling quality	Number of rooms (excluding bathrooms)	5.5	6.5	6.3
	Average number of persons per room	0.2	0.4	0.3
	No hot water	6	2	2
	No central heating	25	15	10
Neighbourhood quality	Graffiti	5	5	7
	Homes/gardens in bad condition	5	4	6
	Vandalism	8	7	8
	Public drunkenness	7	5	8
Reported problems in the dwelling	Dampness/leaks	7	5	5
	Heating	4	3	3
	Sanitary facilities	6	5	3
	Space	0	1	7

Source: Watson and Williams (2003).

Housing costs, affordability and wealth

Table 5.2 summarises the INSHQ data regarding the housing costs and affordability for older people. It reveals that the housing costs of households in this age group are significantly lower than those of their younger counterparts. However, a significant proportion of older people, particularly single adult older households, experience housing affordability problems. For instance, in 2001–2 14 per cent of older people living alone devoted more than one third of their income to rent or mortgage costs, compared to four per cent of multi-adult households and nine per cent of all households. Housing expenditure above this level is regarded a key indicator of lack of affordability (Downey, 2005). In addition, compared with other households, a much larger proportion of older people living alone were unable to afford to replace worn furniture, heat their homes, adequate meals, new clothes or to run a car.

The high levels of housing unaffordability among older households, despite their relatively low housing costs, is related to their relatively low incomes and high levels of income poverty (Layte et al., 1999). Income poverty is also a contributor to older people's poor housing conditions because, as Stratton (2004: 5) points out, many older people have great difficulty paying for housing maintenance and repairs, including those who own their homes outright. While it is important to acknowledge that many older people

Table 5.2 **Housing costs and affordability of older people and all households by household type, 2001–2**

Housing costs and affordability		*One person 65+*	*Multi-adult 65+*	*All households*
Median weekly rent or mortgage	Private rented sector	103	n/a	609
	Local authority rented	57	89	107
	Mortgage	n/a	254	457
More than one third of household income devoted to rent or mortgage		14	4	9
Unable to afford	Replacing worn furniture	42	28	27
	Adequate heating	14	8	8
	Meal with meat	8	4	4
	New clothes	15	7	8
	Car or van	58	24	22

Source: Watson and Williams (2003).
Note: n/a means not available. 'Mortgage' refers only to mortgages granted by commercial lenders, not local authorities.

are income poor, it is also significant that many older people are home owners and relatively rich in capital assets compared with younger people, particularly those who have no mortgage on their home. According to Fahey and Nolan (2005) households headed by a person under 35 have 14 per cent of the housing wealth in Ireland whereas households headed by people aged between 65 and over have 26 per cent of the housing wealth.

Supported home care

Since the late 1960s various policy documents have recommended that older people should be enabled to live in their own homes or in other community-based settings rather than in institutional care. In 1968 the *Care of the Aged* Report argued that adequate housing, income maintenance and community care were required if the objective was to be achieved (Government of Ireland, 1968). Twenty years later, *The Years Ahead* report reiterated these points, in particular calling for better coverage and co-ordination of those services which enable older people to remain living in their own homes, namely: housing repairs; home help; the public health nurse service, physiotherapy, chiropody and transportation (Department of Health, 1988). Although the key health policy statement of the 1990s – *Shaping A Healthier Future* – had little to say about housing issues, it reiterated the importance of promoting community care for older people, setting a target of not less than 90 per cent of those over 75 continuing to live at home (Department of Health, 1994).

Despite these policy aims, supported home care is the least developed aspect of care of older people currently in Ireland as community health and social care services are extremely limited (Convery, 2001a; Garavan et al., 2001; Ruddle et al., 1997). Chapter 5 provides details of the state of current provision in relation to community care. Convery (2001b: 28) argues that this form of care in Ireland is still based on 'the assumption that the family will provide much of the care required by older people with little or no assistance from the state'. Indeed she suggests that the presence of family members who could potentially provide care can reduce the chance of an older person receiving community care and where care is provided the family may have to pay for the cost of such services.

The cost for carers of older people, both financially and in terms of the impact on their own physical and psychological health, can be considerable (Convery, 2001b). Furthermore, it is important to note that with an ever increasing proportion of women in the labour market, the free care traditionally provided by women can no longer be taken for granted in planning for the future care needs of older people living in the community. It is interesting to note that the latest partnership agreement commits government to maximise the use of community and home based care and to support the role of family and informal care (Government of Ireland, 2006).

Owner occupied housing

As was explained above, the vast majority of older people in Ireland own their own homes. This section examines the sources of finance available from government and other sectors to enable older home owners access non-institutionalised accommodation which is appropriate to their needs.

Home improvement supports for older home owners

For older home owners who live in poor quality or inappropriate dwellings and are income poor a number of government-funded schemes are available to assist them with the improvement and adaptation of their accommodation.

The Disabled Persons Grant is administered by local authorities. It funds adaptations to dwellings necessary for the proper accommodation of people with physical or mental illness (Norris and Winston, 2004). In the case of an owner occupied dwelling, the maximum grant available was €20,320 in 2004 or 90 per cent of the cost of the adaptations, whichever is less. While there is no national income limit for eligibility, local authorities can and usually do apply income limits at their discretion.

The Essential Repairs Grant, which is also administered by local authorities, provides assistance with repairs necessary to prolong the life of the house. It is targeted mainly at older people in rural areas. Figure 5.2 reveals that take-up of the scheme has increased in recent years. This increase may be explained in part by a rise in the older population, but it is also due to increased funding for the scheme. There are no nationwide regulations regarding the maximum grant available under this scheme. Individual local authorities apply their own maxima related to the funding which is made available to them by the Department of the Environment, Heritage and Local Government (DoEHLG, various years) to finance the scheme.

Figure 5.2 **Home improvement grants paid to older home owners, 1993–2004**

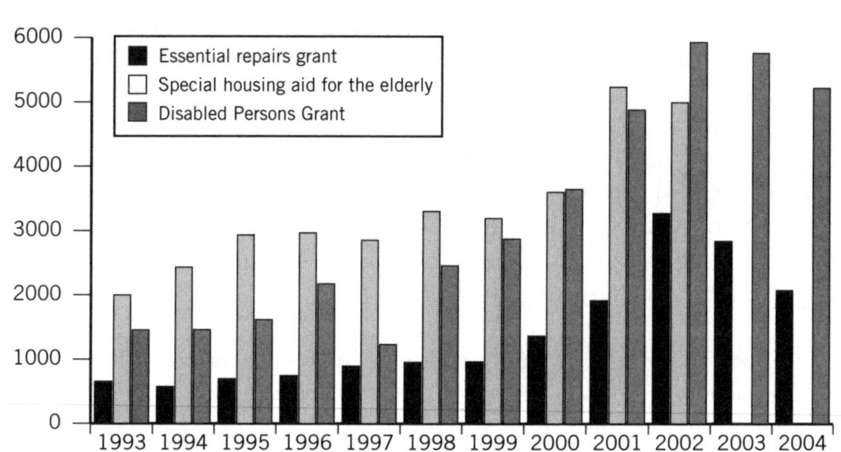

Source: Comptroller and Auditor General (2000) and Department of the Environment, Heritage and Local Government (various years) and unpublished data provided by the Department of the Environment, Heritage and Local Government.

Note: Data on grants paid under the Special Housing Aid for the Elderly Scheme in 2003 and 2004 are not available.

The other main scheme of support for older home owners is Special Housing Aid for the Elderly, which is administered by the Health Service Executive, funded by the DoEHLG and managed by the Task Force on Special Housing Aid for the Elderly. Typically, aid is available for basic repairs to the fabric of the house to secure it from the elements and ensure it remains habitable for the duration of occupancy by the older person. Funding under the scheme has grown significantly over the last decade – from €2.5 million in 1993 to €17 million in 2006 – and as a consequence the number of repairs carried out under its auspices has also expanded, as figure 5.2 demonstrates.

In addition, two smaller schemes to enable older home owners to improve and adapt their homes have been established in recent years. Following a recommendation of the Task Force on Security for the Elderly, the Community Support for Older People Scheme was introduced in 1996. This provides grants to voluntary and community organisations to improve the security of accommodation for older people by installing locks for windows and doors, and security lighting. Furthermore, both Energy Ireland and Sustainable Energy Ireland provide assistance to help older people living alone to insulate their homes.

Several of the schemes described above have been the subject of reviews in recent years as a result of concerns about their increasing cost and the efficiency of their administration. For instance, a Comptroller and Auditor General (2000) review of Special Housing Aid for the Elderly revealed significant problems in all parts of the country such as substantial delays in completing the works to dwellings – with waiting lists of six months to four years, as well as a wide variation in the cost of works and approaches to implementation of the scheme. Nevertheless, the report was largely positive about the importance and value for money of the work carried out. In addition, the DoEHLG (2005) has recently completed a review of both the Essential Repairs Grant and the Disabled Persons Grant. Probably as a result of these reviews, the current national partnership agreement – *Towards 2016* – commits government to 'Reforming the grant schemes for older people in private housing to improve equity and targeting'. It envisages that:

> This reform will build on the experience of a number of local authorities that have been able to prioritise spending through targeting of priority clients and standardised costs. The new arrangements will be more streamlined, cutting down on administration to make the schemes more accessible and provide a more seamless set of responses to the needs of people with a disability and older people (Government of Ireland, 2006: 63).

Equity release and relocation

The preceding discussion has revealed that some older home owners are income poor but asset rich as they own a valuable dwelling. This asset could be used to release equity to pay for community care to enable them to continue living in their own home. Alternatively, it could be sold to facilitate a move to a more appropriate dwelling (smaller and/or more accessible) or to sheltered housing if necessary.

In recent years several financial institutions in Ireland have offered schemes to help people release the equity value of their homes. These involve loans against the dwelling at a rate comparable to mortgage interest, which are repaid posthumously on the sale of the property. However, Stratton (2004) argues that these schemes are rarely in the interest of the older person as the interest may accumulate for many years, eat up most of the equity in the dwelling and the extra income can have tax implications and negative effects on means-tested benefits. In addition, equity release schemes may not offer sufficient income to fund care so the dwelling may have to be sold off altogether. As an alternative, Stratton (2004) suggests that the Health Service Executive (HSE) should establish a scheme to recoup the cost of medical and residential care for older people posthumously on the disposal of their dwelling.

The other option of selling and trading down to a more suitable dwelling can be problematic in a number of respects from the perspective of older people. For instance:

- Many people do not wish to leave their own home
- They may not wish to leave their neighbourhood and may be unable to afford a dwelling in that area
- If they sell their home they will have no asset in the longer term should they require it at a later stage, which raises fears about future financial security
- The costs of relocation, including stamp duty and legal charges, can be a significant disincentive to those who might otherwise consider downsizing
- Older people may be discouraged from this option due to the implications of such a move for eligibility for means tested schemes such as medical card for those under 70 and non-contributory pensions

In an attempt to address this latter concern, the social welfare regulations were reformed in 2001 in order to exempt some of the proceeds from the sale of a family home from the means test for the non-contributory old age pension. However, this disregard is subject to a ceiling of €190,500, which has not been increased since these regulations were originally introduced. Significantly, this provision is not available to older people who release equity from their homes rather than sell it. No data are available on the use of this provision. However, in view of the marked increase in house prices since its introduction – nationwide house prices rose by 63 per cent between 2001 and 2005 – it is likely that it has become increasingly unattractive to older people, particularly those who own properties in Dublin where house price inflation has been particularly marked (DoEHLG, various years).

Social housing

Social housing in Ireland is provided by both local authorities and also by non-profit agencies in the voluntary sector such as housing associations and housing co-operatives (Norris, 2005). In addition to providing social housing, local authorities are also obliged to carry out assessments of the need for dwellings of this type on a regular basis. The number of older people identified in the assessments of social housing need, carried out over the last decade, are set out in figure 5.3. It reveals that in absolute terms the social housing need of older people has remained relatively steady at around 2,500 in each assessment conducted since 1993, although it has fallen in relative terms as total social housing need has increased significantly over this period. However, both Stratton (2004) and the National Council on Ageing and Older People (NCAOP, 2001d) suggest that these figures significantly underestimate older people's housing need. According to the latter, many older people do not apply for local authority housing due to the stigma associated with moving to this tenure in Ireland.

Figure 5.3 **Results of the assessments of social housing need, 1993–2005**

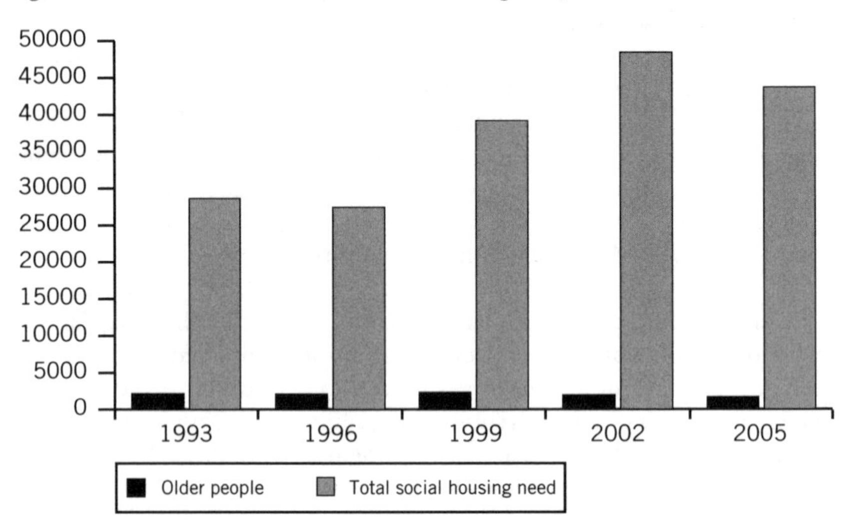

Source: Department of the Environment, Heritage and Local Government (various years).

Local authority housing

The Housing Act, 1988 requires local authorities to 'have regard to' the housing needs of older people in developing their house-building programmes and in allocating local authority housing. Many older local authority tenants have lived in the sector for a significant number of years and may have been allocated their dwellings when they were much younger. In order to ensure that such tenants have accommodation which is suited to their needs and to free up family sized dwellings for letting to larger households, several local authorities have introduced schemes to enable older tenants to transfer to purpose built dwellings for older people. Such accommodation, which is also let to older people who were not originally local authority tenants, is usually in the form of bungalows designed for one to two people or group schemes of self contained dwellings in terraces of apartments. Norris and Winston (2004) estimate that in 2001 local authorities let 15,488 dwellings purpose built for older or disabled people out of a total stock of some 100,000 dwellings. No additional care supports are supplied for most of these dwellings, although some local authorities, such as Dublin City Council, provide schemes for older people which are supervised by a warden (Murray and Norris, 2002). The 2002 review of the National Anti-Poverty Strategy committed the government to ensuring that all local authority dwellings for older people had adequate heating systems by 2007 (Department of Social, Community and Family Affairs, 2002). The DoEHLG introduced a programme to fund these works in 2004 and €15 million was provided during that year for this purpose.

Voluntary and co-operative housing for older people

As was mentioned above, voluntary and co-operative housing associations provide a significant amount of housing for older people and for most of its history the primary focus of the sector has been on housing older people and others with care and support needs (Mullins et al., 2003: 71). In addition to providing and managing dwellings, most voluntary and co-operative housing associations provide a range of ancillary services such as day centres, dining and laundry facilities, counselling, and health care (Mullins et al., 2003). Housing schemes providing a range of these services may be designated as sheltered housing, which is discussed further in the next section.

Most voluntary and co-operative accommodation for older people is funded by the DoEHLG under the Capital Assistance Scheme, which provides up to 95 per cent of the capital (construction) costs of providing these dwellings. Under the terms of this scheme, 75 per cent of the dwellings must be let to households assessed by local authorities as being in need of social housing. In recent years the capital funding for the construction of voluntary and co-operative social housing has been increased significantly. In addition, in 1991 a scheme of grants was introduced for the provision of communal facilities such as dining rooms (Department of the Environment, 1991). As figure 5.4 reveals, these grants have affected a significant increase in the output of dwellings for older people by this sector. This is likely to increase further in future because the current national agreement includes a number of measures to eliminate barriers to the delivery of more housing by this sector (Government of Ireland, 2006). However, funding for the revenue (or management and maintenance) costs associated with providing voluntary and co-operative housing for older people is far less generous than the capital finance available. As is discussed in the next section, this creates particular problems for the provision of sheltered and supported housing for older people.

Figure 5.4 **New dwellings for older people funded by the DoEHLG under the Capital Assistance Scheme, 1993–2001**

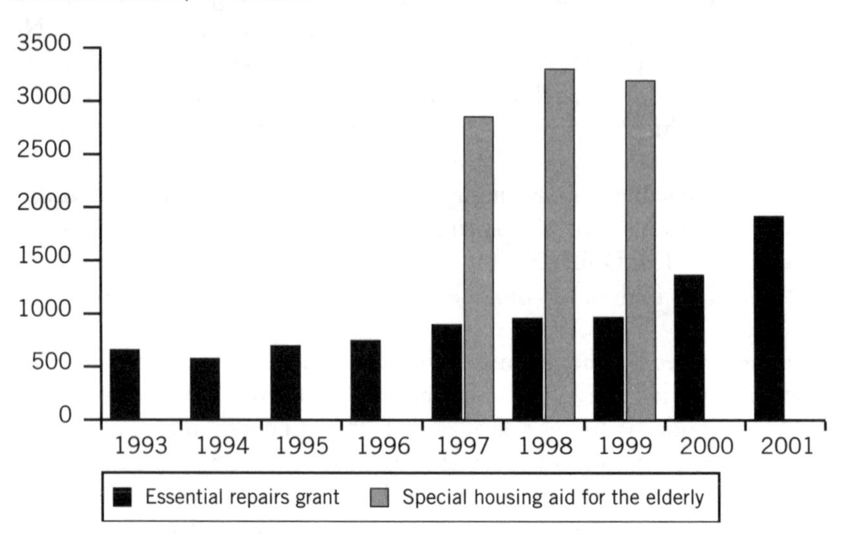

Source: Norris and Winston (2004).

Sheltered or supported housing

Sheltered or supported housing refers to housing wherein older residents have separate, appropriately designed dwellings but share on-site communal welfare areas and have access to on-site support staff. This form of housing usually consists of dwellings with alarm systems to alert wardens or other support staff, a day centre, on-site group meals, meals on wheels options, on-site nursing and medical facilities, visiting support workers and communal areas. Sheltered housing may be part of a cluster of accommodation for older people or it may be integrated with other non-sheltered dwellings. Fisk (2001) argues for more integrated design solutions. The rationale for this is that more segregated schemes have the potential to marginalize older people, reinforce stereotypes of them as frail and dependent, resulting in ghettos of older people and the creation of dependency and isolation. However, developments which only include sheltered housing can be integrated into the wider community and relevant services by being centrally located and/or by having adequate public transport links.

The advantages of sheltered housing include the prevention of institutionalisation, improved housing conditions, assisted independent living and decreased loneliness or isolation. It can also provide an alternative to living at home or living in residential care and it is less expensive than the latter. *The*

Years Ahead Report recommended that, where it was not possible to maintain older people in their own homes, sheltered housing should be the first choice rather than residential care (Department of Health, 1988). Thus, it called for a significant increase in this type of accommodation. The latest national partnership agreement commits government to 'the continued development of sheltered housing options' (Government of Ireland, 2006).

While sheltered housing has been encouraged in many European countries since the Second World War, it is a more recent development in Ireland (Silke, 1994). It is estimated that the first sheltered housing scheme was developed in 1965 by a voluntary agency, the Dublin Central Mission, while the first local authority sheltered housing scheme was built by Limerick City Council in 1973 (Fisk, 2001). In recent years most new projects have been provided by voluntary and co-operative housing associations and to a lesser extent by the private sector. The government has made commitments to expand the latter source of provision (Department of the Environment and Local Government, 2000).

A number of studies indicate that there is an inadequate supply of affordable sheltered housing, especially in the major urban areas (O'Connor et al., 1989; Ruddle et al., 1997; Silke, 1994; Winston, 2002). This means that older people who may be unable to continue living independently, but could live in sheltered housing, may be forced into residential care instead.

In addition, there is considerable variation in the level of support services provided to residents of sheltered and supported housing schemes. In the view of the NCAOP, most of the voluntary and co-operative housing schemes designated for older people could not be defined as sheltered housing (NCAOP, 2001d). In rural areas, for example, most schemes are two to three unit developments providing little or no social care support or communal facilities. There are also a number of small group schemes in both urban and rural areas which have some of the care supports but which have had to scale back other services such as on-site wardens (Ruddle et al., 1997). The Irish Council for Social Housing (ICSH), which is the representative body for voluntary and co-operative housing associations, distinguishes between group housing and sheltered housing arguing that the latter must have on-site staff including a warden and care supports such as the provision of meals and assistance with personal hygiene, while in the former residents live independently with a minimum of assistance but with support from visiting services such as a public health nurse. Its survey of members found that 33 per cent of dwellings provided for older people offer a high level of support and constitute sheltered housing, while 58 per cent are low support (Irish Council for Social Housing, 2005).

The lack of high-support sheltered and supported housing provided by voluntary and co-operative housing associations is related to the inadequacy of the revenue funding available to the sector. Most of the running costs of such schemes are met from a combination of the following sources:

- Rent supplement which is made available by the Department of Social and Family Affairs at a lesser rate for voluntary and co-operative tenants compared to private tenants
- Rents which are related to the incomes of tenants and thus are generally low
- Grants from the HSE (under Section 65 of the 1953 Health Act) which fund some of the welfare, care and support aspects of these housing schemes, including nursing and other care staff, the provision of meals and general maintenance
- Fund raising

However, Mullins et al. (2003) report that in practice many organisations are heavily dependant on fundraising. The Irish Council for Social Housing (2005) attributes this situation to shortcomings in the HSE Funding Regime. It complains about the inadequacy and discretionary nature of the scheme in past years which meant that recipients could not rely on obtaining it. These revenue problems have been worsened by the fact that, like all organisations in the voluntary sector, the decline in voluntary activity has created difficulties for housing organisations because many depend on volunteers to deliver most services to tenants.

A new revenue funding scheme for voluntary and co-operative housing association provided sheltered was introduced in 2005 with an allocation of 0.4 million which increased to 0.9 million for 2006. However, housing associations have raised concerns about the limited extent of this funding and about the standard of its administration by the HSE, while local authorities have requested that access to this finance be extended to include them. These issues will be examined by a cross departmental team on sheltered housing which the *Towards 2016* national agreement commits the DoEHLG to establishing (Government of Ireland, 2006).

Conclusion

This chapter has revealed a mixed picture in relation to the housing situation of older people in Ireland. On the one hand, there are significant high levels of owner occupation among this age group and many of these households own their homes outright. In addition, older people tend to live in relatively good neighbourhoods compared to other groups in the population. However, many older people live in poorer housing conditions than the rest of the population and their ability to address these problems is limited due to their relatively low incomes. Funding for the adaptation of their dwellings and community care supports to enable them to remain living in their own home are limited, as are affordable sheltered housing options. Whereas there are grants to assist with the cost of nursing home care, the absence of similar grants for community care represents a bias towards institutional residential care (Garavan et al., 2001; O'Shea, 2000). This contradicts the key aims of government policy on the housing and accommodation of older people which emphasise the importance of providing appropriate assistance to enable older people to continue living at home (Government of Ireland, 2006).

We have highlighted some concerns about the use of equity release schemes to enable people to make adaptations to their homes and/or sell their dwellings to relocate to more appropriate accommodation. However, it seems likely that older people will be obliged to use these options more often in the future. In the United Kingdom, Malpass (2005) highlights the growth of 'asset based welfare', whereby governments encourage households to accumulate assets such as owner-occupied dwellings during their working years, in the expectation that these will be liquidated if necessary to pay for care in the older years because government support is only provided to the poorest households without assets. The high level of housing wealth among older people in Ireland and the recent direction of policy on the housing and accommodation of this group, indicates that similar developments are likely in this country. Rather than increasing the funding available to enable older people adapt and renovate their homes, the Irish government is committed to stricter means testing of the grants schemes currently available (Government of Ireland, 2006).

The other key issue highlighted in this chapter is the inadequacy of the supply of affordable, community-based, sheltered housing in parts of the country. In part, this is due to inadequate revenue funding for housing associations operating these schemes, which resulted in a strong disincentive to the future development of the sector. The government has recently begun to address this issue. However, in addition to promoting sheltered housing output in the social rented sector, the promotion of private sheltered accommodation for middle and higher income older people should also be considered. The provision of additional sheltered housing would help to cut spending on residential care for older people, extend the housing options available to this group and enable them to remain living in their own localities. Thus, local authorities should be encouraged to plan for the construction of more dwellings of this type as part of the development planning process.

Chapter 6

Older returning migrants

Joan O'Flynn

Introduction

Ten years ago it was observed that return elder migration had attracted less 'scholarly attention' than elder migration in Ireland (Malcolm, 1996). Little has changed. There is limited research and policy focus on the nature, extent and experiences of older Irish return migrants. This chapter opens with a discussion on defining return migration and then older return migration. It goes on to present a short overview of the current data trends relating to inward migration and older return migrants. This is followed by an exploration of some theoretical explanations for return migration. It then outlines key legislative and policy contexts for return migration and includes reference to the range of supports available to potential older return migrants.

The meaning of return migration

More people than ever are migrating around the world. In the context of global migration does 'return migration' have a specific meaning? Irish people have emigrated for centuries, much of it involuntary emigration to escape political, economic, social and cultural oppression and deprivation. This is the context in which return migration is explored.

Return migration is a little discussed concept in Irish public policy. In contrast, there is a rich tapestry of public discourse on return migration in hundreds of Irish songs and ballads (in both English and Irish languages). The dream of loved ones returning to Ireland or emigrants aspiring to return is the theme of countless emigrant songs. This is particularly so for songs that emanated from earlier waves of forced emigration from the nineteenth century, early twentieth century, the post-Second World War emigration of the 1950s and from Australia, Canada, US and Britain (Neville, 2004). The emotional attachment between emigrant and the home country, evoked in the oral singing tradition, finds echo in Winston's study of older Irish emigrants' needs and issues. In a sample of older Irish people in Britain thinking about moving back to Ireland, 54 per cent 'felt that Ireland was home' (Winston, 2002).

Return migration does not have a standard meaning in national or international policy and law. It can mean different things in different contexts and can be measured in a variety of ways. Three issues that are important in defining return migration are:

- The length of time a person is back in the country of origin (home country)
- Whether a return is voluntary or involuntary, as in the case of deportation
- The status of the children of return migrants. Children accompanying returning migrants may have been born in the emigrant's country of destination but may share the ethnic background and affinity with the returning migrant parent's country of origin. Does place of birth preclude them from being considered as return migrants? Or are they immigrants though they may share similar ethnicity and even nationality as that of their parent's country of origin?

Definitions of 'older' in relation to return migration

Establishing when one is older is contentious. Depending on the context, being 'older' can commence at 50 or younger or as old as 75. The question arises as to whether or not it makes any difference if the numbers of returning migrants in the pre-retirement age range of 45–64 is higher or lower than in the 65+ age range and also whether the number of women compared to men in each age category is important. Establishing the scale of older return migration provides more comprehensive data on the composition of a country's population. Understanding demographic composition is relevant to planning for the affordability of future social welfare including: pension provision, housing, public transport and so on. The extent to which the returning migrant is a beneficiary of social welfare provision in their home country is often linked to their previous economic circumstances in their country(ies) of destination. Ireland has a number of bilateral agreements with other countries regarding social security provision. EU Regulations govern the payment of social security for returning migrants within the EU. Ireland is also party to a number of multilateral social security agreements negotiated under the Council of Europe, the International Labour Organisation and the United Nations.

Three age-related issues that may be important are:

- Whether the older returning migrant is likely to be in paid employment on return and therefore generate his/her own independent income to sustain his/her household

- Whether the older returning migrant is likely to have been in 'official' paid employment abroad and therefore have associated social security or occupational pensions or had irregular, insecure employment with associated vulnerabilities
- Whether the older returning migrant is likely to have long-term housing needs

Data on inward migration and older return migrants

Older returning migrants are a subset of the number of Irish born people living outside Ireland. They are also a subset of the overall levels of immigration to Ireland. As observed by research undertaken for the Irish Government's *Task Force on Policy Regarding Emigrants* (Department of Foreign Affairs, 2002) data on return migration is hard to distinguish from:

- Immigration by non-Irish nationals, or
- Immigration by people born abroad who may be of Irish ethnicity or background

The Quarterly National Household Survey (QNHS), administered by the Central Statistics Office (CSO) is a primary method for collecting migration data. It provides the basis for the classification of annual migration flows by sex, age group, origin/destination and nationality. Population and migration estimates are published each year in April, using the results of the QNHS and other migration indicators. The CSO also administers and analyses the data from the national census. The most recent census was in 2006 though data are not available at the time of writing. Since 1986 the Irish Census collects data on the birthplace of immigrants. The Census includes a question on place of residence one year previously and on whether one has ever lived outside Ireland for at least a year. The Census can therefore generate data that provides some insight on the extent of return migration. For example, in 1996 returned Irish-born migrants comprised 5.9 per cent of the Irish population. Foreign-born immigrants comprised seven per cent (Department of Foreign Affairs, 2002: 104). The extent to which some of the latter are of Irish background is not known.

Return migration of Irish nationals has been a sustained feature of Irish demography. Overall, there have been significant increases in the numbers immigrating to Ireland over the last ten years. CSO data suggest that there has been approximately a fourfold rise in gross inward migration from an estimated 17,200 in 1987 to 70,000 in 2005 (NESC, 2006: 7). In the context of an increase in gross immigration, there have also been changes in its composition. Return migration of Irish nationals which was a strong feature of, for example, 1970s immigration, and now represents a decreasing proportion of overall immigration. Table 6.1 outlines the actual numbers of Irish nationals vis à vis other immigrants to Ireland in recent years. The number of return migrants of Irish nationality varies across the seven years 2000–6 (inclusive). The number peaks in 2002 with a high of 27,000, two years later it reaches a low of 16,900 in 2004 before climbing back up again. In the same period the overall number of inward migrants reaches an estimated peak of 86,900 in 2006. In the last five years, the declining proportion of Irish born return migrants as a proportion of the overall is evident. In 2000 almost half of all immigrants were Irish people returning from a period abroad. By 2006 this category of immigrant reduced to less than a quarter of immigrants (FÁS, 2006).

Table 6.1 **Inward migration by nationality 2000–6**

	2000	*2001*	*2002*	*2003*	*2004*	*2005*	*2006*
				'000s			
Irish	24.8	26.3	27.0	17.5	16.9	19.0	19.7
UK	8.4	9.0	7.4	6.9	5.9	6.9	7.5
Rest of EU15	8.2	6.5	8.1	6.9	10.6	7.1	9.6
US	2.5	3.7	2.7	1.6	1.8	1.6	1.3
Rest of World, of which:	8.6	13.6	21.7	17.7	14.9	35.4	48.9
EU10						26.6	37.8
Other						9.0	11.1
Total	52.6	59.0	66.9	50.5	50.1	70.0	86.9

Source: CSO Population and Migration Estimates, April 2006 (FÁS, 2006).

The numbers of Irish born living abroad remains significant. The extended Irish diaspora is also large. It is estimated that in the region of 3 million Irish citizens live abroad and that in the region of 1.2 million of these are Irish born (Walter et al., 2002).

One of the possible consequences of the dramatic fall in emigration levels is that there may be a continuing reduction in return migration. As less people leave Ireland, the 'supply' of potential return migrants is diminished as fewer people abroad are available to return to Ireland to ultimately close their migration circle. Positive net migration (a greater number of people entering the State than leaving) is anticipated for the foreseeable future. The UK appears to be the country of destination from which most return migrants originate. In the period 1986–96 more than 20 per cent of people in Donegal had lived outside Ireland for more than one year, with 75 per cent of them coming from Britain. The UK has consistently provided the highest percentage of immigrants between 1987 and 2001 (Walter et al., 2002). By 2002, 16 per cent of the total population of the state had lived outside Ireland and approximately nine per cent of these were returned migrants (Ní Laoire, 2004). There is little evidence of large numbers of older Irish return migrants (NCAOP, 2001e). Net migration is a term used to describe the difference in numbers between those who immigrate and those who emigrate from Ireland. Table 6.2, using selected data from inter-censal periods since 1945, illustrates average net migration figures for people aged over 65.

Table 6.2 **Net migration of over 65s during inter-censal periods since 1945**

Period	*Total average per annum*
1946–51	1,900
1956–61	1,300
1966–71	1,500
1981–6	1,300
1986–91	1,500
1995	1,900
1997	1,500
2000	2,000

Source: NCAOP, 2001e

Research carried out for the *Task Force Regarding Emigration* (Walters et al., 2002) highlights that, in the 15-year period 1987–2001, amongst people coming to live in Ireland (gross inward migration) men aged 65+ consistently outnumbered women aged 65+. By 2001, the proportion of people aged 65+ continued to reduce as a percentage of the overall total of inward migrants. A similar trend emerged for people in the pre-retirement age category of 45–64. More recent data from the CSO suggest that in the last six years to 2006, there is a little more equalisation in the gross immigrant numbers of men and of women aged 65 and over. Table 6.4 summarises actual numbers of gross inward migrants by sex and age 65 and over. When the above data are considered for outward migration or emigration for the same age group, they suggest a recent reduction in net migration levels for all people aged 65 or over. They also highlight an unusual 'blip' in 2002 when more people aged 65 and over emigrated than immigrated as shown in table 6.5.

A number of key conclusions can be drawn from this review of trends of elder return migration:

Table 6.3 **Men and women by age as percentage of total inward migration, 1987, 1992, 1997 and 2001**

	Aged 45–64		*Aged 65+*	
	Men	*Women*	*Men*	*Women*
	% of overall total of inward migrants			
1987	12.3	10.8	6.2	5.4
1992	11.0	9.4	3.7	3.1
1997	11.1	8.9	3.7	2.2
2001	6.9	6.1	0.9	0.9

Source: Adapted from Walter et al., 2002, table 1.13

Table 6.4 **Inward migration by sex and age 65 and over 2001–6 (000s)**

Year	*Women*	*Men*	*Total*
2001	0.3	0.5	0.8
2002	0.5	0.3	0.8
2003	0.6	0.6	1.2
2004	0.3	0.3	0.6
2005	0.6	0.6	1.2
2006	0.7	0.6	1.3

Source: Adapted from CSO *Population and Migration Estimates, April 2006* (FÁS, 2006), table 6. Data for 2003–6 are preliminary.

Table 6.5 **Immigration and Emigration of population age 65 and over 2001–6 (000s)**

Year	*Immigration*	*Emigration*	*Net migration*
		000s	
2001	0.8	0.7	0.1
2002	0.8	1.2	-0.4
2003	1.2	0.3	0.9
2004	0.6	0.2	0.4
2005	1.2	0.3	0.9
2006	1.3	0.7	0.6

Source: Adapted from CSO *Population and Migration Estimates, April 2006* (FÁS, 2006), table 6. Data for 2003–6 are preliminary.

1. There are small numbers of older return migrants
2. In recent years there has been a decline in the actual number of older return migrants
3. In recent years there has been an increase in the numbers of immigrants to Ireland but a decline in the proportion of immigrants who are return Irish born migrants
4. Historically, more men than women constituted return migrants though there appears to be an equalising of the gender breakdown of older return migrants in recent years
5. Reduced emigration levels may limit the potential 'pool' of return migrants and contribute to reducing levels of future return migration

Explanations for return migration

There are a number of theoretical explanations for return migration. Irish emigrants of the 1950s and 1980s form the current 'pool' for potential elder migration. Irish economic depressions were primary causal factors in these waves of emigration. For some, social, political and cultural repression were also motivating factors but the majority of Irish emigrants of these eras could be classified as economic or labour emigrants.

For labour migrants it is argued that wage differences between the country of origin and the country of destination, the stage a person is at in terms of the different phases of the life cycle, the presence of friends and kin and a familiar social and cultural environment, language and climate are all factors that influence whether migration is a permanent or temporary strategy for individuals and households (Klinthäl, 2006). At the time of emigration, it may be considered a temporary strategy and a return to the county of origin is envisaged after a certain period. Over the whole life cycle, it is assumed that some time spent temporarily in the labour market abroad, and planned savings, can ultimately contribute to building a better life at home. For many emigrants however, their emigration experience may interrupt their plans to return as they become established in their country of destination or, as in the case of many Irish emigrants, their emigration experience leaves them economically and socially vulnerable. Klinthäl also suggests that there is a clear relationship between rates of return migration and structural factors in the country of origin. These include the long-term economic and social situation and short-term issues such as demand for labour, with the latter influencing annual variations in return migration. Walter et al. iterate this when they identify new economic opportunities in Ireland in the 1970s and 1990s as allowing 'reluctant emigrants to relocate, bringing skills and savings with them' (2002, 19).

Even though economic factors are important influences on return migration decisions, family and friends are the most often cited reason given by return migrants themselves. In the case of elder return migration, the duration of absence from the country of origin influences the degree to which family and friends are motivating factors. In a survey of Irish emigrants where the vast majority (70 per cent) were living in Britain for more that 40 years, more than half of them (57 per cent) indicated that they did not want to return to Ireland. Having family and friends in Britain was the main reason given by over a third of the research sample. Fourteen per cent indicated the absence of family in Ireland, 4 per cent indicated that they were living away too long and 12 per cent indicated the cost of living in Ireland as reasons for not returning (Winston, 2002).

Klinthäl (2006) highlights a Swiss study on elderly immigrants, which suggests the family relationships and particularly the location of adult children are important influences on the decision to settle or return. In the Swiss research, women want to settle in the host country to a larger extent than men, primarily in order to keep contact with their children. This finding is also echoed in a 1989 study of Irish emigrants in Britain by Schweitzer (Winston, 2002). In interviews with Irish born London pensioners, women, in particular, were reluctant to lose contact with children and grandchildren living in Britain. Winston's own study (2002) found that men were more likely to wish to return home than women. She found that a third of women wanted to return compared to 42 per cent of men.

Klinthäl (2006) goes on to suggest that economic as well as psychological factors influence the decision to return once people move from a wage income to a pension. When a person has reached a stage in their life cycle where participation in the labour market is less relevant, the purchasing power of pensions and savings assume a greater importance, along with quality of life considerations such as cost of living, access to health care and other services. The extent to which these factors are more favourable in the country of destination, or the country of origin, influences whether return migration or permanent emigration is the outcome.

Nostalgia and emotional attachment to the country of origin are other explanations for return migration, though it may be that they are outweighed by the other factors discussed above. In Winston's study (2002), 54 per cent of interviewees wanted to return to Ireland because they felt it was 'home'. Irish culture and music, renewing community life, country living were amongst other reasons given for wanting to return to Ireland. However, only 27 per cent both wished to return and thought it possible to do so.

People's narratives of their migration experience and their motivation to return provide useful insights. Safe Home is a national organisation that seeks to assist older Irish born emigrants to return to their homeland (Safe Home

Programme, 2000). Its website relates several true-life stories (www.safe-home-ireland.com). Two are reproduced here to illustrate the combination of factors that shape the personal decision to return or not.

Jim's story

Aged 19, Jim left Kerry in 1953 to settle in Birmingham. Here he relates a combination of emotional attachment and family relationships as factors in his and his wife's decision to return to Ireland:

> My wife, Rita, and myself always wanted to go home but the chance was never there. We are hoping that will change now.
>
> Our children (we have six) are all grown up and have moved away to make their own lives. We have two sons living in Dublin for the past half a dozen years and a daughter in Listowel since January 2000.
>
> I suppose we are looking at getting home to be near to my daughter, particularly as she's married with our only grandchildren. One of our sons lives in Brussels. He's with a company based there. Another son lives in London and the youngest lad was killed in a road accident when he was seven. So you can see there are none of them near to us in Birmingham any more. Now that we are both pensioners Rita and myself just about get by. There is nothing Irish about where we live and we long for the day when we can be home again in Kerry.
>
> (*Source*: Safe Home Programme, 2000)

Sarah's story

Aged 14, Sarah left Tipperary for London in 1952. Below Sarah relates how, having secured accommodation in Ireland, she reconsidered and reversed her decision to return to Ireland:

> I was on my way to sign the tenancy agreement for the new home in Ireland. I had been so excited to be going back, but over the past couple of days I started to feel the same fear that I had when I was 14, in 1952, and the loss I felt then has never left me. I know I will never get a chance like this again but wherever I am I will hold the same wonderful memories of days gone by that can never be relived except in my mind. In 1952, the 6th June, when I saw Ireland fading into the distance, from the deck of the ship, the Innishfallon, I was heartbroken. I am too frightened now to go through the same upheaval again and this time youth and a lot of future is something I no longer have. I've had my day. I hope the person who will get the lovely home I was going to have will not be a coward like me and have a long and happy life, second time around.
>
> (*Source*: Safe Home Programme, 2000)

Legislative and policy contexts for return migration

In the twentieth century, Britain was the traditional country of destination for the majority of Irish emigrants. Following Irish independence in 1922, Irish Free State citizens, as members of the Commonwealth, remained free to enter and take up residence in Britain. This was reciprocated to British citizens wishing to live in Ireland. In 1948, Ireland withdrew from the Commonwealth. The British Nationality Act in 1948 and the Republic of Ireland Act 1949 governed the status of Irish people moving to Britain. Under it, the status quo prevailed and it was adjudicated that the 'people of Éire and the people of Britain should not be foreign to one another'. The status of Northern Ireland and post-War labour supply needs in Britain were amongst the factors that influenced this decision (Hickman and Walter, 1997: 10). One of the consequences of this decision was the absence of immigration controls and the creation of, in effect, a free travel zone between Britain and Ireland. Later on, the British Prevention of Terrorism Act 1974 enacted considerable new powers to control the movement of people between Ireland and Britain (Hickman and Walter, 1997).

Until Ireland joined the European Economic Community (EEC) in 1973, Irish emigrants to other parts of the world (including countries now in the EU) were, in general, subject to the immigration and visa controls of their countries of destination. This still pertains for emigration to countries outside the EU. In the 1980s, the phenomenon of the 'illegal Irish' emerged, particularly amongst Irish emigrants to the USA. This refers to circumstances where emigrants breached or overstayed the terms of their stay in the USA. As the generation of 1980s and 1990s Irish illegal emigrants in the US age over the life cycle, their legal status will be a key determinant of their likelihood of ever becoming older return migrants. Unless their immigrant status is regularised, to return to Ireland at any age, with either temporary or permanent settlement intentions, would preclude any return visit or stay to the US.

Freedom of movement of workers in the EU is one of four fundamental freedoms created 50 years ago by the Treaty of Rome in 1957. Of the twelve EU countries in 1992, Ireland, with 12 per cent, had the highest percentage of its citizens residing in an EU member state other than their place of birth (European Social Fund Evaluation Unit (ESFEU), 1996). A range of social security provisions are enshrined under international instruments including those of the EU, International Labour Organisation (ILO), Council of Europe (CoE) and the United Nations (UN). These afford protection in relation to contingencies such as sickness, old age, disability and policy provision relating to taxation, social security credits, pensions entitlement and transferability and so on and mutual access to and recognition of education and training provision and qualifications. In addition, Ireland has a range of bilateral agreements with other countries governing such arrangements.

In the context of the above international facilitation of migration, the Irish Constitution provides a robust context for return migration. Article 2 of the Irish Constitution provides that:

> It is the entitlement and birthright of every person born in the island of Ireland, which includes its islands and seas, to be part of the Irish Nation. That is also the entitlement of all persons otherwise qualified in accordance with law to be citizens of Ireland. Furthermore, the Irish nation cherishes its special affinity with people of Irish ancestry living abroad who share cultural identify and heritage.

Given this constitutional context, Irish-born return migrants and Irish citizens born outside Ireland have a more or less absolute legal right to live and work in Ireland. Support for older return migration is provided both within Ireland and in emigrants' countries of destination, particularly Britain. At Irish Government level, under the Department of Foreign Affairs, Irish embassies and consular offices in emigrant destinations act as key links with emigrant communities.

An Irish Abroad Unit (IAU) is based in the Department of Foreign Affairs. It encourages connections with Irish communities abroad and works to strengthen links with Irish people and people of Irish ancestry. The Irish Abroad Unit manages the financial support that the Department of Foreign Affairs distributes to voluntary organisations engaged in supporting Irish community networks abroad including: Britain, USA, Canada, Australia and Argentina. A key objective is to support the delivery of information and advisory services to vulnerable Irish emigrants. Under its funding provision, a range of voluntary, community and church advice and support services receive grant-aid to work with emigrants, intending emigrants and intending return migrants. There are a range of Irish elderly networks abroad such as the Camden Irish Elderly Network and the London Irish Elders' Forum. The Department of Social and Family Affairs (DoSFA) and the Department of Environment, Heritage and Local Government (DoEHLG) also fund Irish-based voluntary activity supporting return migration.

Information is recognised as a key tool in supporting potential return migrants. Many of the emigrant services at home and abroad provide information and advice to support potential return migrants to make an informed choice about their decision to return home. The Safe Home Programme (2000) is a dedicated service that seeks to assist older Irish born emigrants to return to their homeland. It works to secure housing in the voluntary sector (in housing specifically for the older person) for applicants as near to their 'home place' as possible all over Ireland. Its criteria for application is that people must be aged close to or over 60 years, must be living in rented accommodation and must be seeking to return to their county of origin or a county with which they have close, verifiable links. The Safe Home Programme operates a highly subscribed waiting list.

When older people return, they engage with a whole range of policy contexts. These include: taxation, social welfare and pensions' provision, housing, health and social care provision. It has been recognised that Irish levels of social spending on social protection are low by EU and Organisation for Economic Co-operation and Development (OECD) standards and that is particularly so for services relating to old age (NESF, 2005).

Older returning migrants also engage with a society where public policy development relating to older people is described as having 'a central focus on the medical model of ageing, which addresses ageing in terms of increasing infirmity' (NESF, 2005). The NESF report argues that it is time to develop policies that enhance the social contribution and participation of older people. Such an approach does not consider older people as a problem. It values them and creates public policy and social conditions that seek to realise the full potential and social participation of older people.

Decent and affordable housing is a basic requirement for human dignity. As discussed in chapter 5, home ownership is the dominant form of housing tenure in Ireland. This includes tenure for older people. Data from the 1991 Census shows that 86.2 per cent of non-institutionalised older people lived in dwellings that they owned; seven per cent lived in local authority housing; four per cent in the private rented sector and three per cent in social housing provision (Norris and Winston, 2004). In Ireland, there has been a significant upward trend in house prices for both new houses/apartments and previously owned housing since 1995. This may impact on the accessibility of housing for older return migrants, especially those that may have a fixed income (e.g. pension or social welfare payment), may not have been a home-owner in their country of destination, or may not have a sufficiently valued housing asset to sell in advance of returning home. Irish housing policy recognises the housing needs of older return migrants. Since 2001, following advocacy by the Safe Home Programme an amendment was made to the Capital Funding Scheme for voluntary and co-operative housing, so that up to a quarter of accommodation in a housing project can be made available for allocation to return migrants who satisfy particular eligibility criteria.

As an emigrant, cultural difference in the country of destination can exacerbate the geographical and social displacement of being in a different place to family and friends. Ironically, the experience of being an outsider is also common to people returning to live in Ireland. An international conference on migration heard how British-based Irish emigrants returning to Ireland experienced a racist mentality on return (O'Flynn, 2004). This gives the lie to 'Ireland of the Welcomes'. One participant commented that Irish people's attitudes to emigrants and their families returning to Ireland is a case of: 'come and visit us but don't stay.'

Challenges and conclusions

A number of key challenges and conclusions emerge from this overview of older return migration:

The invisibility challenge

The narratives of older return migrants are an important part of Irish social and cultural history. The extent to which the experiences and needs of older return migrants are distinctive to people who remained in Ireland is largely undocumented. The geographical patterns of settlement of older return migrants are relevant to the development of health, social care, public transport, and housing provision. Yet, there is limited data and limited analysis of the experience of older return migration. This results, first of all, in a certain cultural impoverishment as part of the story of Irish emigration and therefore the Irish nation, remains largely invisible, unheard and undocumented. Secondly, the public policy planning process may not be sufficiently informed by evidence of the needs of older Irish return migrants. Thirdly, knowing more about the process of re-settlement of older Irish migrants could help to address the obstacles that return migrants experience and make it easier for others to come home.

The challenge of defining older return migration

There is no standard meaning of return migration in national or international policy and law. Employing a variable of place of residence one year previously and residence outside for at least a year (previously in Census questions) certainly generates important data but it provides a limited definition of older return migration. This methodology does not capture data on what might have been temporary return migration and it does not identify a form of migration where older people might journey back and forward to family in the country of origin and the country of destination. Establishing at what point 'older' migration is different to pre-retirement migration is a further challenge. Currently, older migration is generally accepted as 65 years of age and over. Numbers in the pre-retirement category aged 45–64 are significantly higher than in the 65+ age group. The dispersion of people in the pre-retirement category towards the upper end of the age range is probably as relevant to defining 'older' return migration as the numbers aged 65+.

Small numbers of older return migrants

The review of data on older return migration clearly suggests that the majority of emigrants, if deciding to return to Ireland, do so before they reach 65 years of age. The actual numbers of older return migrants is in the region of hundreds per annum. The reasons for the low level of older return migrants may reflect stronger family and kinship bonds in their country of destination *vis-à-vis* Ireland, the extent of their economic resources and the cost of living, quality of life issues and health and social care considerations.

In conclusion, while older return migration is an established aspect of Irish demography, it is more often an aspiration than a reality for the vast majority of older Irish emigrants. However, for those that do re-settle here, there is a continuing dearth of data on and analysis of their experiences. This has implications for public policy planning, for how public services engage with the needs of older return migrants and also for planning to support older return migration.

Chapter 7

Ageing and the new communities in Ireland

Joe Moran

Introduction

The preliminary results of the 2006 Census of Ireland notes that almost ten per cent of the population consists of people who classify themselves as citizens from other states (CSO, 2006). This is an increase of four per cent since the 2002 Census (CSO, 2002). The extent of immigration into Ireland over the past decade is one of the most extraordinary aspects of a changing Irish society, only surpassed by the events which have led to this immigration, sustained economic development and wealth creation, which have pushed Ireland close to the top of the league of wealthy nations.

Most migrants, as we know from our own history in Ireland, tend to come from the younger age bracket of the sending society (Conroy, 1999). When we think of immigrants and those who make up new communities[1] we tend to think of younger adults in the prime of their lives. Our image of a typical immigrant does not normally conjure up a picture of an older person. It is undoubtedly true that the vast majority of immigrants are made up of young adults and sometimes their children. Older people, in general, do not make the same journey as their young adult children, to seek work in order to provide for their own and their family's future. Yet some older people do embark on that journey and inevitably, younger immigrants who remain in the country to which they migrate, become older immigrants.

The invisibility of older immigrants is not just in the mind's eye of the individual. Older immigrants are quite often invisible to the state and service providers. In the Irish context we assume that there are relatively few older immigrants, although the exact statistics to support this assertion are not

1 The terms new communities, ethnic minorities, black and minority ethnic groups and immigrants are all used interchangeably in this chapter – while it is not always correct to equate them, to use them with explanations and caveats would cause unnecessary confusion for the reader.

readily available. We do know that amongst the economic immigrant communities there are a small number of older people (CSO, 2006). We also know that among refugee communities in Ireland there is an older population, especially among programme refugees (people invited into the state for resettlement purposes, such as the Vietnamese in the early 1970s and the Bosnians in the 1990s). Likewise a small number of older people claim asylum in Ireland (ORAC, 2004; 2005). The first major problem one is confronted with in trying to address the issue of ageing and new communities is the lack of comprehensive statistical data. The second problem is that there are no services established in Ireland specifically for older people from new communities; nor are there any policy positions, papers, or statements which directly address their needs. Much of what is written in this chapter is therefore, based on materials from other countries. Even this material from these other countries contains regular criticisms from the various authors about the lack of policy development for ageing and ethnic minorities in the contexts of the countries about which they are writing. Therefore, Ireland is not alone in its under-development of this policy area, but we do appear to lag far behind other countries.

Defining 'old age'

Old age is in many respects a socially constructed term based, in western societies, on the ability to be of economic use. One enters old age at 65 years in Ireland, which is determined by the current retirement age from paid employment. This age is not absolute in western countries; we have seen it shift in time, as it has been influenced by a number of different and interrelated factors such as the needs of the economy, social advancement, political necessity and physical capacity. Therefore, while the definition of old age refers to retirement in Europe it refers to family status in other countries (Knapp and Kremla, 2002). The definition of old age is important for older people in new communities. The experiences of economic migrants and refugees require us to take a flexible approach to this definition. The UNHCR (United Nations High Commissioner for Refugees) says in its resettlement manual about older refugees:

> There is no fixed age to define an older refugee as older, largely because life expectancy differs among groups, and the process of ageing is affected by a number of factors, such as an individual's physical and psychological health, along with family and social support, cultural background, living conditions and economic situation (UNHCR 2004: IV 51).

For integration purposes refugee organisations tend to include those of 50 years and older. The reason for this is the potential or lack of potential for economic activity. Knapp and Kremla (2002) argue that the ability to work is crucial for integration in European societies, but that finding a job from this age becomes very difficult and this difficulty increases to near impossibility for refugees and migrants who seek work in the European Union at that age. A further problem in defining 'old age' is noted by Connelly et al. (2006). They say that refugees may come from societies where exact date of birth is not deemed important or where 'an individual's documents show an older or younger age through inaccurate, lost or altered records' (Connelly et al., 2006: 4).

Patel (1999) in her consultations with older people from minority ethnic groups was informed that the challenge was to assist these groups to move socially, economically and psychologically towards the age norm for society. It is accepted that 65 years, the age of retirement, is currently the beginning of old age in Ireland. However, what is important for policy makers and service providers to note is that the ageing process for immigrants, and in particular for refugees, begins earlier than for the majority population. This fact should be recognised and taken into account when decisions about the needs of older people from immigrant groups are being made.

Immigration and population change in the European Union and Ireland

Lanzieri (2006) in his analysis of population projections for Eurostat states that the population of the European Union is likely to decline in the first half of this century, but there are exceptions, including Ireland, where the population is predicted to increase substantially. During the same period the share of the older population in the European Union will increase considerably both in relative and absolute terms. The number of persons 80 years and over is projected to nearly triple from 18 million in 2004 to approximately 50 million in 2051 (Lanzieri, 2006). In Ireland the trend is for increased population growth, to almost 5.5 million by 2050 and for an increase in the older population from 11.9% to 25.9% during the same period. Ireland's population is ageing but in comparison to most of the other EU countries it is still relatively young (Eurostat, 2006; NCAOP, 2005).

In 2004 the total number of non-nationals (people from outside the EU) living in the EU was around 25 million or 5.5 percent of the total population (Eurostat, 2006). In the 2002 Irish Census 5.8% of the population was non-Irish nationals (just above the comparable EU figure). This has increased to an estimated 10% of the population in the 2006 Census (CSO, 2006). According to the 2002 data the non-national population in the EU was dominated by young adults, while the most significant relative difference in age structure to be observed was for the age group over 65 years. The relative differences for this age group were 17 percent of the total EU population is over 65 while only nine percent of the immigrant population was above that age (Eurostat, 2006). Thus, immigration tends to rejuvenate populations in the short term but inevitably in time these populations also contribute to the older population.

What these trends in population change and immigration mean for Ireland is that in the short to medium term the number of immigrants who are older will continue to be substantially less than for the population as a whole. Statistical details show that approximately 1% of all immigrants who came to Ireland between 2001 and 2006 were 65 and over, that is 3,534. However, this does not mean that they are all from new communities, as many of these people are returned Irish emigrants. Of the total number of 353,400 people who immigrated into Ireland between 2001 and 2006 almost 36% or 126,400 were Irish nationals returning to Ireland (CSO, 2006).

In short we do not know with any accuracy how many older people from new communities live in Ireland. Such a scenario brings with it many challenges to meeting the needs of older people from these new communities. In Great Britain in 2000 it was estimated that just over 7% of the population were people from the minority ethnic population and of that population just over 7% were older people and yet 'the ethnic dimension with regard to social inequalities among older people has been largely overlooked in public policy' (Age Concern, 2002). There is no evidence to show that older people from minority communities in Ireland fare any better. Just as in Britain, there is little national data available about our population of ethnic minority older people. As highlighted in other contributions to this volume, there is much neglect of older people from the majority population, and on that basis it is unlikely that a smaller sub-section of older people from new communities will enjoy better lives than their majority population counterparts.

International policies on older people and migrant communities

United Nations and World Health Organisation

There are a number of international instruments, principles and action plans that refer to older people and within these there are some references to migrant older people. The *Vienna International Plan of Action on Ageing* in 1982 was the first instrument on ageing endorsed by the United Nations General Assembly. This instrument had the aim of strengthening governments' and civil societies' capacity to deal effectively with the ageing of the population. Recommendations for action were made in areas such as:

- Health and nutrition
- Protection of elderly consumers
- Housing and environment
- Family
- Social welfare
- Income security and employment
- Education

(UN, 1982)

While the *Plan of Action* consists of broad guidelines and principles it suggests that more specific approaches and policies must be determined 'in terms of the traditions, cultural values and practices for each country or ethnic community, and programmes of action must be adapted to the priorities and material capacities of each country or community' (UN, 2006). The endorsement of the plan was followed eight years later with the adoption of the *United Nations Principles for Older Persons.* The eighteen principles are clustered into five key areas relating to the status of older people: independence, participation, care, self-fulfilment and dignity (UN, 1990)

In 2002 the Second World Assembly on Ageing held in Madrid called for 'changes in attitudes, policies and practices at all levels in all sectors so that the enormous potential of ageing in the twenty-first century may be fulfilled' (UN, 2002b). The Assembly developed a plan, which promotes an intergenerational policy approach that pays attention to all age groups with the objective of creating a society for all ages and a shift from developing policy *for* older people towards the *inclusion* of older people in the policy-making process. The UN identified three priority directions: older persons and development, advancing health and well-being and ensuring enabling and supportive environments for older people.

The *Madrid International Plan of Action on Ageing* (UN, 2002b) document extensively lays out how ageing should be treated in the new millennium, primarily linking ageing to other more general frameworks for social and economic development and human rights. The document also includes an objective directly related to the integration of older migrants in their new communities. Under 'Goal 34, Objective 3: Integration of older migrants within their new communities', there are a number of recommendations:

- Encourage supportive social networks for older migrants
- Design measures to assist older migrants to sustain economic and health security
- Develop community-based measures to prevent or offset the negative consequences of urbanization, such as the establishment of centres for older persons

- Encourage housing design to promote intergenerational living, where culturally appropriate and individually desired
- Assist families to share accommodation with older family members who desire it
- Develop policies and programmes that facilitate, as appropriate, and as consistent with national laws, the integration of older migrants into the social, cultural, political and economic life of countries of destination to encourage respect for those migrants
- Remove linguistic and cultural barriers when providing public services to older migrants (UN, 2002b)

The World Health Organisation, in its policy document *Active Ageing: A Policy Framework* (2002), provides an international framework by stressing 'active ageing', the process of optimising opportunities for health, participation and security in order to enhance quality of life as people age. Eight determinants guide this framework. Two of them, culture and gender, are crosscutting, in that they influence the other determinants and shape responses to them. The other six are:

- Health and social services
- Behavioural
- Personal factors
- Physical environment
- Social environment
- Economic determinants

European commitment

Following the *Madrid International Plan of Action on Ageing* (UN, 2002b) the United Nations Economic Commission for Europe (UNECE) held a Ministerial Conference on Ageing in Geneva. Ireland was represented at that conference. This Conference committed the European countries that participated to take many significant measures in the interests of older people. These included a reference to migrant workers. Under Commitment 5, which is 'to enable labour markets to respond to the economic and social consequences of population ageing', paragraph 37 specifically addresses the issue of older migrant workers as follows:

> In many countries, migrant workers who arrived in earlier decades in the host country are now growing older. Special needs of ageing migrants should be taken into consideration, as appropriate, and consistent with national laws in the design and implementation of programmes to facilitate their participation in the social, cultural and economic life of countries of destination. As migrants and as older

persons, they may face further disadvantages, which may be exacerbated by poor economic conditions. Governments should strive to develop measures to assist older migrants to sustain economic and health security. It is especially important to promote a positive image of their contribution to the host country and respect for their cultural differences. (UNECE, 2002b: Para. 37)

The European Union supports the approach taken by the UN and has developed a variety of policy responses to the needs of older people beginning with *Towards a Europe for All Ages* (Commission of the European Communities, 1999) suggesting that closer co-operation between Member States would be of benefit to this issue. The EU policy approach to ageing is set out in a communication from the European Commission and the European Parliament in its response to the 2nd World Assembly in 2002. It says that ageing should not be treated as a separate issue to be tackled in isolation from others. The EU response to ageing is addressed through the Lisbon Strategy which encompasses 'the economic, employment and social implications of ageing' (Commission of the European Communities, 2002: 5). The approach is to ensure that ageing is part of the broader development of social protection within the EU.

Ireland's policies on older people

The first policy document on older people in Ireland was *The Care of the Aged Report* (Government of Ireland, 1968). Twenty years later, *The Years Ahead: A Policy for the Elderly* (Department of Health, 1988) was published and this remains the 'most significant national policy document exclusively dedicated to older people' (NCAOP, 2005: 32). The National Health Strategy, *Quality and Fairness: A Health Strategy for You* (Department of Health and Children, 2001a) includes the development of health care for older people. Two very important documents which have added to the debate on ageing in Ireland were published in 2005. They were the National Council on Ageing and Older People's *An Age Friendly Society: A Position Statement* (NCAOP, 2005) and the National Economic and Social Forum's *Care for Older People* (NESF, 2005). Through these documents one can see that the trend in Ireland on age issues is to move towards international best practice and the incorporation of international instruments and principles in policies as they apply to older people. Yet to date there is almost no reference to the needs of older people from new communities.

Only one of the documents, *Care for Older People* (2005), says anything at all about the needs of ethnic minority groups (Travellers are not included in this category, they are categorised on their own). In a chapter on those it describes as groups of older people at particular risk, the NESF states that policies for the majority of older people must be balanced with those who have specific needs. Ethnic minority groups are identified as one of those groups. The report says 'as Ireland becomes a more multi-cultural society it is important that services are delivered in a culturally and linguistically appropriate manner' (NESF, 2005: 82). While it is important that there is at least a reference to ethnic minority communities, what is said is very limited and certainly falls far short of the commitments sought in the *Madrid International Plan of Action on Ageing*. It is evident from the materials available on the needs of older people in Ireland that the needs of those in new communities barely register on the policy agenda.

The socio-economic needs of older people from new communities

National Council on Ageing and Older People (NCAOP, 2005) refers to the inadequacies in information for planning purposes for older people. The older people referred to here are older people from the Irish population. Information on the socio-economic circumstances of older people from ethnic minority groups (including older Travellers) is non-existent in Ireland. The lack of such information is not only a feature of Irish public policy; it is also problematic in the UK where the population of black and minority ethnic older people as a proportion of the population is far greater than it is in Ireland. Age Concern (2002: 1) claims that this is because the ethnic dimension of inequalities among older people has been 'largely overlooked' in public policy. Butt and O'Neil (2004: 5) remark on the 'sheer quantity' of research material available in Britain on older black ethnic minority groups but point out that much of it is 'small scale local studies' and that it does not address the 'incidence and prevalence of need'.

Older people from new communities have at the very least the same needs as the general population of older people and, as we shall see, more than those needs. From a review of various research documents and writings on the needs of older black and minority ethnic groups in the UK and other European countries a number of common themes emerge. These are: family, isolation, income and poverty, health, accessing welfare services and accommodation and care (Barnard and Pettigrew, 2003; Evandrou, 2000, 2003; Evandrou and Falkingham, 2004; Age Concern, 2002; Butt and O'Neil, 2004; Caritas Europa, 2006; Office of the Deputy Prime Minister (ODPM), 2006; Livingstone and Sembhi, 2003; Bowes, 2006; Grundy, 2006; PRIAE, 2004; Yu, 2000).

Family support

Family members, both within and outside of households, are important for support of older people from ethnic minority communities. However, it cannot be assumed that such support is uniformly available across all ethnic groups. A variety of distinctive social and family patterns exist within migrant groups reflecting different demographic structures and cultural differences across the immigrant population (Evandrou, 2000). There is evidence which shows that older people from minority ethnic groups prefer to be supported by their family in their own home (PRIAE, 2004). Yet it is not always possible for this to happen as it is shown across Europe that increasing numbers of older women from ethnic minority communities are living alone, reflecting patterns in the wider population (PRIAE, 2004).

It is not always the case that older migrants have their families with them as the act of migration may have separated close relatives (Grundy, 2006; PRIAE, 2004). There is also evidence to suggest that not all immigrant families wish to look after their older members (Yu, 2000; Butt and O'Neil, 2004). Yu (2000) found in her study of Chinese older people that their middle-aged children's ability to provide care for them was often exaggerated. Changing family patterns at the end of the twentieth century in the western world have impacted not only on the majority community but also on minority communities, even if to the outside world they appear to be stable and less influenced by change. Therefore, there can be no assumptions made that older people will automatically be taken care of by family just because they are from an ethnic minority community (Butt and O'Neil, 2004). Multi-generational households are often not places of support for ethnic minority older people, as conflict, loneliness and containment can replace care (Butt and O'Neil, 2004).

Isolation

Butt and O'Neil (2004:10) point to a number of studies which suggest that many older people from minority ethnic communities experience a 'lack of support, isolation and loneliness'. Yu (2000) found that Chinese older people were not only isolated from the mainstream community but they are also detached from the Chinese community. This is due to a number of factors relating to economic and cultural issues. The isolation experienced by older black and ethnic minority groups is also experienced by those who care for them. Butt and O'Neil (2004) refer to studies which state that, just as in the white community, black and ethnic carers are 'unsupported and isolated' and these carers are mostly women. Age Concern (2002) states that there is evidence to suggest that older people from black and ethnic minority groups who lack access to public services and information can be isolated from their peers. Through a number of consultative meetings with black and ethnic minority older people Age Concern learned that these older people 'felt less lonely and isolated when they were able to meet up with people who shared similar experiences and spoke the same language' (2002: 6).

Income and poverty

In the UK people from ethnic minority communities are more likely to experience unemployment than their white British counterparts and when in work are more likely to be in low paid work with no occupational pension schemes (Age Concern, 2002; Evandrou and Falkingham, 2004). As a result older people from new communities are likely to experience an increased risk of poverty. This problem is likely to be worse for first generation ethnic minority immigrants as they usually migrate during their working life and thus make fewer contributions towards their pensions (Age Concern, 2002; Evandrou and Falkingham, 2004). It would not be true to say that all of those from new communities will experience poverty or the same degree of poverty. In the UK there are specific minorities that have better employment outcomes than others with its consequent impact on levels of poverty (Age Concern, 2002; Office of the Deputy Prime Minister ODPM, 2005). Such variations have been found in other countries too. However, PRIAE (2004) found, in its comparative study of a number of European countries, that there were significant numbers of older people from ethnic minority groups on lower incomes than the average for older people.

Health

There is evidence that people from ethnic minority groups are likely to be in poor general health and more likely to have specific health conditions (ODPM, 2005; PRIAE, 2004; Age Concern, 2002). Evandrou (2000) found in her analysis of six years of data from the British General Household Survey that older people from ethnic minority communities are more likely to report poor health during the previous year. Between ethnic groups differences in health also emerged; there is 'significant diversity in the prevalence of chronic ill-health and disability in later life by ethnicity' (Evandrou, 2005: 19). People from ethnic minority communities have been shown to be the highest users of primary care services but are less likely to gain access to appropriate health services (Age Concern, 2002).

Health problems are not restricted to physical health. Butt and O'Neil (2004) say that there is evidence that ill health may be accompanied by a risk of dementia and depression. It is suggested that ageing, relative socio-economic deprivation and immigrant status may lead to a greater vulnerability to mental ill-health in these groups (Rait et al., 1996 referred to by Livingstone and Sembhi, 2003; Moran, 2005). Livingstone and Sembhi make the point that the changes in the lives of immigrants influenced by a new cultural environment are not given sufficient consideration; there is a lack of consideration of how these lives are affected by a range of factors which make for different experiences of migration.

Accessing welfare services

A recurring theme through the literature on ethnic minority older people is the difficulty they have in accessing services from which they would benefit. In Yu's (2000) study 97 per cent of respondents found it difficult to use social services claiming that inability to speak English, lack of information about social and public services and the costs of these services were common difficulties encountered by the Chinese older people. Barnard and Pettigrew (2003) carried out a study for the UK's Department for Work and Pensions, to explore the barriers to the take-up of benefits among black and minority ethnic older people. They found that a number of barriers existed which prevented these older people from claiming benefits. These included: language barriers, concerns about the impact of making a claim on residency status, lack of a social insurance number, literacy problems, ignorance about the benefits system and fear of contacting statutory service providers.

Other barriers to accessing services are identified by Age Concern (2002: 4) such as racism – 'overt and often inadvertent', inadequate support from family, negative experiences of retirement and lack of consultation with relevant communities in the planning and delivery of services. Bowes (2006: 743) refers to other research which highlights 'the unsuitability of services for people with distinctive cultural systems'. The problem of accessing welfare services seems to be widespread. Butt and O'Neil (2004: 9) say that 'much of the available literature demonstrates lack of knowledge and under use of social care services by black older people irrespective of age and disability'. Furthermore, service providers are at times directly at fault for the poor take-up of services through their lack of responsiveness to the needs of service users. Bowes (2006: 750) makes the point that services tend 'to stereotype the needs and wants of older people'.

Accommodation and care

'For many immigrants lack of adequate housing forms a huge obstacle to integration into the host society' (Caritas Europa, 2006: 41). The lack of good accommodation is a serious problem for many ethnic minority groups. They often live in the worst type of accommodation with the poorest of amenities (Butt and O'Neil 2004). Evandrou (2000) highlights that older people from ethnic minority backgrounds live in households with the greatest number of people, and as a result within some groups there is overcrowding. Despite changes in family structure many of the older people from black and ethnic minorities live with their extended families. Where long-term care may be needed existing services are too often ill-prepared to meet such needs – 'historically there have been difficulties in recognition of the needs of [black and ethnic minorities], in service design, planning, assessment and delivery' (Patel, 1999: 269).

For these groups a lack of supply of culturally appropriate care facilities may prevent older people and their families from using existing services and thus add stress to carers as well as accentuate feelings of guilt (Patel, 1999). Furthermore, good care is 'not about being culturally sensitive to the exclusion of competence, quality and value of care' (Patel and Traynor, 2006: 18). Those with particular care needs, such as those with dementia or suffering from elder abuse are especially vulnerable in services which do not adequately meet their full range of needs. One of the problems related to the area of accommodation and care is that the whole 'area of aspirations and expectations of older people from minority ethnic groups is largely unexplored by researchers' (ODPM, 2003: 3). Nonetheless, some basic issues to consider in providing older people from new communities with appropriate accommodation and care include: acknowledging cultural, ethnic and religious identity; the location; engaging with minority communities; engaging with the wider community; and consideration of the physical and social environment of care facilities so that they meet the differing needs of the service users (Patel, 1999; Patel and Traynor, 2006).

Refugees and asylum seekers

Many of the issues outlined in the previous section are relevant to refugees and asylum seekers but there are some features of the lives of these forced migrants which need to be considered separately. United Nations High Commission for Human Rights (UNHCR, 2004) identifies older refugees as 'particularly vulnerable' having possibly been separated in flight from their families, friends and community. They may have witnessed relatives being killed and are also vulnerable to the impact of the hardship of flight, especially if they were already frail.

'Refugees are more at risk of severe illness than nationals and migrants' (Knapp and Kremla, 2002: 24). By its very nature forced exile brings some stresses which tend to be different from those of economic migrants (Moran, 2005). Health – physical and mental – is one particular area that is impacted on by the experience of forced migration. Individuals may have been tortured or witnessed torture or death. The physical effort to flee from one country to another in fear of being caught, the experience of uncertain status and future in the country in which one arrives, separation from cultural familiarity, language and homeland, living conditions in the host country and discrimination experienced both on grounds of age and ethnicity, all add to physical and mental health problems for older asylum seekers and refugees (Knapp and Kremla, 2002).

While there is some literature on the housing needs of asylum seekers and refugees in Ireland there is none on the specific housing needs of older asylum seekers and refugees (Bradley and Humphries, 1999; Moran, 2005). Many of the issues which confront minority ethnic groups in relation to accommodation are also applicable to asylum seekers. However, forced dispersal and direct provision policies by government are particular to asylum seekers. Direct provision accommodation provides basic accommodation for asylum seekers but it has been found to be inadequate to meet the needs of this group (SONAS, 2005).

Information on older refugees and asylum seekers in Ireland is difficult to obtain as there is very limited statistical or other data available on these groups in general, never mind on specific sub-groups such as older people. The Office of the Refugee Applications Commissioner (ORAC) in its Annual Report for 2004 said that only one per cent of asylum seekers for that year were over 55 years of age. In its 2005 Annual Report ORAC reported that the figure was at almost half of the 2004 number – 0.6%. Thus clearly the majority of asylum seekers who come to Ireland are younger people. Once asylum seekers obtain refugee status they may bring close relatives to Ireland under the state's family reunification scheme as outlined in the Refugee Act 1996, as amended. However, this scheme is restrictive and only older people (such as parents or other close relatives) may be granted permission to join their relatives if they can be shown to have been 'dependent' on them in the past (Government of Ireland, 1996). Programme or quota refugees, those invited by the government to come to Ireland for resettlement, are more likely to have older people in their midst, as they are more likely to enter the state in family groups. Examples of these programme refugees who have come to Ireland over the past 30 years are the Vietnamese, Bosnians, Kosovars and more recently, in 2006, a group of Iraqi Kurds who have all been given permission to resettle in Ireland (Sheridan, 2006). These groups of invited refugees are relatively small amidst an increasing immigrant population since the mid-1990s.

Conclusion

The main limitation on attempting to write about older people and new communities in Ireland is that there is little information to assist in this work. Statistics and data are in short supply; the usual social and economic policy commentators have as yet to turn their attention to this issue; agencies working to support older people in Irish society have to date said nothing about the needs of older migrants in Ireland (apart from returning Irish emigrants); and there are no academic papers written on the subject. It is therefore only possible to highlight the key issues for older minority ethnic groups from the experiences of other countries. While this is helpful it does not provide an Irish angle and is therefore ultimately limited. Even where it is possible to find international materials on the needs of older ethnic minority groups, the paucity of such information is frequently raised.

What is evident though is that at international level some efforts have been made to place the needs of older minority groups and migrants on the international agenda in the context of ageing in general. But this appears to have made little impact on policy makers in Ireland since the first international plan on ageing, the *Vienna International Plan of Action on Ageing*, was launched in 1982. An argument may be made that the number of older immigrants in Ireland is small even now, and to focus on such a small group would have been unwarranted from a policy perspective given the requirement to address the broader issues that increased immigration merits. The problem with this argument is that the broader issues have not been addressed either.

In 1999 the Department of Justice, Equality and Law Reform published a document entitled *Integration: A Two Way Process* (Department of Justice, Equality and Law Reform, 1999b). At the time this was to be the blue print for refugee integration into Irish society. This document has never been implemented. Little has occurred since then to assist with the integration of refugees into Irish society. The same can be said regarding economic immigrants – despite the fact that much is made of integrating these new workers into Irish society there is no strategy to do so. Ireland, along with other countries within the EU, has failed to live up to its commitments to combat poverty and social exclusion of immigrants. In its analysis of the National Action Plans for Social Inclusion 2003–5 the European Commission states that more determined action is needed across Europe to assist immigrants who are at risk of poverty and social exclusion. The Commission says that 'many countries still fail to provide in-depth analysis of the factors leading to this situation. Little attention is given to promoting access to resources, rights, goods and services, in particular to appropriate healthcare' (Commission of the European Communities, 2004: 20).

There is no doubt that Ireland has some way to go in promoting the welfare of economic immigrants, refugees and asylum seekers. Older people from these new communities may be small in number now but they will increase in the coming decades. There is as much diversity within this group as there is within any other sector in society; some will do well and live out their lives into old age happily and fruitfully, but many will not, as the evidence from all western countries shows that immigrants are more likely to be poor than the general population. It is therefore time for government agencies and the voluntary and community sectors to begin taking into account and planning for the needs of older people from new communities. That is the immediate challenge ahead.

Chapter 8

Alzheimer's disease, activism and the pharmaceutical industry

Orla O'Donovan

Introduction

As part of a general upsurge of health activism and groups of people who identify themselves in biological terms, organisations mobilised around Alzheimer's disease have flourished internationally and in Ireland in recent decades. Throughout the western world, there has been a proliferation of 'NGOised' Alzheimer's disease movement organisations – well-resourced and professionalised organisations that speak on behalf of people with the disease and their carers. Closely allied to the Alzheimer's biomedical research enterprise, the Alzheimer's disease movement has played a crucial role in gaining biomedical and civic recognition of Alzheimer's as a disease (Fox, 1989; Moreira, forthcoming). In the politics of nosology, or the classification of diseases, the movement has triumphed in its mission to recast what was once regarded as a normal and routine aspect of ageing as a specific neurological disease entity. No longer is the cognitive decline associated with ageing something to which we should be resigned as part of a more general acceptance of the fragility and contingency of the human situation (Illich, 1994). In keeping with currently pervasive discourses on risk that assume human suffering can be averted through technical intervention, dementia has been reframed as a biomedical condition to be pre-empted, measured and managed (Lupton, 2000).

This chapter considers another but related sphere in which the Alzheimer's disease movement is proving to be a formidable political force in the pharmaceutical policy domain. Over the past few years Alzheimer's disease movement organisations in Europe, including the Alzheimer Society of Ireland, have been embroiled in a controversy about the public subsidisation of antidementia drugs. Struggles over the delineation of the boundaries between public and private responsibility for the payment of medicines, knowledge about the effectiveness of drugs and the appropriateness of pharmaceutical industry sponsorship of patients' organisations are just some of the dimensions of this controversy. It is one of a number of such controversies involving calls by pharmaceutical industry sponsored patients' organisations for greater access to medicines, calls that have been denounced as irrational because of the absence of sufficient scientific evidence of the drugs' effectiveness and their high costs. I use this controversy to explore the dynamics of Alzheimer's disease movement activism in Europe and the frames of understanding it promotes. It is also used to highlight the profound challenges entailed in patient participation in official processes of health technology assessment and decision-making about the public subsidisation of drugs. The antidementia drug controversy underscores tensions in contemporary state and EU discourses that extol patient participation in health policy making, but that also eulogise 'cost containment' and 'evidence-based' policy making. This controversy has particular relevance in the Irish context, where the state has historically shown an unusual willingness to subsidise medicines and where public expenditure on drugs has escalated dramatically in recent years (Barry et al., 2008), but also where recent reform proposals have called for a more stringent approach to public pharmaceutical expenditure and recognition of the adverse side effects of pharmaceuticals (see Commission on Financial Management and Control Systems in the Health System, 2003; Joint Oireachtas Committee on Health and Children, 2005).

The brief analysis presented here builds on a recent study of health activism in Ireland that considered dimensions of the 'cultures of action' (Klawiter, 1999) of Irish patients' organisations, including the constructions of their health cause, the identity banners they adopt, their political action repertoires and their framings of protagonists and antagonists (O'Donovan, 2007).[1]

The Alzheimer's disease movement

The heterogeneity of political mobilisations around health, which have multiplied in many countries in recent decades, is considered by Kyra Landzelius (2006: 529) who prompts us to think about the varying ways in which articulations of health activism are contributing to 'new metamorphoses in patienthood'. One current of health activism is 'moves to author and authorise patienthood', efforts to get recognition for disputed diseases and quests for a patient identity for people previously not recognised as being 'sick'. Another current is moves involving 'mutations in the category of the patient', as in the anti-ageing medicine movement, the euthanasia movement and health activism organised around preterm babies. Other currents of health activism push in the opposite direction and involve efforts to shed biomedical

1 This study was supported by the Royal Irish Academy's (RIA) Third Sector Research Programme.

definitions that exceptionalise and pathologise what are deemed normal life events and ways of being such as: birth, mental distress and deafness and constitute 'mutiny from patienthood'. The Alzheimer's disease movement is a clear example of a movement that has prevailed in its struggles to gain biomedical and civic authorisation of a previously unrecognised disease. It has succeeded in redefining people once regarded as just getting old as being diseased. This rapid definitional transformation is considered by Patrick Fox in an essay on the rise of the US Alzheimer's disease movement. In 1989 he noted that 'the disease has emerged from an obscure, rarely applied medical diagnosis to its characterization as the fourth or fifth leading cause of death in the United States in little more than 12 years' (Fox, 1989: 58). According to Fox, the transformation was the result of a coalescing of a number of factors, but crucial amongst these was the establishment of the National Institute on Aging in 1974, as an institute of the US National Institutes of Health, and the efforts of a small number of scientists to build up the research status and funding of the institute and justify its existence. When Fox interviewed Robert Butler, the first director of the National Institute on Aging, a psychiatrist and 'issue entrepreneur', Butler spoke about his efforts to establish Alzheimer's disease as a major biomedical research priority and thus attract federal funding for the newly established institute. He said

> I decided that we had to make it [Alzheimer's disease] a household word. And the reason I felt that, is that's how the pieces get identified as a national priority. And I call it the health politics of anguish. People don't die from basic research; they don't suffer from basic research. They suffer from specific diseases.
>
> (Fox, 1989: 82)

An essential strategy in this 'health politics of anguish' identified by the director of the National Institute on Aging was the mobilisation of carers of people with Alzheimer's disease and the establishment of a national voluntary organisation devoted to the disease. Hence, the US Alzheimer's Association which was subsequently established in the late 1970s (initially under a different name – The Alzheimer's Disease and Related Disorders Association) has its origins not so much in the 'grassroots' as its formation was largely 'led from above' by influential biomedical professionals and scientists. The interests and influence of these actors on the national organisation, which grew out of a sometimes tense amalgamation of a number of existing organisations, is evident in the definition of the organisation's cause which prioritised advocating for more investment in biomedical research into the disease.

In 1979 the first Alzheimer's disease organisation was established in Europe and since then there has been a spawning of similar organisations mobilised around the disease. By 2005, there were over 30 national associations in

Europe (Alzheimer Europe, 2005). Unlike their US counterpart, the first organisations established in Europe, in England and Ireland, were founded by carers and were not, initially at least, concerned with supporting biomedical research. The Alzheimer's Society in England was founded in 1979 by two women motivated by their personal experiences of caring for relatives with dementia. The Alzheimer's Society of Ireland was founded in 1982, again by two women caring for family members diagnosed with the disease. Initially, it operated out of an office in the home of one of the founders, but in 1987 it moved to an 'official office' in a nearby hospital and appointed its first employee (Bligh, 2003). By 2006, it employed almost 800 staff and had an annual income of €8 million, making it one of the largest disease-specific NGOs in Ireland and the biggest service provider for older people other than the state (interview with CEO of Alzheimer Society of Ireland, 21 November 2006). Activities of the organisation include: a helpline, information provision, a range of day centre, home care and respite services for people with the disease and their carers, and carers' support groups.

Transnationalisation has been a feature of Alzheimer's disease organisations in Europe over the past two decades and was formalised in 1990 when the Irish, Belgian, Dutch and Spanish Alzheimer's disease organisations established Alzheimer Europe. In 2007, the Luxembourg-based pan-European organisation had 31 member organisations from 26 countries (Alzheimer Europe, 2007). This organisation was established to promote collaboration between national level Alzheimer's disease organisations, but was also impelled by recognition of the increasing significance of EU institutions as policy-making arenas. In pharmaceutical policy the move away from national level decision-making, which has led some commentators to declare the nation state moribund as a chief site for the exercise of power (Robinson, 2003), is evident in the establishment of institutions such as the European Agency for the Evaluation of Medicinal Products (EMEA). The EMEA was established as an EU institution in 1995 with the introduction of a European system of licensing medicines for sale on the market; it is central to the move towards a single European market for pharmaceuticals. Alzheimer Europe strives 'to raise the awareness of all European institutions about Alzheimer's disease and other forms of dementia' (Alzheimer Europe, 2007), reminiscent of efforts to make Alzheimer's disease 'a household word' in the US during the 1970s. With the disease status of Alzheimer's now widely recognised in Europe, the organisation now strives (in competition with patients' organisations mobilised around other conditions) to establish the disease as an EU public health priority. The organisation has succeeded in having its representational claims legitimised by EU institutions and in its endeavours to get political presence in key EU decision-making fora. For example, in February 2006, it became one of the first organisations deemed to fulfil the criteria for patients' organisations to be involved in EMEA activities and was one of only two patients' organisations represented on the board of the EMEA.

The Alzheimer's disease movement has differed from other health movements, such as those mobilised around AIDS and breast cancer, in its general absence of self-advocacy and patient activists. Renée Beard's (2004a: 798) analysis of the US Alzheimer's Association reminds us that 'the Alzheimer's Disease (AD) movement was not initiated by, or originally intended for, people with the condition'. Similarly in Europe, carers and medical and other professionals have tended to be the instigators of and key actors in Alzheimer's disease organisations. A survey conducted by Alzheimer Europe (2005) found that of 31 national associations, only one (Alzheimer Scotland – Action on Dementia) had a person with dementia represented on its board of directors.

The movement's construction of the disease as involving a form of patienthood in which 'sufferers' are deficient has been identified as an obstacle to self-advocacy and as rendering these recently authorised patients mute in public life (Herskovits, 1995). Evident in the British Alzheimer's Society slogan 'Your brain is what makes you you', the movement's construction of the disease is rooted in dominant western perceptions of brain functioning as defining humanness. The movement has not challenged the norms of acceptable modes of communication; instead its construction of the disease renders the speech of people with the condition meaningless. As Elizabeth Herskovits (1995: 53) puts it, a 'debased personhood', a 'loss of self' and a 'monsterising of senility' have been implicit in the movement's construct of the disease. This construction of Alzheimer's disease patienthood is akin to the understanding of madness in the classical period, discussed by Michel Foucault (2001: 109) as 'nothingness' and 'non-being'. Not only does the disease stop you 'being you', as suggested by the Alzheimer Society of Ireland's disease awareness slogan that emphasises the potential for antidementia medications to 'keep you being you', it stops you from being; it is a living death. Below, I discuss how this initial construction of the disease and its associated patienthood is currently being reimagined within the movement. Early diagnosis and medical treatment of the disease are now widely believed to be enabling a new and active form of Alzheimer's disease patienthood.

The antidementia drug controversy

In 1996, the first antidementia medication was launched on the US market, not as a cure for Alzheimer's, but as a means of stemming the progression of the disease. Belonging to a class of drugs known as cholinesterase inhibitors, donepezil's launch was accompanied by its acclaim in medical journals for having produced 'highly significant improvements in cognitive and clinical global assessments' (Maggini et al., 2006: 1) in clinical trials. Since then, other cholinesterase inhibitors have been licensed for sale (galantamine and rivastigmine), but donepezil remains the number one selling drug for Alzheimer patients worldwide and in Ireland. According to its manufacturers, more that 3.8 million people have been treated with the drug (Aricept.com, 2006). In Ireland it is widely prescribed and compared to other countries' public subsidisation of the drug is largely unrestricted. Unlike elsewhere, it does not have to be prescribed by a medical specialist and it is publicly subsidised for medical cardholders who are deemed to be in any stage of the disease. In 2004, donepezil was number 18 in the top 100 drugs in terms of expenditure under the medical card scheme. Under this scheme, public expenditure on the drug in 2004, excluding the dispensing fee paid to pharmacies, was in excess of €7 million and 61,296 prescription items for the product were issued (Director of the National Centre for Pharmacoeconomics, 2006).

Despite the widespread prescribing and consumption of antidementia medications, and the active involvement of Alzheimer disease organisations in disease awareness campaigns that promote them, their effectiveness is highly contested. In 1997 the independent *Drug and Therapeutics Bulletin*, which analysed published clinical trial data on donepezil concluded the evidence of its effectiveness was unconvincing (Collier, 1998). A systematic review of clinical trial data, published in 2005, concluded that because of flawed methods and small clinical benefits, the scientific basis for recommending the three drugs licensed for the treatment of mild to moderate Alzheimer's disease was questionable (Kaduszkiewicz et al., 2005). Public bodies in some countries have refused to subsidise the drugs (such as the provincial government in British Columbia, Canada) and in others such as Britain and Romania, restrictive measures have been introduced on the grounds that they do not work for many patients and are a waste of money. Draft guidance was issued in 2005 by the British National Institute for Health and Clinical Excellence (NICE) to restrict NHS prescribing of antidementia drugs to people with moderate Alzheimer's disease, and to discontinue the prescribing of them for people in the early and late stages of the disease became the eye of a storm about antidementia drugs. This institute is commissioned by the British Department of Health to develop clinical guidelines for public health, health technologies and clinical practice. Not only did this draft guidance, which was based on a review of data on the drugs' clinical and cost effectiveness, provoke angry opposition from the London-based Alzheimer's Society, which argued the decision amounted to 'counting pennies' while 'destroying lives', it also prompted irate patients' organisation rumblings further a field, from Alzheimer Europe and its member organisations including the Alzheimer Society of Ireland (Alzheimer Society, 2006b). Despite the mobilisation of a very high profile and active campaign to oppose the NICE guidance, it came into force in November 2006 thereby reducing the level of public subsidisation of antidementia drugs in Britain. At the time of writing, the storm continues as Eisai and Pfizer, the manufacturers of donepezil, together with the Alzheimer's Society, are taking legal action to seek a judicial review of the NICE guidance. Pressure to reverse the NICE decision has also come from other (arguably connected) sources. During an official visit, the US Deputy Health Secretary explained his conviction to the British Health Secretary that NICE rationing mechanisms were misguided and that 'a free market for the largely US-based major drug companies was a better idea' (Boseley, 2007). Presumably this is a 'free market' in which doctors can prescribe as they see fit, but where the state picks up the tab.

The involvement of Alzheimer Europe and its member organisations, including the Alzheimer Society of Ireland, in opposing the NICE guidance appears to have been driven by a fear that the NICE ruling could set a dangerous precedent for other European countries and also by the transnationalisation of Alzheimer disease movement activism mentioned earlier. Although the public subsidisation of drugs remains a preserve of national level policy, a press release from Alzheimer Europe cautioned other European countries against following the example set by Britain (Alzheimer Europe, 2006). Similarly, a statement from the Alzheimer Society of Ireland noted that 'the Society would not like this type of restriction applied in Ireland' and called on Irish general practitioners to disregard the directions from NICE (Alzheimer Society of Ireland, 2006a). The involvement of organisations outside Britain in the controversy can also be seen to reflect the extension of the 'field of contention' (Crossley, 2006) in which national-level organisations are involved as a result of the 'Europeanisation' of their activities, bringing them into new sites of struggle and interaction with more agents and organisations mobilised around similar concerns.

A puzzling aspect of the antidementia drug controversy is how Alzheimer's disease organisations' mobilisation around demands for the subsidisation of antidementia drugs can be explained, given the inconclusive scientific evidence of their efficacy? Let me briefly consider three possible explanations.

Patients' organisations enabling the covert pursuit of corporate interests

The consequences of patients' organisations acceptance of sponsorship from pharmaceutical corporations, a form of sponsorship that is now widespread, have come under increasing critical scrutiny. Defenders of such sponsorship highlight the mutual interests of the industry and patients' organisations and contend sponsorship has been a crucial enabler for many patients' organisations' advocacy activities (Kent, 2007). But critics point to inherent conflicts of interest and the potential for patients' organisations to enable the covert pursuit of corporate interests, particularly in respect of marketing masquerading as education (Mintzes, 2007). Marcia Angell (2004), former editor of the *New England Journal of Medicine,* argues that pharmaceutical industry sponsorship, frequently given to patients' organisations in the name of patient education, is simply a disguised form of marketing. She and many others regard the marketing activities of the pharmaceutical industry as a crucial force driving the expansion of the realm of biomedicine and the market for drugs, and cultivating a 'technoconsumption mindset'. This mindset interprets health as being advanced primarily through innovative medical technologies and promotes a reliance on costly new treatments that, according to these critics, are often marginally effective and sometimes dangerous (Deyo and Patrick, 2005). Marketing that turns previously healthy people into patients has been dubbed 'disease mongering' by its critics. For them, this 'selling of sickness' is exemplified by industry-funded disease awareness campaigns, which frequently involve alliances with patients' organisations. Disease mongering, it is argued, fosters unrealistic expectations about drugs and constitutes 'opportunistic exploitation of both a widespread anxiety about frailty and a faith in scientific advance and "innovation"' (Moynihan and Henry, 2006). Some commentators consider the promotion of antidementia drugs as a case in point of disease mongering (Maggini et al., 2006).

Specifically in the context of the antidementia drug controversy, the Chairman of NICE has cautioned that industry sponsorship of patients' organisations 'could lead to excessive pressure and unfair rulings about which medicines were made available' and that it undermines confidence in the organisations' independence (Mintzes, 2007). Alzheimer's disease movement organisations have also been singled out in media accounts of drug companies' efforts to 'enlist a major new ally in their struggle for profits' (Boseley, 2007). Alzheimer Europe is one of a number of organisations identified as supporting industry efforts to change EU legislation that restricts the advertising of medicines to members of the public.

Reflecting what has become the norm for Alzheimer's disease movement organisations throughout Europe, the Alzheimer Society of Ireland and Alzheimer Europe receives funding from pharmaceutical corporations that manufacture antidementia drugs. The two organisations frame these corporations as their allies in the fight against Alzheimer's disease and have long-established 'partnership' arrangements with them. Alzheimer Europe appears to be less shy about relying on the pharmaceutical industry than its national level equivalent, a trend that is also apparent in respect of patients' organisations mobilised around depression (O'Donovan, 2007). The Alzheimer Society of Ireland's disease awareness raising activities rely on grants from drug companies, as do some other activities. Its disease awareness campaign, launched in 2005, which includes: mass media advertisements, the distribution of information packs and an online 'health clinic', is supported by an educational grant from Pfizer, the marketing authorisation holder for donepezil in Ireland. Up to recently, Shire Pharmaceuticals sponsored the Alzheimer Society of Ireland's newsletter and its Dementia Recognition Awards – annual awards made to healthcare staff, carers and volunteers. Shire manufactures galantamine, another one of the controversial antidementia medications. Documents available on the Alzheimer Europe website provide ample evidence of the friendly relations between the pan-European organisation and pharmaceutical corporations on whom it relied for 37 per cent of its income in 2005 (Boseley, 2007). It provides details of network links with all of the manufacturers of antidementia drugs and outlines meetings with various pharmaceutical corporations at which 'barriers to access to treatment' (Alzheimer Europe, 2005c) and 'inequalities between European citizens' (Alzheimer Europe, 2005b) with regard to their access to drug treatments were discussed. The irony of these discussions is highlighted by the work of organisations such as Médécins Sans Frontières ('t Hoen, 2002) who struggle to expose the role played by the pricing and intellectual property rights policies favoured by the industry in denying millions of the world's poor access to essential medicines.

While acknowledging the significance of these alliances with the pharmaceutical industry, there is little evidence to support the suggestion that the Alzheimer organisations are simply hoodwinked into being 'fronts' for the pharmaceutical industry. The Alzheimer Society of Ireland relies on the industry to fund its disease awareness raising activities, but this sponsorship makes up a tiny proportion of its overall income. Unlike most other Irish patients' organisations, the Society receives substantial state funding. The same is true of the Alzheimer's Society in Britain; between 2002 and 2004, donations from the pharmaceutical industry amounted to just over 0.1 per cent of the Society's income (Alzheimer's Society, 2004). Furthermore, in the conversations I had with staff in the Alzheimer Society of Ireland, the quandaries associated with pharmaceutical industry sponsorship were acknowledged and spoken about at length. The rationale underpinning acceptance of the funding was that it enables the organisation to undertake important public awareness work that it could not otherwise afford to do and that the Society has procedures in place to ensure it is not compromised by the relationship. All in all, the partnership with Pfizer was constructed as reflecting a concurrence of interests, in which potential conflicts of interests are managed. Here, it is important to note that our study of patients' organisations in Ireland found that almost half of them receive pharmaceutical industry sponsorship. It provided evidence of a strong and growing cultural tendency in these organisations to frame pharmaceutical corporations as their friends and allies in their quests for better health. Furthermore, there is a widespread belief that organisation's autonomy can be protected through proper management of their relations with the pharmaceutical industry and adherence to voluntary codes of conduct.

This suggests that while relationships with the pharmaceutical industry are important, our analysis needs to consider not only the consequences of industry sponsorship, but also the cultural consonance that makes such friendly relations seem appropriate and possible in the first place.

Competing forms of knowledge?

As seen above, friendly relations with 'Big Pharma' are a feature of the cultures of action of many Alzheimer's disease organisations. However, these same organisations have been to the fore in highlighting the shortcomings of the kind of scientific knowledge produced with the assistance of the pharmaceutical industry. The British Alzheimer's Society, for example, has argued that significant benefits of antidementia medications are not the outcomes typically measured in clinical trials and that conventional scientific research fails to heed user-defined outcomes (Blume and Catshoek, 2002). That said, Alzheimer's organisations' opposition to the NICE guidance has emphasised weaknesses in the interpretation of the scientific data on the clinical efficacy of the drugs rather than weaknesses in the actual data, and also NICE's failure to adequately consider patients' and carers' assessments of the health technologies. For example, in the British Alzheimer Society's appeal submitted in June 2006, it argued that 'the conclusion that there is insufficient evidence to determine the clinical efficacy of memantine is perverse in light of the evidence' (Alzheimer Society, 2006c: 13). This view is echoed by Alzheimer Europe in its assertion that 'Enough clinical evidence exists to support the use of anti-dementia drugs and clinical trials have shown them to be effective not only in improving memory, but also for beneficial effects on behaviour and activities of daily living' (Alzheimer Europe, 2005). Alzheimer Europe goes on to say that the clinical data on the drugs' efficacy, data deemed by NICE to be of mixed quality and largely inconclusive, 'is supported by testimonies of great numbers of people with dementia and their carers.' In this regard, the CEO of the Alzheimer Society of Ireland described the NICE controversy as a clash between 'the lived experience' of carers of people with the disease and 'the intellectual argument' (Alzheimer Society of Ireland, 2006b). Alzheimer's disease organisations and others present patients' personal testimonies and assessments as key to resolving the impasse in the debate about the effectiveness of the medications (Moreira, 2007). Struggles to claim status and recognition for knowledge that is currently dismissed as being merely anecdotal are thus a significant dimension of the NICE controversy.

A further challenge to the NICE guidance concerns the decision to base prescribing decisions on MMSE (Mini Mental State Examination) scores.

NICE recommended that these scores be used to determine if a patient has mild, moderate or severe Alzheimer's disease and thus their NHS eligibility to drugs. In their opposition to the guidance, Alzheimer's organisations highlighted the absence of an 'exact science' for measuring the severity of the disease and argue the MMSE tool is unreliable and inappropriate. Here, it is important to note that Alzheimer's disease organisations promote an understanding of the disease that recognises difficulties not only with determining its severity but with the diagnosis itself. For example, in its disease awareness raising materials, the Alzheimer Society of Ireland states 'As there is no straightforward test for Alzheimer's disease, making a diagnosis is often difficult, particularly in the early stages' and that diagnosis is usually made by excluding other possible causes (Alzheimer Society of Ireland, n.d.: 10).

Resistance to the knowledge underpinning the NICE guidance has also involved rejection of the approach adopted for determining the drugs' cost effectiveness. Echoing the ongoing calls of many (especially feminist) commentators for recognition of 'love labour', according to the British Alzheimer's Society, the NICE guidance is based on a flawed economic model that fails to take the true costs of care services and the quality of life of carers into consideration (Alzheimer's Society, 2006a). Similarly, Alzheimer Europe makes the charge that the 'cost-effectiveness models used by the National Institute of Clinical Excellence fail to duly take into account effects on quality of life of carers of people with Alzheimer's disease' (Alzheimer Europe, 2006).

Alzheimer's disease movement organisations have not just argued that the model of cost-effectiveness employed by NICE was technically flawed, but that it was imbued with institutionalised ageism. The CEO of the Irish organisation has discussed the NICE dispute as evidence of the devaluing and stigmatisation of the 'grey army' and asks 'Is it because of age that it becomes less important to take the risk or spend the money?' (O'Connell, 2005: 4). The struggle against ageism and the paucity of interest in the field of biomedical research on older people's health has long been conceived as part of the mission of Alzheimer's disease movement organisations (Fox, 1989). Alternatively and paradoxically, the movements' endorsement of and entanglement with the biomedical quest for a cure for the disease can also be interpreted as fostering ageism. As articulated by Renée Beard (2004b: 416), biomedicine 'threatens to exacerbate an anti-aging mentality where biomedicine ultimately aims to "cure" aging itself. Such attempts to combat aging are symbolic of a cultural unwillingness to ascribe positive meaning to aging'. On these terms, the involvement of Alzheimer's disease organisations in the NICE controversy can be read as challenging ageism in the form of exposing and opposing a lack of official willingness to invest public money on healthcare for older people, but also, paradoxically, as promoting ageism through their engagement with medicalised efforts that construct old age as a sickness.

From the discussion so far, it can be seen that a complex set of logics underpinned Alzheimer's disease organisations' resistance of the NICE guidance. Let me now finally turn to a further changing dimension of the culture of action of the organisations that I regard as crucial to understanding their opposition, namely their reconstruction of Alzheimer's disease patienthood.

Reimagining Alzheimer's disease patienthood

Recent years have witnessed the imagination of a new form of Alzheimer's disease patienthood, enabled by the medicalised preservation of self. Shifts in the Alzheimer's disease biomedical research enterprise have been largely responsible for this expansion and reconfiguration of the movement's construction of patients. There has been a 'curbing of expectations' in the search for a cure and a move towards strategies that promote early diagnosis and drug therapies believed to modify and prevent progression of the neurodegenerative disorder (Moreira, 2007). Emphasis has shifted from the quest for a cure to damage limitation medical technologies and strategies that enable disease 'management'. As noted earlier antidementia drugs are now widely prescribed. Moves towards greater diagnostic expansion are currently afoot in efforts to have these drugs also licensed for the treatment of the new clinical entity Mild Cognitive Impairment (MCI) (Maggini et al., 2006). Renée Beard (2004a: 815) argues that these contemporary biomedical initiatives make 'organisational habits of paternalism' more difficult to sustain and will potentially transform Alzheimer's disease activism. Echoing the optimistic biomedical narratives of many Alzheimer's disease organisations, she talks about the 'vast contributions' that have been made in trying to eradicate the disease (Beard 2004a: 805). These include advances that allow much earlier diagnosis and the development and licensing of medications 'thought to slow decline in the early to moderate stages' of the disease. Consequently, she says 'For the first time in its history, it is possible that the AD movement will have to actively incorporate the voices of those afflicted with the disease' (Beard 2004b: 426).

These sentiments are very much in evidence in the pronouncements of European Alzheimer's disease organisations. In the 2004 Annual Report of Alzheimer Europe (2005: 22) it is noted that 'Early diagnosis has led to people with dementia being diagnosed at a stage when they are able to understand the diagnosis and take an active role in decisions affecting their lives'. It goes on to say that consequently Alzheimer's disease organisations 'can no longer merely focus on the needs of carers'. According to the Alzheimer's Society (2005: 3), in Britain 'Earlier diagnosis drugs for Alzheimer's disease and better awareness mean that more and more people with dementia are able and willing to speak out for themselves.' Commitment to the belief in antidementia medications as a means to empowering people, promoting their autonomy and enabling them to preserve their selfhood underpins the Alzheimer Society of Ireland's disease awareness raising activities. The new Alzheimer's disease patienthood is evident in one of the organisation's Pfizer-funded leaflets which states that along with a healthy lifestyle and other measures, 'medication can slow the progression of the symptoms of Alzheimer's disease – and keep you being you' (Alzheimer Society of Ireland, n.d.b). Therefore, alongside the advanced stage Alzheimer patient who is incapable of self-advocacy has emerged the patient in the early stages of the disease whose speech is meaningful and who has the capacity to be a patient activist.

There has also been a move away from ways of talking about Alzheimer's disease and those who have the condition that featured in the 'health politics of anguish' pursued in the early days of the Alzheimer's disease movement. The staff in the Alzheimer Society of Ireland described the organisation's efforts to promote positive representations of people with the disease and to change the way the condition is spoken about. It has circulated a guide for journalists writing about the disease that discourages the use of terms such as 'sufferers' of the disease, the 'burden of care', and euphemisms such as 'the long goodbye' and 'the living death' (Alzheimer Society of Ireland, 2006d). Furthermore, transformations in the action repertoires of Alzheimer's disease organisations that are occurring due to the reconstruction of patienthood include the establishment of support groups for Alzheimer patients themselves, the involvement of patients as 'partners' in steering biomedical research, and novel formats for conferences in which patients speak for themselves.

Alzheimer's disease movement organisations promote the idea that access to diagnostic and treatment technologies is not just an option resulting from biomedical advances, but a right. Publicising this idea is a key priority in the mission to advance the autonomy of people with dementia in the current business plan of Alzheimer Europe (2005: 9). Similar to many other patients' organisations, such as those formed around conditions such as asthma and diabetes, Alzheimer Europe and its member organisations operate on the assumption that there is a significant disparity between the prevalence of the disease and the number of people diagnosed. In other words, there is a large population of people who have the disease but do not know it, and these people are missing out on the self-preserving opportunities afforded by early diagnosis. The pan-European organisation argues that, amongst other reasons, the widespread under-diagnosis of the disease is why most Alzheimer's disease organisations 'rarely manage to represent as much as five per cent of their target population' (Alzheimer Europe, 2005a: 19).

In sum, belief in the efficacy of the drugs at the centre of the antidementia controversy is fundamental to the cultures of action of some Alzheimer's disease movement organisations in Europe. The conception of patienthood that they actively promote through disease awareness raising activities reflects a departure from previous movement constructs and underpins new ways of taking political action. The NICE guidance does not just threaten people with dementia's access to the contested medical technologies, it also poses a challenge to what has become a foundational truth of these health movement organisations.

Conclusion

This discussion of the antidementia drug controversy highlights a series of recent transformations in the cultures of action of certain Alzheimer's disease movement organisations in Europe. It shows how changes have occurred in organisational thinking and talk about the disease and those who have it, and in organisational practices. Many of these shifts have coincided with alterations in the Alzheimer's disease biomedical research enterprise, particularly the change in emphasis from the search for a cure to strategies of early diagnosis and medical 'management' of the disease. Changes both internal and external to the Alzheimer's disease movement, particularly the 'Europeanisation' of drug policy and movement organisations, have also transformed the 'field of contention' in which national organisations such as the Alzheimer Society of Ireland are players.

Recognition of these cultural shifts goes some way towards understanding puzzling aspects of the antidementia drug story, particularly the steadfastness of Alzheimer's disease organisations' belief in the efficacy of the controversial drugs. It is a certainty in a sea of scientific uncertainty that surrounds the disease, uncertainty about its diagnosis, methods of determining the stages of its progression and its treatment. The organisations recognise some of these uncertainties, but not others. The above discussion points to a complex set of logics underpinning the organisations' opposition to the NICE guidance to restrict NHS prescribing of the drugs. However, I have argued that crucial to understanding the organisations' perspective on the drugs is an appreciation of the investment they have made in belief in the ability of antidementia drugs to stave off the loss of self that is associated with the disease. It has become a core cognitive commitment of the movement organisations. Historically, this belief can be seen to emanate from optimistic biomedical narratives that have been a feature of the organisations since their genesis, but also it is a belief that has shaped the organisations' recent historical trajectories, and begot new institutional thinking and practices especially in respect of the novel Alzheimer's disease patient activist. A sceptical attitude towards the potential of antidementia drugs flies in the face of these significant organisational cultural shifts that are currently taking place. Viewed in this light, the NICE controversy is about much more than access to publicly subsidised antidementia medicines.

In the contemporary context in which public drug bills are spiralling and in which many governments are attempting to control and 'rationalise' this expenditure, this story raises profound questions about how the health policy-making process should proceed when there are significant discrepancies between 'expert' and patient assessments of medical technologies. Tensions arising from such discrepancies are likely to come more and more to the fore, not just because state institutions are increasingly extending invitations to patients' organisations to be 'partners in healthcare planning and evaluation' – to use the language of the 2001 Irish National Health Strategy (Department of Health and Children, 2001c), but because such organisations, with the support of their various allies, are demanding such political presence.

Chapter 9

Health care for older people

Suzanne Quin

Introduction

With increasing life expectancy, many can now expect to spend between one-fifth and one-quarter of their lifespan within the category of older people. Good health is of crucial importance in old age as it is at any other stage of the lifespan, but for older people it is 'the key determinant of their ability to remain independent and autonomous (Feldman, 1999: 272). As yet, the health system in Ireland has not had to deal with significant increases in the proportion of the population over 65 as has been the case in other countries within the EU and elsewhere. This is largely because of substantial emigration from Ireland in the 1930s, 1940s and 1950s (Fitzgerald, 2004). However, as Fitzgerald points out, this will change and by 2026 there will be a much higher proportion of the population over 65. While overall, older people have greater need for and greater usage of health care, the common assumption that an increasing proportion of older people within the population inevitably means substantially increased spending on health care is not necessarily the case. Fahey (1995), in his study of health expenditure across a number of countries found that the most important determinants of spending on health care was the relative wealth of the country and the way in which it funds its health services. In addition, while the proportion of older people in the population is predicted to grow (see chapter 3 above): most of them will be healthy for much of their lifetime. In relation to the older population in the UK for example, Pollock (2005: 167) comments that 'the vast majority of people over 65 are fit and healthy and able to look after themselves . . . Older people do consume more health care than younger people, but this is mainly because most health care expenditure takes place within the last year of life, as is equally true for people of all ages'. It is therefore the old within the older category that have the most needs and usage of health and it is this group (over 80) that is increasing at a greater rate than the older population as a whole (Department of Health and Children, 2001a: 41).

It is difficult to make comparisons between spending on health for older people in Ireland and what is spent in other countries on the same age cohort.

Clearly, the differing proportions of older population must be taken into account in any such comparison. A more important issue, however, is that in Ireland expenditure on personal social services is subsumed under the overall umbrella of health, structurally as well as in terms of funding. This obviously is of importance in relation to spending on services for older people whose need for personal social services would be much greater than the population as a whole (see chapter 11 below).

Complexity of need

One reason why older people use more health care is that in the later stages of life they may have more complex health needs in that they are more likely to suffer from long-term conditions such as chronic lung disease, heart disease and diabetes (Dr Foster Intelligence, 2006). Moreover, they may have a number of conditions simultaneously. This can result in dilemmas of treatment in that the appropriate treatment for one condition may be counter-indicated for another. In addition, their recovery time may be slower compared with a younger person, such as following surgery or rehabilitation after a stroke.

Eligibility for health care

Entitlement to publicly funded health services is determined by income. All Irish residents belong to Category 1 or Category 2 eligibility. Those in Category 1 hold what is known as a medical card which entitles the holder to free general practitioner service with a choice of doctor, providing that the practitioner of choice is listed to take medical card patients and has not exceeded their quota. In addition the medical cardholder is entitled to prescribed medicines free of charge, to all hospital out-patient and in-patient services (in a public ward, including consultant charges). They are also entitled to free dental, ophthalmic and aural services and appliances, though the provision of these services is limited and often involves long waiting periods. Those in Category 2 are also entitled to hospital care in a public ward (subject to limited charges), but must pay for their general practitioner services and for prescribed medicines. There is provision for those suffering from a limited range of conditions to get free those prescribed medications necessary for that condition and, in addition, a drug refund scheme is available to all in Category 2 who spend more than a specified amount per month on prescribed medicine.

It will be evident from the description above, that eligibility for Category 1 is of considerable importance for older people, given their greater need for and use of health services. In addition, in the context of the increasing focus on health promotion of older people, which will be discussed in more detail later in this chapter, ready access to primary care is central. Since 2001, those aged 70 years or over are now entitled to a medical card regardless of income. This increased the number of medical cardholders by 80,000 by 2003 (Tormey, 2003: 420), and has continued to rise commensurate with the increasing numbers of people over 70 years of age in the population. Those between the ages of 65 and 70 must qualify on income grounds like the rest of the population. The decision to grant medical cards regardless of income was a controversial one. On the one hand, there is the argument that it offered free services to older people, some of whom could well afford to pay. In addition, given that older people as a whole require more health care than the adult population as a whole (a point discussed in more detail below), it increased the loss of payment from those who could afford it. The new provision was contrasted with the situation of low-income families where the low threshold is a particular issue for those whose income is just above the threshold of eligibility (Wren, 2003: 204). On the other hand, it can be argued that the best way to maintain older people's health is a preventative approach coupled with immediate access to primary care to deal with as many ailments as possible at this level. This can help prevent the necessity of accessing the very costly as well as overstretched, acute hospital sector. Overall, the strongest argument could be that in the resource rich country that Ireland has become, it should not be a matter of choosing between extending medical cards to older people or raising the threshold for low-income families but of doing both in the interest of good health care.

The private sector

The extent of commitment to the public/private mix is illustrated by the following comment in the recent Statement of Strategy (Department of Health and Children, 2005: 23) which reads:

> In the same way as private sector interest has significantly benefited hospital and long-term developments; there is similar potential for such developments in primary care to complement investment by the State.

In the Irish health care system, public and private care is intertwined in terms of both funding and provision. Payment for private care is largely through insurance. The Voluntary Health Insurance (VHI) Board was set up by the State in the 1950s to provide cover using a community rating system for the wealthiest 15 per cent of its citizens who, at that time, were not eligible for acute public hospital care. It held a monopoly position as a health insurer until the introduction of the Health Insurance Act 1994 arising from the Third Directive on Non-Life Insurance for the European Union. Over the years, health insurance proved a popular option with over one-third of the population in the late 1990s (Nolan and Wiley, 2001) choosing to pay into its schemes, in spite of the extension of public hospital cover to all the population in the interim and the rising costs of cover. It is estimated that over half of the population, including over two thirds of non-medical cardholders, now have some form of private health insurance (Tussing and Wren, 2006: 130). Since the 1994 Act, other health insurers such as BUPA (who have recently sold out of the Irish market) and Vivas have offered alternative cover. The issue of risk equalisation has been to the fore, the basic issue being related to the older population. As VHI has been long established and for many years the only provider, it has a high proportion of members who are older and, therefore, on average likely to be higher users of health services. At the same time, the community rating system does not allow discrimination between different members once they have joined and neither can membership be refused on the basis of increasing health need. The VHI points to increases in the volume of claims, identifying the fact that 'the nation has an ageing population' as one of the key variables.

Ageism and health care

'Any ageism in medicine', argues Bowling (1999: 1353), 'is simply a reflection of ageist attitudes that exist in the wider society'. Minichiello et al. (2000: 253) define ageism as 'a set of social relations that discriminate against older people and set them apart as being different by defining and understanding them in an oversimplified, generalised way'. These authors discussed the variety of ways in which ageism has been researched in relation to health care: For example, whether misconceptions about ageing on the part of health professionals can have a detrimental effect on the ageing process; if therapists apply stereotypical negative attitudes about ageing prevalent in society towards their patients; and whether health care workers are less inclusive, engaged and respectful of older people. In their own small, qualitative study, Minichiello et al. (2000) found that their respondents could recount a number of negative incidents with health professionals. Their experiences were less about overt ageism than situations where they had felt neglected or treated as 'unimportant' or where they were given inadequate information or had not been included in important decisions regarding their own or a 'significant others' health care. Indirect ageism is 'subtle and often covert or invisible, and very often individuals and organisations practice it unawares, making it difficult to challenge' (Adams et al., 2006: 305).

An important aspect of ageism in relation to health care resources is the danger that there will be a propensity to give youth priority over old age, rather than on the basis of individual assessment. Nord et al. (1996) distinguish between two different types of thinking in relation to health care, both of which are based on ageism. Egalitarian ageism is the view that the right to life and its enjoyment should be greater for those who have lived fewer years. The idea of 'fair innings' (Tsuchiya et al., 2003) would be associated with this view. Utilitarian ageism is the idea that the greater duration of health benefits should be an important consideration in the distribution of scarce resources. There is evidence that ageism does exist overtly as well as covertly in health care. Williams (2000) offers examples of this in different spheres such as: excluding older people in clinical trials and from standard screening such as breast cancer, offering less intensive treatment for conditions such as cardiovascular disease and elective surgery being cancelled too readily because it is not rated as high priority. Robb et al. (2002) cite evidence that older people with cancer may not be diagnosed as early as younger people with the same symptoms. 'When age related decisions are irrational or inequitable, they may reflect ageism' according to Sutton (1997: 1,032). 'The crux of ageism,' he argues, is 'the stereotyped negative view of older people that leads to policy decisions that disadvantage them' (1997: 1,033).

In a situation of finite resources, Grimley Evans (1997) argues, older people may be victims since they are less likely to complain and tend to be politically inactive. He looks at the sources of ageism in health care, suggesting that they can arise from well-intentioned ignorance, or straightforward prejudice on the part of health care professionals. In regard to the practices of primary care doctors in the UK and USA, for example, Adams et al. (2006: 317) found 'some systematic differences in their clinical decision-making processes during consultation with older as compared to midlife patients who present with identical CHD (coronary heart disease) clinical symptoms'. Overall, however, the same study found 'little evidence of indirect ageism, particularly in relation to intervention decisions' (2006: 317). On the other hand, Bowling (1999) reported higher rates of intervention for cardiovascular disease among young in comparison to older people. Robb et al. (2002) suggest that ageism practices may go unrecognised by physicians because the bias is implicit rather than explicit. Regarding health professionals working full time with older people, Feldman (1999: 273) points out that 'working in aged care is not widely valued by health professionals'. Feeling undervalued in the professional role may, in turn, affect the professional response to service users.

The issue of ageism in the health care of older people is one to be specifically addressed in the training of health professionals. Robb et al. (2002: 8), for example, cite training programmes which incorporate practice-based exposure to older people and empathy-oriented exercises to enhance understanding of ageing. These, they suggest, 'when partnered with contact with healthy, functioning older people may be successful in changing attitudes or improving knowledge or both.' Such programmes would help to combat any tendency on the part of staff to stereotype older people which demeans them, diminishes their individuality and, potentially, reduces the quality of care they receive (NCAOP, 2005b).

Ageism and ethnicity

The changing demographic profile of the Irish population will present new challenges for the care of older people from a number of ethnic, racial and religious groups (see chapter 7 above). Already, the issue of ethnicity and ageing is a factor in the health care of older people given the number of medical, nursing and paid carers that are recruited from outside Ireland. According to the Irish Nurses Organisation (INO), for example, from 1998 to 2006, over 10,000 nurses from outside the EU have registered in Ireland. Over a decade ago, Lookinland and Anson (1995: 55) suggested that as more care will be provided by nurses from minority/ethnic groups in the future, attitudes and behaviours in these groups require investigation.

Older women and health

Any discussion of ageing and health must consider the particular position of women and ageing. In the first place it is of importance because women, on account of their greater life expectancy, comprise the majority of the older population in virtually all countries including Ireland. While they have a longer life expectancy than men, women have a higher morbidity rate, particularly in the later years of their lives. There are some conditions with marked gender differences in older age. Osteoporosis, for example, a major cause of morbidity, disability and death, largely affects women. According to WHO (2006) figures, women suffer 80 per cent of all hip fractures, they have a lifetime risk of 30 per cent to 40 per cent for fractures occurring as a result of osteoporosis while it is estimated to be 13 per cent for men. Robb et al. (2002: 9) point to the dual disadvantage for women when ageism and sexism combine. They refer to evidence that this combination is responsible for the higher reported rates of mental disorder in older women.

Mental health and older people

The Psychiatric Services: Planning for the Future (Department of Health, 1984) differentiated between three groups in relation to mental illness in old age. The first group was those who developed a mental illness such as depression for the first time after they had reached 65 years. The second was the very specific condition associated with old age, that of dementia while the third was those with an existing condition (such as schizophrenia) who were 65 years or more. This subdivision was useful in identifying the range of conditions and differing needs of older people with mental health problems. The Expert Group on Mental Health Policy (Department of Health and Children, 2006a: 115) comment on the relatively recent development of specialist teams providing mental health services for older people (Mental Health Service for Older People (MHSOP)) which have as their particular remit three main conditions:

1. Functional disorders, depression being the most common
2. Organic brain disorders (dementia in particular)
3. Other disorders such as anxiety, substance abuse and (less commonly) late-onset psychosis.

'Dementia and depression represent the two most serious challenges to mental health faced by people as they age' (Drury, 2005). Dementia is a global term used to describe a range of conditions which cause brain cells to die, resulting in progressive deterioration in memory. It affects the person's capacity to undertake activities of daily living and can also affect personality and mood. The Mental Health Act 2001 included dementia in its definition of a mental disorder for the purposes of the Act. It defined severe dementia as 'a deterioration of the brain of a person which significantly impairs the intellectual function of the person thereby affecting thought, comprehension and memory and which includes severe psychiatric or behavioural symptoms such as physical aggression'. It is estimated that more than 35,000 people in Ireland have dementia, it's most common form being Alzheimer's disease (see chapter 8 above). The risk of Alzheimer's disease increases markedly with age with less than one per cent of the population under 65 to more than 25 per cent of those over 80 years of age (Alzheimer's Society of Ireland, 2006c). The increasing numbers of older people in the population, particularly of those over 80, has obvious implications for the development of care for those with dementia (O'Shea and O'Reilly, 1999). The Dementia Services Information and Development Centre was created by the Department of Health and Children in 1999 for professionals, policy planners, family members and other parties interested in this area. Its purpose is to provide education and information on dementia and to facilitate the development of national and international research on the many aspects of dementia and its care.

While depression can occur at any stage of life, it is associated in a particular way with old age. Deteriorating physical health, lack of social contact and/or loss of spouse and close family members add to hazards of developing an emotional response of sadness and despair to warrant some treatment intervention. The Expert Group (Department of Health and Children, 2006a: 115) estimates that the numbers of older people with depression will increase from around 47,300 in 2001 to over 95,000 in 2026 rising further to approximately 122,500 by 2036 based on a prevalence rate of 11 per cent. During the same period, those with dementia are expected to rise from 21,500 to 55,750 based on prevalence of 5 per cent of those over 65 years. This growth, it points out, will have considerable impact on the numbers of older people requiring mental health services resulting in a substantive increase in the resources presently devoted to this sector, especially in view of its current shortfall in staffing and in designated resources. The Expert Group (Department of Health and Children, 2006a: 117) itemised some of the 'major gaps in current mental health services for older people'. These included: the absence of specialist services in many catchment areas, lack of multidisciplinary representation on existing MHSOP teams, lack of specialist assessment/ treatment in acute facilities, inadequate accommodation in continuing facilities and lack of day hospital facilities. Importantly, the Expert Group included in this list the 'lack of emphasis on recovery and positive coping skills in existing service provision' (2006a: 117).

Health promotion

The Expert Group (Department of Health and Children, 2006a: 117) pointed out that 'the literature on ageing tends to over-emphasise the medical difficulties and cognitive decline that can be a feature of later life'. To counteract this tendency, the Group stated the importance of preserving 'a respect for the potential in older people to grow and flourish in later life and to counter negative myths of ageing that can become self-fulfilling prophesies'. 'Active ageing is the process of optimising opportunities for health, participation and security in order to embrace quality of life as people age' (WHO, 2006). The Health Strategy also acknowledged the need for 'active health maintenance programmes for continuance of health in the elderly' (Department of Health and Children, 2001c: 149).

The National Health Promotion Strategy (Department of Health and Children, 2001c: 44) raised concerns about the findings of the SLAN data that 36 per cent of older people in the study reported taking no exercise, a figure that rose to over half (51 per cent) of those over 75 years. The overall aim of the health promotion strategy was to improve quality of life and longevity by means of lifestyle changes, creating supportive environments and providing appropriate services to meet the needs of the older population. Key principles in the approach were community-based partnership and consultation with service users in the development and implementation of service provision.

Primary care

Commitment in theory at least to the development of primary care services is expressed in the Statement of Strategy 2005–7 (Department of Health and Children, 2005: 23). It points out that 'a strengthened primary care system has the potential to have a major impact in reducing demands on specialist services and the hospital system, particularly accident and emergency and out-patient services'. Plans for the development of the primary care sector in Ireland were laid out in the policy document *Primary Care: A New Direction* (Department of Health and Children, 2001d). It emphasised its importance in the promotion of good health as well as ensuring early intervention at the most cost-effective level when ill health occurs. General Practitioners, who provided independent services paid for by the State for those on medical cards and privately by the rest of the population, had been separated structurally and spatially from the rest of the community care team. In the new system, the General Practitioners were to be the team leaders of a multidisciplinary team which would provide one point of entry other than Accident and Emergency (A & E) to comprehensive community based care and to specialist health services. The Primary Care Team, with its brief of health and personal social services provision in the community, has clear relevance for the older population.

Acute hospital care

The 'lion's share' of public spending on health care in Ireland goes on acute hospital care. Just under half of the total budget for health goes to the acute hospital sector (Department of Health and Children, 2006b) and there is no reason to presume that this will diminish in the foreseeable future. Indeed, the current focus on the inadequacy of A & E services to meet demand indicates that, along with improving primary care, there will be considerable pressure to increase the number of inpatient beds available in acute hospitals.

Certain chronic conditions, more prevalent in older people such as congestive heart disease and respiratory illness, can lead to repeated emergency admissions to acute hospitals. The term, 'high-impact users', has been coined to refer to patients who have more than three emergency admissions to an acute hospital in a given year (Dr Foster Intelligence, 2006). The suggestion is that identifying and targeting such patients for preventative and early intervention primary care could reduce their need for repeated acute hospital admissions.

The provision of acute hospital beds is of particular import in regards to older people. Drawing on OECD data for 2002, Tussing and Wren (2006) state that Ireland had 26.9 beds per 1000 over-65 year olds compared to an EU average of 25.9. They found marked variance across Europe in this respect with Germany highest at 38.4 beds per 1000 over 65; UK at 23.2 while Finland had as low as 15.3 in 2002. However, the comparison must take account of such factors as length of stay, out patient provision and population distribution. Tussing and Wren (2006) point out that the overall figures are no grounds for complacency taking account of the growing population and the particular demands facing Dublin and the East of the country overall. Moreover, Tussing and Wren (2006: 185) stress the importance of not assuming that 'the hospitals whose beds make up the Irish acute bed count are all truly acute, when many offer less than comprehensive services'.

Extended care

By far the greatest resource expended on extended care is that of unpaid family care of older relatives. Writing in relation to the National Health Service in the UK but of equal pertinence to Ireland, Pollock (2005: 165) points out that 'when the state does intervene it is mainly when this informal network is unable to cope'. A Supreme Court challenge to the Health Amendment No. 2 Bill resulted in substantial repayments having to be paid to older people who were medical cardholder but nevertheless were charged for publicly provided extended care over a number of years. Following the publication of the *Review of the Nursing Home Subvention Scheme* (Department of Health and Children, 2003c), a Working Group was set up to produce policy recommendations on the financing of long-term care for older people in Ireland. This area of health care is discussed in more detail in the chapter concerned with personal social services (see chapter 11 below).

Palliative care

Another very important area of health care for older people is the availability of care for those with terminal conditions. Often used interchangeably with the term 'terminal care', palliative care encompasses this and more. It is essentially treatment that is about alleviation of symptoms caused by a life-limiting condition. It is also used in place of the term 'hospice care' which is more accurately related to care when illness is at an advanced stage. Hospice care, while often associated with a place of death, can be used to also describe a philosophy of care that is applicable to a range of settings including the acute hospital and the dying person's own home. Palliative care encompasses a holistic view of the person and their illness. Hence, the trajectory of care encompasses the care of the dying person's family, before, during and after the death has occurred.

While by no means only of relevance for older people, the provision of palliative care is an essential element of health care for this section of the population. The increasing numbers of older people, especially in the proportion of those over 80 years will increase the need for palliative care services in the coming decades. This will require rapid and substantial investment in the development of such services. O'Síoráin and Ling (2005: 204) comment that 'the Republic of Ireland has started from a low base in terms of service provision' in that 'there are currently only 67 specialist palliative care beds serving the population of the greater Dublin area'. At the same time, 'some parts of Ireland, namely the midlands, the south east and the north east have no specialist palliative care in-patient beds'.

The *Report of the National Advisory Group on Palliative Care* (Department of Health and Children, 2001b) had highlighted the gaps in what was provided, pointing to the differentials based on diagnostic condition and geographical location. For example, a study by Igoe et al. in 1997 found that less than 10 per cent of patients receiving palliative care had a diagnosis other than cancer. Community-based, consultant led, palliative care teams were seen by the National Advisory Committee (2001b) as the key to enabling people to die at home, the place of choice for most. A study by the Irish Hospice Foundation (2004), found that 67 per cent of respondents wanted to die at home while the most important factor (rated higher than freedom from pain) was to be with people they loved. This has particular implications for older people, particularly for those in the 80 + category. In such cases, their carer may be also an 'old, older' person with serious health issues and families can have more than one relative who is dying within the same timeframe (2001b).

In a review of palliative care services nationally, the Irish Hospice Foundation (2006) noted the expansion in the provision of home care services since the National Advisory Committee Report in 2001 (Department of Health and Children, 2001b). However, overall it was found that

> access to specialist palliative care remains far too dependent on where a person lives rather than on medical need . . . four years on from the findings and

recommendations of the NACPC National Advisory Committee on Palliative Care (2001b) there remains a wide regional divergence in the range of services and care options available (Irish Hospice Foundation, 2006: 110).

Conclusion: Ongoing challenges

The growing number of older people in the population, and in particular the projected increase in the proportion of 'old, older' people (i.e. those aged over 75 years) within this cohort will provide challenges for the funding and delivery of health care in the coming decades. In this chapter, three points noted were: the need to redefine what is old age in the context of health care, as well as the importance of focusing on health promotion and primary care to minimise the stress for older people (and the cost) of unnecessary dependence on acute hospital care. In addition, the further development of adequate and appropriate mental health services for older people was identified as a priority.

Given the importance of facilitating good health for older people, and the concern about ageism in this sector, O'Shea and Gillespie's (2006) argument for the need to introduce a health-proofing framework and to focus equalising opportunity for health is worth noting. This could involve positive discrimination and the provision of material and structural support of individuals whose choices in relation to health are limited by their economic and social circumstances. The National Economic and Social Forum (NESF) Report Number 32 calls for the development for a new national strategy on ageing and highlights the need to root out ageism. It supports the notion of policy proofing and ensuring that the needs of older people get greater attention in service provision. It proposes the creation of a Working Group on Positive Ageing to develop new approaches to the health care of older people in Ireland. To quote the World Health Organisation (WHO, 2006) 'ageing is a privilege and a societal achievement. It is also a challenge which will impact on all aspects of 21st century society'.

Chapter 10

Disability in old age

Anne O'Connor

'Ageing has traditionally been associated with physical and mental decline . . . conceptualized in terms of loss of faculties'

(NDA and NCAOP, 2006: 4).

Introduction

As the world's population experiences longer life expectancy, people are also experiencing increased risks of acquiring disabilities as they age. Exploring the issue of disability in old age is a relatively new and neglected phenomenon. This chapter examines the issue of older people who experience the late onset of disability, specifically, people who have acquired a disability due to the ageing process. It also examines issues relating to a separate cohort, people who had a disability present at birth or acquired it during childhood or young adulthood. This cohort is also experiencing longevity. As with the general population, people with a lifelong disability are benefiting from improvements in medical and social advances, resulting in increased life expectancy (WHO, 2000). For some living with a lifelong disability, the onset of ageing, is not only premature but also brings with it additional complications (Bigby, 2004). Associated 'syndrome specific' symptoms include early onset dementia for those with Downs Syndrome or reduced energy levels and emergence of chronic pain for people with Cerebral Palsy (Evenhuis et al., 2000). However, discrepancies in the availability and level of care are impacting on the quality of life for people ageing with lifelong disabilities. While many theorists and practitioners currently argue for the need for a combined focus on the area of disability and ageing, for those who 'age with a disability' and those who experience 'disability with ageing', little progress has been made for a joint focus. The WHO states that only if the same specialised supports, health care and access to mainstream services are made available to people with lifelong disabilities, will the common goal of universal healthy ageing be achieved (2000). For a more detailed discussion on ageing with a lifelong disability, see Redmond and D'Arcy, 2003.

The chapter begins by examining the factors which define disability in old age, focusing on both the physical and mental health factors. It then highlights international policies and research regarding encouraging healthy ageing. It concludes with a brief examination of current Irish policy and research focusing on disability in old age, and highlights the future developments and challenges facing this emerging cohort of older people.

Defining disability in old age

Currently in Ireland, disability is defined as 'a substantial restriction in the capacity of a person to participate in economic, social or cultural life on account of an enduring physical, sensory, learning, mental health or emotional impairment' (Department of Justice, Equality and Law Reform, 1999a). This is a contentious definition of disability, in that it requires a 'substantial' restriction limiting the individual, which may have implications for entitlement to services. In comparison, the WHO defines disability as where an individual has 'difficulties' carrying-out everyday tasks in their daily lives. Here disability in old age is defined as, 'difficulties in one or more basic self-care tasks, often called "physical activities of daily living", or PADLs (bathing, dressing, toileting, continence, feeding, transferring from chair to bed) or in one or more instrumental activities of daily living or IADLs (using the phone, shopping, preparing meals, housekeeping, laundry, public transportation, taking medication, handling finances)' (Health Evidence Network (HEN), 2003: 6). PADLs and IADLs encompass an individualistic approach in defining disability, which considers the limitations on everyday activities for the person experiencing disability in old age.

According to the WHO, the most prevalent chronic conditions affecting older people throughout the world include: cardiovascular disease, hypertension, stroke, diabetes, cancer, mental health conditions, blindness and visual impairment (WHO, 2002). Increasingly, research is indicating that the origins of the risks for chronic conditions, such as diabetes and heart disease begin in early childhood or even earlier (2002: 16). In addition, other factors such as: tobacco use, lack of physical activity and nutrient-deficient diet can place individuals at relatively greater risk of developing non-communicable diseases (NCDs) at older ages. In 1990, 27 per cent of the burden of disease for the general population in developing and newly industrialised countries was due to NCDs. This figure is expected to rise to 43 per cent by 2020 (WHO, 2002). NCDs are not contagious and cannot be passed from person to person, but they limit the individual in their everyday activities. Factors such as obesity, high blood pressure, high cholesterol, alcohol and tobacco use can lead to the onset of a NCD. Therefore, some of the disabilities associated with ageing and the onset of chronic disease can be prevented or delayed. Culture, gender, personal attributes and behaviours, the physical environment, social structures and economics are further determinants identified by the WHO as significant contributors to the active ageing framework (2002). WHO state that long-term physical activity can enhance the independence of those ageing, even those with chronic diseases (HEN, 2003).

While physical factors tend to dominate the literature on disability in old age, mental health and ageing is an emerging area, which up until recently received little attention. According to the WHO, depression is one of the most common mental health disorders in older people (HEN, 2003). Depressive symptoms are more frequent among the oldest, which could be explained by factors associated with ageing, such as depression being more prevalent for females than males overall and more physical incapacity (HEN, 2003). Despite a favourable response to treatment, late-life depression remains largely undetected and untreated (Department of Health and Children, 2006a). Current data demonstrates that physical activity and exercise may reduce depressive symptoms and delay the onset of disability (HEN, 2003).

International policy regarding ageing populations and its implications

As the world's population ages, the onset of disability in old age is an emerging phenomenon. This concern is echoed in policies first put forward by the United Nations in the 1980s, and then by the European Union which resulted in: *Ageing at Work* (European Commission, 1993), *Towards a Europe for All Ages* (European Commission, 1999a), *Active Ageing: Promoting a European Society For All Ages* (European Commission, 1999b), *Survey on the Current Status of Research into 'Ageing' in Europe* (European Commission, 2000), *Europe's Response to World Ageing: Promoting Economic and Social Progress in an Ageing World: A Contribution of the European Commission to the 2nd World Assembly on Ageing* (European Commission, 2002). The Organisation for Economic Co-operation and Development (OECD) followed suit with such articles as: *Urban Policies for Ageing Populations* (OECD, 1992), *Ageing in OECD Countries: A Critical Policy Challenge* (OECD, 1996), *Maintaining Prosperity in an Ageing Society* (OECD, 1998), *Ageing and Income: Financial Resources and Retirement in 9 OECD Countries* (OECD, 2001). The driving force behind all policies relates to the idea of preventing illness and disability, and encouraging people to engage in healthy behaviours which will ensure extended good health. Two countries – the United States and Japan (which incidentally has the oldest population in the world) – have demonstrated a successful reduction in rates of disability among the older population. Factors such as: improved educational levels, standard of living and the management of chronic conditions, support the concept of 'Active Ageing', the policy encouraging older people to stay healthy longer (WHO, 2002).

In 2002, the Second World Assembly on Ageing was held in Madrid, Spain. From this, *The Madrid Plan of Action on Ageing* (2002) was established. This action plan places great emphasis on adequate access to primary health care for older people to ensure that they remain in good health, or if they do need treatment for a particular condition, that they are treated effectively and ultimately with an aim to rehabilitation. Following the World Assembly on Ageing, the WHO developed a strategy document entitled *Active Ageing: a Policy Framework* (2002). 'Active Ageing' is the 'process of optimizing opportunities for health, participation and security in order to enhance quality of life as people age' (WHO, 2002: 12). This policy document defined 'older people' as anyone over the age of 60 years, but acknowledged that in the developed world, this may be regarded as relatively young, while in the developing world it may not. The document acknowledged that 'population ageing is one of humanity's greatest triumphs' while also being one of the greatest challenges to face modern societies (2002: 6). Furthermore, the WHO asserted that a comprehensive policy framework required action on three specific areas, namely: health, participation (to support the participation of older people within society so that they can continue to make a productive contribution to society as a whole) and security (policies and programmes needed to ensure the protection, dignity and care of older persons).

To meet the new challenges that this demographic change brings to the world stage the WHO have put forward a number of policy recommendations in regard to adequate provision for older people. Firstly that the *United Nations Principles for Older Persons* (UN, 1990) of independence, participation, care, self-fulfilment and dignity are maintained, and to ensure that each society is prepared to deal with these challenges. As part of the health recommendations, the WHO states it is necessary to:

1 Prevent and reduce the burden of excess disabilities, chronic disease and premature mortality.
2 Reduce risk factors associated with major disease and increase factors that protect health throughout the life course.
3 Develop a continuum of affordable, accessible, high quality and age-friendly health and social services that address the needs and rights of women and men as they age.

The WHO categorically states that it is the responsibility of policy makers to initiate programmes that will halt the massive expansion of chronic diseases through policies focusing on prevention and health promotion (WHO,

2002). In response, it has developed an Ageing and Health Programme which focuses on the development of policies to ensure 'the attainment of the best possible quality of life for as long as possible, for the largest possible number of people' (2002: 54). Recent findings show that a reduction in age-specific disability is possible. Evidence from the USA, England and Sweden, show a significant decline in age-related disability over the last twenty years (2002). While education levels and better standards of living are key factors in this improvement, advances in the medical field has resulted in better management and treatment of chronic conditions, early and accurate diagnosis and the increasing use of aids including services and technologies, all of which have impacted on the management of disability in old age (2002).

Employment

The Organisation for Economic Co-operation and Development (OECD) has also been concerned about the reality of ageing populations, in terms of the economic and social burden that this places on societies. In its document, *Live Longer, Work Longer* (OECD, 2006b), the OECD carried out a review of policies in 21 member states, including Ireland, and acknowledged the fact that older people can still actively contribute to the fiscal strength of a society, by working for longer. Their report focused on the policies that would improve the employment prospects of older workers. Recommendations put forward by the OECD Report go hand in hand with many of the policy recommendations put forward by the WHO and the European Commission. All conclude that by encouraging older people to stay in the workplace, they are imbued with a sense of purpose and remain active physically and mentally. In essence, they contribute to the fabric of society while at the same time engaging in activities that promote good physical and mental health and well-being which have been shown to delay the onset of age-related conditions which can lead to disability.

Healthy ageing in Europe

In 2003, the Health Evidence Network (HEN) which is coordinated by the WHO Regional Office for Europe and is an information service for public health and health care decision makers, published a report looking at the main risk factors that contribute to disability in old age and how this may be prevented. The purpose of the HEN Report was to consider the evidence relating to disability in old age and discuss the ways in which policies and policy makers can positively impact on the quality of life for those older people living with a disability (HEN, 2003). It has been estimated that between 1995 and 2015, there will be a 40 per cent increase in the number of people aged 80 and over in the European Union member countries. According to the

HEN Report, the years up to 2023 will see an increase of 17 million people over the age of 65 years, the 'prevention of disability in old age is therefore a matter of great humanitarian and economic concern' (2003: 2).

The HEN identified certain risk factors which can be addressed throughout the life cycle which may delay the onset of a condition leading to a disability. By knowing that there are certain modifiable factors which can delay, if not lessen, the impact of a certain condition on a person, prevention strategies can be employed to reduce the incidence of illness and disability in old age (2003). Therefore, according to the HEN, policies addressing 'disabling chronic illness, depressive mood, functional decline and sedentary lifestyles are among the most important prevention strategies' (2003: 4). The development of strategic preventive plans at national and community levels, the promotion of training in gerontology and geriatric medicine for relevant professional groups, the development of programmes to enable older people to cope effectively with disability risk factors and manage chronic illness and the creation of initiatives to stimulate research and development on old age disability are all recommended by HEN (2003: 5)

ActivAge Project

In 2002, the ActivAge Project was launched focusing on ageing in Europe. Led by the Interdisciplinary Centre for Comparative Research in the Social Sciences (ICCR), this three-year project compared the data of ten European countries considering the challenges posed by demographic ageing. The overall aims of the project were to 'identify and analyse the socio-institutional, economic, political realities facing the implementation of active ageing policies in Europe' (ICCR, 2005). According to the final report of the ActivAge Project: 'we are far from meeting the requirements of a substantive policy reform as foreseen by the active ageing paradigm and recommended by the European Commission's Communication Towards a Europe of All Ages' (ICCR, 2005: 4). The report stated that the biggest challenge facing Europe over the next ten years would be the care needs of older people. Furthermore, this challenge would be further compounded by the current ethos within the medical field to practice 'curative' rather than 'preventative' health care (2005). The Report argued that health promotion must dominate future policies in order to tackle the implications of an ageing population in Europe.

Burden of Disease in Old Age Network Project

In 2001, the Burden of Disease in Old Age Network Project (BURDIS) was established with funding from the European Commission. The resulting report based on the project *Disability in Old Age* was published in 2004 by the Finnish Centre for Interdisciplinary Gerontology. While this report identified both the physical and behavioural factors contributing to disability in old age, it also acknowledged the role society plays in limiting the individual with a disability (Finnish Centre for Interdisciplinary Gerontology, 2004). Some of the physical and behavioural factors identified included: 'inappropriately treated diseases, depression, cognitive, sensory, and physiological impairment, smoking, unhealthy dietary habits . . . and insufficient social support' (2004: 8). The report also acknowledged the impact of discrimination on particular cultural groups, which may limit the range of activities available to them. As with previous research explored in this chapter, this report also concluded that 'disability in old age should be a focus of all public health policy and programmes and cover the whole continuum of services aimed at both preventing disability and restoring functional capacity through rehabilitative measures' (2004: 3). The key recommendations from BURDIS were: promoting physical activity through inter-sectoral collaborations, providing comprehensive geriatric services, increasing clinical skills in geriatric medicine, screening for conditions which affect elderly people in the community and the provision of adequate housing and pensions for older people preventing prejudice and discrimination (2004: 3).

Current policy in Ireland

While there is no specific legislation protecting older people who are ageing with a disability, the Equal Status Acts 2000 and 2004 and the Employment Equality Acts 1998 and 2004 (Department of Justice, Equality and Law Reform, 1998; 2004) provided protection against discrimination in relation to age and disability, the provision of services, access to employment and education. The Disability Act 2005 also provided statutory obligations in relation to disability. In particular by providing people with disabilities the right to an assessment of need and access to both information and the physical environment. Since *A Stategy for Equality: Report of the Commission on the Status of People with Disabilities* (Department of Justice, Equality and Law Reform, 1996), there has been very slow progress in relation to research into disability in old age. The first National Disability Survey, which was suggested by the Commission ten years ago, was only scheduled to take place in September 2006. This is the first time in the history of the state that baseline data has been collected which will have a significant impact on policymaking.

The Years Ahead: A Policy for the Elderly (1998)

In 1988 a policy document *The Years Ahead: A Policy for the Elderly* was launched which set forth the ways in which older people were to be cared for and treated (Department of Health, 1988). The key principle of this report was to provide comprehensive and cost-effective care for the elderly, preferably in their own homes. By supporting the individual in their own home, their wishes and independence would be maintained. This was the first important policy document that addressed the needs of this distinct group.

National Council on Ageing and Older People (NCAOP)

The majority of research and information available in relation to the status of older people in Ireland is provided by the National Council on Ageing and Older People (NCAOP). The policy regarding disability in old age is largely subsumed within the overall policy, legislation and services provided to those with a disability and those over the age of 65 years. There is no single stand-alone policy dealing with the phenomenon of disability in old age. However, in February 2006, the NCAOP and the National Disability Authority (NDA) published a joint paper entitled *Ageing and Disability: A Discussion Paper*. This paper acknowledges that within the Irish health and social services, people with disabilities and older people are treated as two separate groups, receiving support from two separate government agencies. Furthermore, it recognises the changing demographic structure and implications for the structural organisation of Irish society. The NCAOP is working towards an 'Age Friendly Society' in Ireland, through 'optimising opportunities for health, participation, and security of citizens as they age' (NDA and NCAOP, 2006: 12).

Expert Group on Mental Health

Mental health and ageing is a neglected area of research despite people with long-term difficulties being at a higher risk of mental health difficulties 'in so far as they are socially excluded' (NDA and NCAOP, 2006: 16). However, in 2003 the Expert Group on Mental Health Policy was established and published its first findings in January 2006, *A Vision for Change: Report of the Expert Group on Mental Health Policy* (Department of Health and Children, 2006a). This report was based on consultation with a variety of stakeholders in the disability field and focussed on the range of services available for people with mental health difficulties in Ireland. Within this report attention is paid to the mental health needs of older people. The report suggests that mental health services, including those for older people, should be person-centred and promote self-determination (2006a). It further concludes that the majority of older people with mental health difficulties would prefer to remain in their own home and be treated within that context. The Expert Group also emphasises the importance of ensuring that the over-medicalisation of older persons is not practiced, and that society's thinking that disease is an inevitability of ageing is challenged (2006a).

Dementia and depression increase in the population as the number of adults over the age of 65 increases (2006a). According to the population and labour force projections for 2036, nearly 20 per cent of the Irish population will be over 65 (CSO, 2004). Ultimately then, it is important that the dynamic of 'Active Ageing' as put forward by the UN and WHO is adopted and reflected in policy and service provision so that older persons can remain in good health for longer, and simultaneously, that society as a whole has a positive and constructive attitude towards ageing and older people.

The Expert Group on Mental Health Policy has put forward recommendations regarding the care of older people with mental health difficulties. These include:

1. Any person aged 65 years or over, with primary mental health disorders, or with secondary behavioural and affective problems arising from experience of dementia, has the right to be cared for by mental health services for older people (MHSOP).
2. There should be targeted health promotion programmes.
3. Primary health care teams should play a major role in assessment and screening for mental illness in older people.
4. There should be eight acute assessment and treatment beds in each regional acute psychiatric unit for MHSOP and carers.
5. Families should receive appropriate recognition and support including education, respite, and crisis response when required.

(Department of Health and Children, 2006a: 123).

Future challenges facing Ireland's ageing population and possible developments

In 2001, the NCAOP undertook a research project entitled *Health and Social Services for Older People (HeSSOP): Consulting Older People on Health and Social Services: A Survey of Service Use, Experiences and Needs* (Garavan et al., 2001). This study found that 37 per cent of those found to be 'severely impaired' in carrying out PADLs had not received any home service in the past year. This finding highlights the limited and inadequate role that health and social services were providing for older persons within the community.

The HeSSOP study (Garavan et al., 2001) identified key areas that needed to be addressed. These include:

1. The delivery of home-based care. Older people express a very strong desire to remain in their own home when asked about future long-term care options. However, the research found that home support services were lacking or unknown to those who may have a need for them. All services must be designed so that they are comprehensive and flexible and person-centred.

2. Strategies to combat stigma as a barrier to care are urgently needed. The research found that many older people were reluctant to avail of aids and services due to the perceived stigma attached to these services. It identified a surprising amount of stigma attached to many of the services that are provided to older people.
3. Lack of access to transportation was a potential barrier to the uptake of services by older people. According to the HeSSOP, the first step in changing this is to develop a liaison between those with responsibility for health and for transport.
4. Inclusion of older people in the workforce. The research found that 10 per cent of those interviewed would like to return to the workforce.

In 2005, the NCAOP conducted a follow-up study which focused on changes in health and the mortality of older people, together with changes in their health, behaviour and service usage over a four-year period (O'Hanlon et al., 2005). Participants from the 2001 Report were re-interviewed, along with additional participants both from the Republic and the North of Ireland. Despite the Report finding one in ten participants experiencing major difficulties in physical and psychosocial health, uptake of many health and social services remained low (2005). In line with the 2001 study, the majority of participants (89 per cent) chose home care as their preferred support, but as the NCAOP note, a multi-disciplinary support team providing a range of services is essential to meet this need (2005). In conclusion, prevention, services, information and financial support are necessary for an ageing population to achieve an optimum quality of life.

As health, social support and long-term care use are closely related to disability, it is important to develop both health and welfare organisations to provide older people with efficient services for disability prevention. According to HEN, it is essential to address 'the old myth that the risk of disease is a normal part of old age' and to explore the idea that an ageing body can respond positively to change. The growing burden of old age disability includes reduced independence, an increased use of various services and decreased quality of life. There is emerging evidence that many of the risk factors for old age disability are modifiable. However more research is required to address knowledge gaps in effective intervention strategies. Several reports have noted that the key factor in the delivery of services to those ageing is that services must be based on home care (Department of Health, 1998; Garavan et al., 2001; WHO, 2002; O' Hanlon et al., 2005). However, the development of such services is dependent on a number of factors including the collaboration between supports for home carers, respite services, community care services and most importantly the needs and wishes of the individual. Furthermore, the provision of adequate housing or assistance in making homes more accessible is also an important factor.

In 2003, the Department of Health and Children approved the establishment of a new agency The Health Information and Quality Authority (HIQA, Department of Health and Children 2003b) which aims to develop better health information for older people and for people with disabilities. Its role includes providing accessible material relating to health matters and ensuring standards are achieved and maintained within the health service sector. HIQA was formally established under the Health Act 2007. Such information to be provided by the HIQA will not only be invaluable to those ageing with a disability but also essential for carers so they can provide adequate and efficient care. It will also enable carers and those with a disability in old age to access information on treatment options and health and social welfare entitlements (Garavan et al., 2001). A carers' allowance is payable to people on low income who are looking after someone in need of support, because of age or disability. This allowance not only provides financial support for the carer but also helps the individual being cared for to retain their dignity, knowing that their carer is receiving some remuneration for their work. It goes some way in ensuring that people ageing with a disability have greater choice in decided to receive care in their own home. However, as this payment is means tested, an excessive burden is still experienced by carers not qualifying for this support.

As the world's population ages, the late onset of disability is becoming a real challenge for policy makers trying to develop strategies which will limit the impact on the individual and society. What appears to be emerging is a drive for greater awareness and prevention strategies in relation to healthy ageing, and at the same time a call for an individualistic approach to the delivery of services, which sees the individual first and the disability second.

Chapter 11

From community care to residential care: personal social services and older people

John Brennan

In Ireland, the policy rhetoric in relation to older people continues to hark back to the ground breaking *Care of the Aged* Report (Government of Ireland, 1968) and its follow-up, *The Years Ahead: A Policy for the Elderly* Report (Department of Health, 1988). The latter document became the cornerstone of government policy that stated, amongst other things, that older people should be supported to live at home whenever possible and that high quality residential care should be provided when home was no longer a sustainable option (Department of Health and Children, 2001a).

Context for personal social services

Today, the vast majority of older people in Ireland live independent lives at home (as was the case in 1988). However for the minority who require care, the reality of service delivery is such that it is still trying to live up to the laudable aspirations of the 1988 Report. Despite a substantial increase in recent years, funding for care services is below the European average (National Economic and Social Forum (NESF), 2005: 5). As a consequence, personal social services in the community remain patchy, inconsistent and inequitable. There has been little attempt to underpin service provision with legislation. The NESF suggests that the lack of legislation has possibly arrested the expansion of community-based care services (2005: 57). Policy appears to be developed in a reactionary way and there have been many changes in direction along the road since 1988. This ad-hoc approach can be seen in the current Health Service Executive (HSE) moves to engage with the private sector via the new home care packages in providing community-based care services. The traditional mix of public, private and voluntary provision is thus further complicated because the roles and responsibilities of these sectoral providers and entitlement issues have not been fully clarified.

Layte et al. (1999), in their review of Irish income inequality, argue that the gaps in the provision of personal social services have serious consequences for those older people who are on low incomes. They suggest that in Ireland, inadequate access to health and social care services is largely a function of income inequality because those who are less well off cannot afford to buy health insurance (1999: 133). This echoes Angel and Angels' view of informal support in America which suggests that care support is predicated on income (1997: 92).

Personal social services

Personal social services will be defined for the purposes of this discussion, as those services provided in response to 'social care' needs. Social care is a contested notion (Blackman, 2001; Fine, 2007). However, Blackman suggests that social care 'encompasses personal care such as washing and dressing, practical assistance with preparation of meals and house cleaning and opportunities for socialising and leisure activities' (2001: 10). Such services can be provided in one's own home or in a residential care setting.

In Ireland, community-based personal social services are provided directly by the HSE via, home care attendants, chiropodists, with minimal respite, physiotherapy, speech and language, occupational therapy services and an almost complete lack of social work services. Respite services were drastically cut in 2003 and have not recovered. It is now difficult to access public respite care. A respite care grant is available, but limited to those carers who qualify for a means-tested Carers Allowance. Services, such as home helps, meals-on-wheels and day centres, are generally provided by the voluntary sector (non-profit) with funding from the HSE. However, such voluntary provision is in many instances patchy. In regard to day centres, for example, the National Council on Ageing and Older People (NCAOP) argue that this service is inconsistent and underfunded (Haslett, 2003: 7). In recent years, there has been a growing trend to use the private sector to provide personal social services (Converya, 2001: 87). The so-called 'cash-for-care' scheme, that is, in Ireland, the Home Care Grant has enhanced this position (Timonen and McMenamin, 2002).

The following gives an indication of what some of these services entail. The home help service undertakes shopping, light cleaning duties and meal preparation, for usually one or two hours a day, for up to five days a week. The home care attendant service undertakes personal care such as bathing and dressing. This service is, in practice, generally only available once a week. There are two types of respite service; the first and more usual one is institutional care for overnight, or for one to two weeks, provided to give a carer a break. The second type is supplied in the older person's own home. This second type is mainly delivered by the voluntary sector to persons suffering from a dementia, where institutional respite would be too distressing for the person. It consists of approximately four hours of care, once or twice a week and again, it is provided to give a carer a break. Day centre care provides meals, bathing, respite, social networking opportunities and sometimes physiotherapy and in practice, it is usually offered one or two days a week, depending on care staff levels. Meals-on-wheels services provide a dinner in the middle of the day for up to five days a week, depending, usually, on the supply of volunteers with cars, or budgetary constraints.

Public Health Nurses (PHNs) while having a statutory duty to provide a home nursing service, nevertheless, in the absence of other service providers, do provide some personal social services. General Practitioners (GPs) provide free health/medical services via the General Medical Scheme to those older people with a medical card.

Unlike the United Kingdom experience, almost all community services are delivered on a Monday-to-Friday basis between the hours of 9 a.m. to 5 p.m. Some positive change in out-of-hours services have been brought on by the introduction of the Home Care Grant Scheme. This scheme will be discussed later. In sum, there are many gaps in services and waiting lists apply to several instances.

Charges, sometimes called 'contributions', are often levied for personal social services. Charges differ from service to service and from area to area. Most services are free, but again, there is no uniformity. Private sector services are supplied by 'for-profit' organisations who charge the same rates to all.

Informal personal social services: the role of family, friends and neighbours

Despite the growth in formal personal social services in Ireland, actual use is very low (Timonen and McMenamin, 2002; O'Hanlon, et al., 2005). The bulk of care is offered by what Fanning describes as the 'informal sector' (Fanning, 1999: 52, 53). This is not unique to Ireland. O'Connor, for example, states that in the UK, 85–90 per cent of support to older people is provided by families (O'Connor, 1999: 71). In Germany, Scharf comments that the family 'is of paramount importance' in the provision of care and support to older people (1998: 128). Older people themselves provide care for one another and others (Phillips et al., 2006; Wilson, 2000). In Ireland, most people prefer informal care (Garavan et al., 2001; Timonen and McMenamin, 2002). In comparative terms, Ireland can be likened to Italy and Greece in having strong cultural support for informal care. On the other hand, Scandinavian countries rely much more on formal paid care services. Use of formal care services can give rise to more positive interpersonal relationships between carer and cared-for person, because the stress of caring can be mediated by the formal service (Blackman, 2001).

The informal sector consists of unpaid, or underpaid, family carers, usually women (Timonen and McMenamin, 2002), who are sometimes offering care because of the absence of any alternative. However, most informal care is provided out of a sense of family altruism and solidarity and this is echoed in other countries (Fine, 2007: 7). It can regularly cause great strain to the carer because of the lack of formal support (O'Shea and O'Reilly, 1999; Timonen and Doyle, 2006). Indeed, for many, information on services and entitlements is not available in any accessible way (Garavan et al., 2001), a situation that further isolates older people and carers. Many commentators suggest that across Europe and elsewhere, informal care is coming under threat because of the alterations in family life caused by changing economic and other factors (Fine, 2007; Taylor and Donnelly, 2006). This has been contested (Fine, 2007) and indeed, in the Irish context, O'Hanlon et al., in their recent study, found that informal care was still strong (2005).

Ageism

The numbers and proportion of older people are growing across the globe (Hugman, 1994: 1). This phenomenon is less pronounced in Ireland because of its relatively young population. The response from many policy makers has been to suggest that huge costs will be generated that will be a colossal economic burden on the state (Lymbery, 2005: 24). Such reactions can be described as 'ageist' in that they view old age as merely a time of dependency and decline and ignore the positive contributions that older people make to society (Wilson, 2000; Lymbery, 2005) and the fact that the majority of older people live independent lives (O'Hanlon et al., 2005). Biggs et al. argue that ageism can be 'seen as a mechanism for producing, sustaining and justifying abusive action towards older people . . . through infantilisation, negative stereotyping and institutional priorities and practices' (1995: 95). Ageism, widespread in Ireland, as elsewhere, in many ways is manifested in personal social services and leads to negative discrimination against older people, disempowerment and abuse (NESF, 2005: 33). The NESF suggests that the lack of services for older persons is a reflection of the inherent ageism in policy and practice and that traditional models of service delivery need to be evaluated to ensure that age discrimination is eliminated (2005: 33–5).

Cognitive impairment

In the case of older people with a cognitive impairment, such as a dementia, the voluntary sector has historically played a major role in providing personal social services. The Alzheimer Society, for example, provides home respite, day care and overnight respite. This is of benefit, in particular, to informal carers who can often be under severe strain. However, as O'Shea and O'Reilly suggest, the voluntary sector does not play a meaningful role in policy formation, so that its contribution is not fully realised (1999). Personal social services for older people with a cognitive impairment are generally similar in nature to those for other older people and despite the efforts of voluntary groups, availability is patchy. In their strategy document *An Action Plan for Dementia*, the NCAOP noted the underdevelopment of services and argued that the underlying cause for this was the lack of a statutory mandate for most community care services for older people (1999).

Multiculturalism

Ireland has become a multicultural society over a short space of time. Older people from different ethnic backgrounds are beginning to require personal social services. Alongside this, formal carers from many ethnic origins are now being employed by the various sectoral care providers. This situation throws up many issues relating to cultural norms and expectations for service providers. Racism may become a problem in the future. There is anecdotal evidence that some Irish older people refuse to have carers from non-Irish backgrounds.

Home care grants

The stated policy in Ireland has been to enable older people to live at home for as long as possible. There is now an attempt to give greater effect to this by increasing personal social services through the introduction of the Home Care Grant to buy personal care services. This echoes the shift away from institutional care towards community-based care experienced in other European countries (Hugman, 1994) and in the United States (Binstock and Cluff, 1999). The HSE Home Care Grant is offered on the basis of a means test related to income and a 'needs assessment'. However, when a state Old Age Pension is taken into consideration, the maximum amount of money offered (approximately €500 in 2006) buys only a few hours care a day given the cost of such care. However there is clearly discrimination in accessing care at home as those with limited means cannot afford to pay for any extra care required to help the older person remain at home in a dignified manner, while those with abundant means can afford to buy in high levels of care. This highlights Layte et al.'s (1999) comments above, on income inequality and access to services.

To date, in some areas, private care agencies have delivered this grant funded personal care while in others, the voluntary sector has had a greater involvement (Prendergast, 2006: 89). Regardless, the Home Care Grant has given a significant boost to the expansion of the private sector in the provision of personal social services.

The introduction of the Home Care Grant Scheme has also given rise to the concept of the package of care. This concept was advocated by Ruddle et al., in their *Review of the Years Ahead Report* (1998). It is more fully realised in the UK where care and case management are now well established under legislation. In Ireland, in some areas, home care grants are focused on the acute hospital sector because of the well-documented 'A & E crisis'. A package of care is designed on a case-by-case basis to meet the individual needs of the older person requiring care at home. Alongside the means test already mentioned, there is a needs assessment carried out by a 'case manager', who, to date, has been a PHN. However, the assessment can only deliver care services within the confines of the maximum grant. This fact, plus the discretionary nature of the grants, driven by budgetary imperatives, limits the effectiveness of the scheme. The concentration on the acute hospital sector has, in some areas, resulted in delaying access to the grant to many living at home. Without extra funding, this situation will persist.

Needs assessments

In Ireland, unlike the UK, there is no standardised assessment tool in use across the country. Much of the effort to date here appears to be of an ad-hoc nature. While in the UK the assessment process is well developed, its emphasis on rote form filling has been criticised. Taylor and Donnelly argue that the process there does not always allow for the complexities of emotions that drive an individual older person's decision making regarding his or her own care (Taylor and Donnelly, 2006). The NESF argues 'that the absence of a right to assessment of need is a significant gap in the Irish system'. It states, however, that the right to assessment 'does not necessarily mean that the service will then be provided' (NESF, 2005: 61). The consequence of such a situation can be seen in the UK, for example, where Burton, speaking of empowerment and choice in dementia care, argues that such empowerment is subverted by the 1990 legislation requiring needs assessments to stay within 'available resources' (Burton, 1997: 194). In these circumstances, needs assessments can be a futile exercise for those who require a good deal of support.

Significance of dependency

Stevenson echoes Taylor and Donnelly when she raises the issue of the emotional and social significance of dependency amongst older people. As Taylor and Donnelly (2006) have pointed out in relation to admission to long-term care, this is not a topic that has been fully addressed in the rather mechanical and indeed, ageist, way in which personal social services have been planned and delivered to date. Stevenson rightly argues that when planning personal care interventions, the older person should be canvassed as to what activities of daily living hold most significance for them (Stevenson, 1989). Fenton and Mitchell echo this sentiment when they suggest that the older person must exercise control in relation to service provision if his or her dignity is to be maintained (2002: 19–21). That such control is not always exercised in the Irish context was highlighted by Garavan et al., who, in a study of older persons' preferences for health and social services, found that 20 per cent of older respondents did not believe that their views were listened to in relation to the services they received (2001: 212). In the UK, Peace et al., in discussing entry to residential care, suggest that often the older person has little say over the decision because it usually occurs at a time of hospitalisation when the older person is most frail and vulnerable (1997: 40–4).

Garavan et al. have highlighted the stigma that many older people attach to certain personal social services (2001). O'Hanlon et al. in a follow up to Garavan et al.'s 2001 study, reported that up to 10 per cent of a population of older people they studied would not use home help, personal care, or meals-on-wheels services even if they were required, because of the perceived stigma attached (2005). This phenomenon requires closer examination to see if such stigma can be overcome. However, the principle of allowing older people the 'dignity to fail' by refusing the help that, objectively, they require, is very important in this context. While stigma is reducing in respect of dementia (O'Shea and O'Reilly, 1999: 73), nevertheless, this factor, plus the fear engendered by the condition, can have negative consequences in terms of diagnosis, treatment and take up of services for those with dementia.

Residential care

Government policy in Ireland echoes popular public sentiment, summed up in that well-worn phrase, 'there's no place like home.' Historically, residential care has a very negative image (Phillips et al., 2006). It is seen by most people as a last resort (O'Hanlon et al., 2005) and this belief is reinforced by nursing home scandals such as the Leas Cross affair. In the UK, residential care has been seen by many as the only option given the dearth of community-based personal social services (Peace et al., 1997: 17). This applies equally to Ireland today. However, in reviewing personal social services as part of a continuum of care, residential care may in some cases be a far better option than continuing to live at home. In research on decision making and long-term care, Taylor and Donnelly suggest that the perspectives of older respondents with similar physical needs varied greatly regarding what were acceptable care options and that communal living could be viewed as an appropriate way to meet certain social needs, for example, loneliness or boredom (2006: 815, 816). Blackman notes with concern that very dependent people, being cared for in the community, may be 'denied the quality of care, security and opportunities for social interaction that good nursing home care should be able to provide' (2001: 21).

Despite the policy rhetoric about maintaining older persons in their own homes, funding still favours institutional care over community based care (NESF, 2005: 26). Residential care in Ireland is provided by a mixture of the public, private and voluntary sectors. The HSE is now engaging with the private sector to make up the serious shortfall in public long stay facilities. The provision of public community units for older people providing residential care, day care and respite facilities at the local level have not developed. This is despite, for example, in 1998, the now defunct Eastern Health Board issuing a 10-year plan to provide 29 such units in the greater Dublin area (Eastern Health Board, 1998). To date, only a handful has been provided, with little indication that there will be any increase. As it is, many older people going into residential care must move many miles from their own homes and community networks. An opportunity has, therefore, been lost in this region to develop local residential care where older people would have been able to maintain their local community links and a sense of continuity with their past.

Inspection of services

The span of the inspection process in Ireland lags way behind the United Kingdom where there is routine inspection of social care services for older people. The inspection of nursing homes, an issue put under the spotlight since the Leas Cross affair, has been addressed by the government with the establishment of HIQA. The recognition that elder abuse occurs not only in institutional settings, but also in informal relationships, reminds us of the need for comprehensive inspection processes. The rise in the number of private home care agencies, together with the general rise in care at home, gives added impetus to the need for action on inspection. Such inspection must include all personal social service providers.

Discussion: challenges

The current state of affairs has given rise to situations where many older people and their carers live in great distress. The existing system of social care is under-resourced, inequitable, fragmented and ineffective. The system impacts on quality of life to the extent that it denies many individuals their basic human rights. In redressing this situation, we must begin to move forward in some coherent fashion. The time is long overdue for a uniform structure of services across the country that allows access in a transparent and fair way for those that need support and care.

Among the number of challenges with which we must grapple to move towards a system of appropriate care are:

Legislation: The dearth of legislation in relation to personal social services must be tackled in a comprehensive manner, to ensure that essential services such as home help, meals-on-wheels, day care and respite care are provided as of right. Greater access to services for those on low incomes must be achieved to overcome the income inequalities in Irish society. The then government's strategy, *Shaping a Healthier Future* (1994), acknowledged that the inequity in the provision of personal services was due to the lack of legislation and a commitment was made at that time to implement national guidelines underpinned by legislation. However, this commitment has not yet been realised.

Quality standards: National quality standards must be agreed and implemented under legislation in relation to: objectives, quality of care, education and training, values, staff-client ratios and alongside the above, physical environment issues in the case of residential care. Monitoring and evaluation processes must also be put in place.

Anti-ageist policy: Public policy relating to personal social services must become overtly anti-ageist so as to move away from the traditional paternalism of service providers and policy makers. It is imperative that more positive conceptions of old age are accepted. It is quite possible that future recipients of services, now more educated and affluent, will be less accepting than previous generations of ageist philosophies and practices. However, in the meantime, we must challenge ageism in a manner that, as Phillips et al. (2006) suggest, does not further marginalise older people who are already frail and dependent.

Involvement in decision making: A consequence of ageism is the exclusion of older people in the decision making about their use of personal social services. Such services, as Stevenson (1989) has pointed out, often involve intimate areas of one's life and can shape our sense of identity and worth. The older person, including those with a cognitive impairment, must be brought into the decision-making process if some control is to remain with him or her. Also, by being inclusive, there is an acknowledgement of the two-way nature of the caring relationship, particularly between the carer and the cared-for person within informal care. Involvement may also help to reduce the stigma attached to using some services, although, as Garavan et al. (2001) suggest, this phenomenon will require further enquiry. In relation to older persons with a cognitive impairment or dementia, the issue of cognitive 'capacity' must be addressed, preferably by legislation, if the voices of older people are to be heard.

Eligibility and entitlement: Eligibility and entitlement issues must be resolved satisfactorily. Legislation to address this is promised, but it can only be effective if it overcomes the gross inequities in the current system of provision. Ways must be found to disseminate information on entitlements and services to those who need it if informal carers are to receive appropriate and timely support. While a standardised assessment process is required, the question of the right to such assessments should be reviewed in the light of the inevitable budgetary issues. As has been discussed in relation to the UK experience, undergoing a 'needs assessment' is not a panacea.

Formal services: Approaches must be developed in which family carers can be facilitated and supported to continue in their role as carers given that this is the wish of the majority of older people. At present the capacity of informal carers to offer care in the future may be waning, although O'Hanlon et al.'s recent study suggests that in Ireland the willingness to offer informal care is undiminished (2005). However, the stress and strain is often immense. Therefore, formal personal social services must be available to all who require them in the future in a flexible, timely and co-ordinated fashion. It is also essential to ensure that cultural diversity issues are factored into future service planning and delivery. In this way, service delivery as a whole, can move away from being crisis driven as it regularly is today.

The public, private and voluntary sector mix: The introduction of the Home Care Grant Scheme has underlined the need for greater clarity about roles and responsibilities between the public, private and voluntary sectors so that there is some meaningful sense of 'joined-up services'. This of course has to be achieved in the context of a planned approach to the provision of a comprehensive range of formal personal social services.

Inspection processes: A wide-ranging inspection scheme is required that encompasses all personal social services, such as is the norm in the UK. Without this, standardised, high quality care cannot be ensured, nor the abuse of older people diminished. The plan to expand the remit of the Social Services Inspectorate to cover residential care facilities is welcome as an initial starting point in providing a comprehensive inspection service. Provision of national quality standards is essential in order to benchmark any new inspection processes.

Funding: Older people and their families bear the brunt of the cost of care, often in an inequitable way. Formal services need to be resourced to a greater degree than at present. Spending should increase, as the NESF argues, to at least match that of the OECD average. There must also be a shift in the balance of funding that currently prefers residential care, in favour of community-based care in order to achieve this.

Conclusion

In conclusion, it can be said that the policy issues about personal social services throw up common themes across Europe and beyond. It appears that in all countries, there are concerns and debates about the quality and extent of and, indeed, the future provision of these services. Ireland is no different. Here, to date, the policy rhetoric relating to personal social services for older people has not been matched by the reality on the ground. This scenario leaves serious gaps in services for older people in Ireland. There are many challenges in implementing social policy in what is an increasingly changing policy landscape. O'Hanlon et al. sum up the situation well when they suggest that 'vision in planning for health and social services for older people in Ireland . . . is something that the older people of today deserve. It is, at the same time, the legacy that the rest of Irish society will inherit, for better or worse, in the coming decades. It, thus, is in everyone's best interest that we provide the ageing services we ourselves aspire to receiving' (2005: 28).

Chapter 12

Elder abuse

Anne O'Loughlin

Introduction

This chapter outlines international developments in elder abuse policy and strategies. The emergence of elder abuse policy in Ireland is discussed within the context of current Irish policy and its implementation. Significant events and developments that have had an impact in the emergence or shape of responses to elder abuse are analysed. Challenges facing the response to and ultimately the prevention of elder abuse are put forward.

International context

The growing interest and increasing attention to elder abuse on the world stage was first reflected in a publication entitled *Elder Abuse: International and Cross-Cultural Perspectives* (Kosberg and Garcia, 1995). The focus was on the vulnerability of those dependent on care by families. In the concluding chapter the authors identified both the unique and common experiences regarding elder abuse within the countries represented. Issues raised were the lack of an adequate definition of elder abuse and the paucity of research regarding its extent. The dependency of the older person, the decline of the welfare state and privatisation of resources and socio-cultural changes were the three common explanatory themes presented. The authors argued for more rigorous reporting and the development of treatment and prevention programmes. They also highlighted the importance of the involvement of older peoples' engagement in advocacy and the need for wide spread publicity to heighten public, political and professional awareness. It was their view that elder abuse 'will probably increase as a worldwide problem' (Kosberg and Garcia, 1995: 183–97).

It is now recognised that elder abuse is a universal phenomenon, which reflects the growing worldwide concern about human rights, gender equality, domestic violence and population ageing (Krug et al., 2002). The *International*

Plan of Action on Ageing (UN, 1982) did not refer to elder abuse which was in marked contrast to the Second World Assembly on Ageing in 2002. The Action Plan arising from this Assembly (UN, 2002b) held that the economic, social and cultural rights of older people, as well as their civil and political rights should be ensured and that this included 'the elimination of all forms of violence and discrimination against older people' (UN, 2002b: par. 12 (e)). The Recommendations for Action included the elimination of all forms of neglect, abuse and violence and the creation of support services to address elder abuse (UN, 2002b: par. 107–11).

Prior to the 2nd World Assembly in 2002, the *Valencia Forum*, brought together researchers, educators and practitioners to identify priorities for policy related research and data collection. The *Research Agenda on Ageing for the 21st Century* was designed to support the implementation of the *Madrid International Plan of Action on Ageing* (UN/IAG, 2002). The Research Agenda identified critical research arenas, which included the violation of human rights and age discrimination factors (socio economic, structural, attitudinal) which influence social participation and integration in different societies (UN/IAG, 2002: Section 2, par. 2.1.13) and research on elder abuse, neglect, violation and exploitation (UN/IAG, 2002: Section 2, par. 2.1.14).

The World Health Organisation (WHO) has also recognised the need to develop a global strategy for the prevention of the abuse of older people. An initial step in the development of this strategy was a qualitative study conducted in eight countries – Argentina, Austria, Brazil, Canada, India, Kenya, Lebanon and Sweden. This was a cross-cultural exploration of elder abuse from the perspective of older adults its aim being to identify the components of elder abuse as identified by older people and by primary health care teams. The importance of the cultural context in defining elder abuse was highlighted, challenging an individualistic focus 'by documenting the vital importance of structural-societal factors, underpinning virtually all aspects of elder abuse reported from developing countries' (WHO, 2002: 8).

As part of the global response to elder abuse, the WHO and International Network for the Prevention of Elder Abuse (INPEA), founded in 1997, along with the national co-ordinators of the study, agreed to a number of strategies. These included: the development of educational programmes and screening and assessment tools with a focus on primary health care professionals, a research methodology 'kit' for the study of elder abuse in developing countries, intergenerational studies, awareness raising, developing a global inventory of good practice and a Minimum Data set on elder abuse (WHO/INPEA, 2002: 20). The WHO is also one of the parties at the *Toronto Declaration on the Global Prevention of Elder Abuse* (WHO, 2004: 3).

The *World Report on Violence and Health*, published by WHO (Krug et al., 2002) is the first comprehensive summary of the overall problem of violence on a global scale. In the chapter on the abuse of older people, the developing concern about and research on elder abuse in a number of countries is tracked. The priorities for confronting the problem of elder abuse are greater knowledge about the problem, stronger laws and policies and more effective prevention strategies (2002: 141).

INPEA aims to increase society's ability, through international collaboration, to recognise and respond to the mistreatment of older people. Its current initiatives include: a Five Nation Study (Canada, Finland, Norway, United States, and Japan) exploring intercultural and intergenerational perceptions of elder abuse and older people's rights, a Worldwide Environmental Scan of Elder Abuse, gathering information on public policy, services, educational resources and training available on elder abuse and the collaborative project with WHO and Geneva International Academic Network, *Global Response to Elder Abuse and Neglect* (WHO/GIAN). To further highlight the issue, a World Elder Abuse Awareness Day was held on 15 June 2006, focusing efforts across the globe to raise awareness of elder abuse in a co-ordinated fashion for the first time. This event represented an unprecedented exploration of elder abuse across the world.

Elder abuse policy in Ireland

Several factors have paved the way for the increasing recognition of elder abuse in Ireland. The growing emergence of child abuse as a social problem has had a major impact on public receptivity to recognising violence within the family in all its forms as well as in institutional care settings. A new commitment to confront the problem of violence against women began in the early 1990s. This influenced concern about the abuse of older people. The first attempt to document violence against women (Cronin and O'Connor, 1993) looked at 119 female admissions to an Accident and Emergency unit. It was found that three of the women who were victims of domestic violence were over the age of 65 years. The authors (1993: 5) concluded that 'close co-operation between organisations working on assault of women and those working with the elderly must be developed if we are to have any realistic assessment of the number of elderly women suffering physical and sexual abuse in the family'. A similar project in another hospital found that of 45 identified cases of domestic violence, two were women over 65 years (Kelleher et al., 1995).

In March 1996, the *Domestic Violence Act* came into effect, providing protection for spouses, children and older persons. The 1996 Act introduced new categories of persons who could apply for legal remedies such as safety orders, barring orders and protection orders. These categories include a parent in respect of a non-dependent adult child and any adult in respect of co-resident adult, where the basis of the relationship is not primarily contractual. Powers given to the Health Boards, now Health Service Executive (HSE), under *Section 6* of the Act are very significant. These enable the HSE to apply on behalf of a person, who is deterred as a consequence of molestation, violence or threatened violence by the perpetrator or fear of the perpetrator from pursuing an application for a safety or barring order. This applies where there is reasonable cause to believe the person is being assaulted, ill-treated, sexually abused or seriously neglected.

Elder abuse policy: first steps

The Years Ahead (Department of Health, 1988), a report now twenty years old, currently forms the basis of official policy for older people in Ireland. The Report acknowledged that the problem of elder abuse had not been recognised. It contained only one specific reference to elder abuse, in the context of care-giver stress, stating that 'in a small number of cases, intense strain on the carer can result in the physical or emotional abuse of elderly people' (1988: 98). As discussed earlier, internationally, attention to elder abuse would appear to have accelerated since the mid-1990s.

In 1995, the Minister for Health commissioned a report on Elder Abuse in Ireland from the National Council for the Elderly, the predecessor to the National Council on Ageing and Older People (NCAOP) – the statutory advisory body on all aspects of ageing and the welfare of older people. Following the production of a preliminary briefing on elder abuse (1996), the NCAOP commissioned a more in depth study to explore the views of service providers and to formulate recommendations for the development of a comprehensive policy on elder abuse in Ireland. The subsequent report entitled *Abuse, Neglect and Mistreatment of Older People: An Exploratory Study* (O'Loughlin and Duggan, 1998) marked a significant step forward in the recognition of elder abuse and the formulation of an official plan to respond to the issue in Ireland. It presented a wide range of recommendations regarding: professional training, public awareness, use of the legal process, reform of the inspection process and the development of innovative areas of work such as community responses to elder abuse, telephone help lines and shelters for older people who are victims of abuse. The report also emphasised the importance of making links with those working in the fields of child protection domestic violence, substance abuse and mental health (1998: 103–15).

Working Group on Elder Abuse (WGEA)

A major recommendation of the report was the establishment of a Working Group on Elder Abuse 'to coordinate the development of policy on elder abuse and to give national guidance on procedures and guidelines' (Department of Health and Children, 1998: 104). The role of the Working Group, set up in

1999, was to advise the Minister on the requirements to effectively address incidents of elder abuse. It had a wide membership of social and health care professionals, as well as administrators and representatives of older persons' groups and carers. Draft policies and procedures and guidelines were developed and pilot training programmes were established in two Health Board areas to evaluate and test these. The final report of the WGEA, entitled *Protecting Our Future*, 'provides a foundation for the development of policy and procedures to respond to actual or alleged cases of elder abuse' (Department of Health and Children, 2002b: 7). The report opted for the explicit age of 65 as being the age beyond which 'abuse may be considered to be elder abuse' and defined elder abuse as 'a single or repeated act or lack of appropriate action occurring within any relationship where there is an expectation of trust which causes harm or distress to an older person or violates their human and civil rights' (2002b: 25).

It acknowledged the value of a UK policy document (Department of Health UK, 2000) as providing the basis for the development of policies in the Irish setting (Department of Health and Children, 2002b: 5). In common with the UK Department of Health's document, many forms of abuse are recognised (2002b: 26). These are: physical abuse (including the misuse of medication, restraint, or inappropriate sanctions); sexual abuse; psychological abuse, financial or material abuse (including pressure in connection with wills, property or inheritance), discriminatory abuse, as well as neglect and acts of omission (such as ignoring medical or physical care needs).

The report recommended that the response to elder abuse be placed in the wider context of health and social care services for older people. Key principles underlying service provision were empowerment, rights, the adequate protection of those unable to protect themselves and the adoption of the principle of 'least restrictive alternative' where intervention is required in the best interests of the older person (2002b: 30).

Implementation of recommendations of the Working Group on Elder Abuse

The brief of the Elder Abuse National Implementation Group (Department of Health and Children, 2003a), established in 2003 is to plan and advise on the implementation of the recommendations of *Protecting Our Future*. Its priorities have been the establishment of Elder Abuse Steering groups in each regional area, the appointment of senior elder abuse case workers and dedicated officers. Local Steering Groups have been established in most areas. The Health Service Executive (HSE) has also established a National Steering Group on Elder Abuse. The recruitment of staff did not commence, despite rising concern about elder abuse, until October 2006 when the advertisements were placed for Senior Elder Abuse Case Workers (Professionally Qualified Social Workers) and Regional Officers for Elder Abuse. Funding had also been made available in 2006 for the setting up of a National Elder Abuse Centre. Other priorities for the National Implementation Group are: public awareness campaigns, dealing with financial abuse, advocacy programmes and elder abuse in professional curricula.

Other developments relevant to elder abuse in Ireland

Health (Nursing Homes) Act 1990

The Health (Nursing Homes) Act 1990, the Nursing Homes Regulations 1993 and the Nursing Home (Subvention) Regulations 1996 are the legal framework for long-stay care in the *private* sector. The act and regulations provide for a system of registration, regulation and inspection of private nursing homes and also specify situations where financial subventions for long stay patients may be provided. However, the Nursing Homes (Care and Welfare) Regulations (Statutory Instrument 226 of 1993) do not cover standards of care and are in need of reform. Article 23 deals with inspection of nursing homes by designated officers. Inspections are required to be made not less than once in every period of six months. These officers must be permitted to enter, inspect the premises and conduct interviews 'where the officer has reasonable cause to believe that a person in the nursing home is not or has not been receiving proper care, maintenance or medical or other treatment' (Article 23d). Proposals for reform of this legislation, in particular in relation to the inspection process have been prompted by two significant events. Firstly, the case of Rostrevor Nursing Home in Dublin highlighted serious difficulties. It involved efforts by the South Western Area Health Board to close down the nursing home, which it found in breach of the Nursing Home (Care and Welfare) Regulations, 1993. However, the High Court ruled in August 2004, that the Health (Nursing Homes) Act 1990 did not confer on the Health Board an entitlement to close the home, while it remained on the Register of Nursing Homes. This case underlined the need for new legislation and stronger powers. Secondly, in May 2005, the Leas Cross Nursing Home in North County Dublin became the centre of major controversy when the RTÉ *Prime Time* programme revealed serious lapses in the care of residents. This led to increased public awareness about elder abuse and a commitment by Government to an urgent review of the operation of the Health (Nursing Homes) Act, 1990. Of the four separate 'inquiry' reports on Leas Cross, to date three have remained unpublished. The main emphasis in the media coverage has been on the need for an independent inspectorate.

In November 2006, the Leas Cross Review Report was published (O'Neill, 2006). This report was a review of the deaths of residents of Leas Cross through an analysis of written documentation. In summarising the report, the author stated: 'The overall documentary findings are consistent with a finding of institutional abuse' and 'deficiency in the regulatory process' (2006: 4). The report recommended urgent action to remedy 'system failure', in particular in the recognition of the complex needs of older people in long term care, legislative reform and the introduction of an independent social services inspectorate. In April 2007, the Minister for Health and Children announced the establishment of the Commission of Investigation into the Management, Operation and Supervision of Leas Cross Nursing Home.

Report of Human Rights Commission

The Human Rights Commission published a report entitled *Older People in Long Stay Care.* This important report provides an analysis of the admission and treatment of older people in long stay care, 'having regard to standards of human rights law, constitutional and international' (Mangan, 2003). The main findings of the report outline the concerns of the Commission about the lack of legislation and information about entitlements and quality of care, inadequate complaints and appeals procedures and lack of transparency about access to care. In particular, the report notes the failure to implement commitments to establish an independent inspectorate and the lack of systematic analysis of existing inspection reports on private nursing homes. It also highlights the fact that inspection does not currently cover public sector care.

'Trust in Care' policy

In May 2005, the HSE Employer Representative Division issued the report entitled: *Trust in Care: Policy for Health Service Employers on Upholding the Dignity and Welfare of Patient Clients and the Procedure for Managing Allegations of Abuse against Staff Members* (HSE, 2005). The aim of this policy document is to highlight the importance of the proper operation of human resource policies in maintaining high standards of care amongst health service staff and to ensure proper procedures for reporting suspicions or complaints of abuse and managing such allegations. The definition of abuse used in this report is: 'any form of behaviour that violates the dignity of patients/clients' (Health Service Executive (HSE), 2005: 7).

Health Service Reform Programme

In March 2005 the interim Health Information and Quality Authority was established and the permanent Health Information and Quality Authority (HIQA) was established under the Health Act 2007. It is proposed to place the Irish Social Services Inspectorate on a statutory basis (as part of HIQA) and to extend its remit to cover community and residential services for older people provided by the HSE as well as services for older persons in private nursing homes.

The Health Act 2007 established the Health Information and Quality Authority in May 2007. HIQA has responsibility for the development of standards for health and social care services. The Social Services Inspectorate, as part of HIQA, will undertake inspections. The extension of the Inspectorate to include services provided in the public sector is a major change. Draft National Standards for Residential Care Settings for Older People were published in August 2007. These include a standard and criteria on protection from abuse. The Health Act 2007 also includes protection for employees making disclosures of information about risks to health and welfare of a person or the public, or failure to comply with legal obligations.

Investigation by the Ombudsman of complaints regarding payment of nursing home subventions

In 2001, the Ombudsman reported on a special investigation into the payment of grants for nursing home care by Health Boards and found 'little evidence that notions of the rights of applicants were paramount' (Office of the Ombudsman, 2001: 72, 73). This resulted in the Government having to repay over £6 million as Health Boards failed to pay arrears despite allocation of funds for that purpose, a process which was characterised by yet further exploitation of older people (Comptroller and Auditor General, 2001). This report presented an analysis of exploitation and emotional abuse of older people at a corporate level (Office of the Ombudsman, 2001; O'Loughlin, 2005). It stated that the maladministration of the process of payment was 'a clear example of Health Boards' deliberately ignoring the law in preference to their own practices. Elderly patients' property rights were simply not a priority' (Howlin et al., 2006: 509).

Management of charges for long-stay care

In October 2004, following a question in the Dáil, the illegal charging of long-term care patients in the public sector first came into the pubic arena, such charges having been levied since 1976. The Minister for Health and Children sought the advice of the Attorney General on the legality of these charges. The response was that the practice of charging elderly people (and others in long-term care) had no basis in law and that new legislation would be required. New legislation was prepared – the Health (No. 2) (Amendment) Bill 2004; its purpose being to allow charges for long-term care to be levied. The Bill was passed in December but was referred to the Supreme Court by the President. It found that the provisions of the Bill (which sought to *retrospectively* legalise the illegal charges imposed over 29 years) to be repugnant to the Constitution. As a result, the Government accepted that substantial compensation, thought to be in the region of €1 billion, would have to be repaid to older people who were systematically and illegally overcharged in long stay institutions. Legislation, the Health (Repayment Scheme) Act 2006 was passed to regulate the repayment of the money and to regulate the property accounts of those in long-stay care. It introduced a statutory framework to protect patients' interests, particularly in the context of large repayments, which may be placed in these accounts. The Health (Amendment) Act 2005 and Health (Charges for In-Patient Services) Regulations 2005 were subsequent legislation that was passed providing for charges in public long-stay institutions.

In 2004, the Minister for Health and Children set up an independent evaluation into the long stay charges issue. The '*Travers Report*' concluded that 'overall systemic corporate failure occurred within the Department of Health and Children at the highest levels over more than 28 years'. The Report was presented to the Joint Committee on Health and Children, which then issued a final report in 2005 (Joint Oireachtas Committee on Health and Children). Kinsella and Kinsella (2006) place this scandal in the framework of a betrayal of trust between the Government and its citizens.

Law Reform Commission

The Law Reform Commission published a consultation paper, *Law and the Elderly* (Law Reform Commission (LRC), 2003). Proposals for law reform included an integrated system dealing with substitute decision making for those without general legal capacity and the protection of vulnerable adults from abuse. Recommendations included abolishing the current Ward of Court system (which dates back to Lunacy Regulation Ireland Act 1871) and its replacement with guardianship and the establishment of the Office of the Public Guardian. The new system of guardianship offered protection to those who lack legal capacity. The Commission also proposed that an adult may be in need of protection, even if legally capable. In this regard the Commission's new system included provision for specific orders (service orders, intervention orders and adult care orders) for those who had legal capacity but needed protection and were unable to obtain this themselves, and for those who did not have legal capacity but who did not need guardianship (Law Reform Commission, 2003: par 6.07). An Adult Care Order was an order that an adult could be removed from their residence and taken to another home or care facility. The order could only apply to an adult without legal capacity (Law Reform Commission, 2003: par 6.88).

A further Law Reform Commission Consultation Paper, *Vulnerable Adults and the Law: Capacity* (Law Reform Commission, 2005) examined important issues relating to capacity, including the capacity to make health care decisions. The Commission is working on a final report detailing what it recommends in proposed legislation. These consultation papers represent significant attention to the protection of vulnerable adults, in particular older people.

The final report, *Vulnerable Adults and the Law* (2006) deals with reform of the law on mental capacity, (including a Draft Scheme of a Mental Capacity and Guardianship bill) and the establishment of a new institutional decision-making structure – Guardianship – to replace the current Wards of Court system. The proposed frameworks diverge from the Consultation Papers in that Guardianship Orders and the Intervention Orders are to be confined to adults who do not have capacity. This report represents significant attention to the protection of vulnerable adults from abuse and exploitation.

The challenges ahead

It is clear from the discussion above that there are a number of major challenges ahead in regard to abuse of older people in Ireland. First of all, there is a need to address ageism in Irish society that has been at the root of sustaining abusive action towards older people. Policy makers must hear the voice of older people about the lived experience of abuse and the meaning of abuse. This may challenge the individualistic focus and show the importance of structural–societal factors underpinning elder abuse.

The location of a response to elder abuse within a health and social care context needs to be extended to widen the ownership of elder abuse across a range of organisations. This should be informed by the principles of citizenship and social inclusion. National coordination is required to guard against inconsistency, particularly with regard to definitions of what constitutes elder abuse and information about service developments. As the awareness of the abuse of 'vulnerable adults', such as those with disabilities increases, the question of how 'elder abuse' will be distinguished from or subsumed under 'vulnerable adults' policy will have to be addressed.

The first steps in providing a staff structure to respond to elder abuse will also require appropriate resources for training and service development. The establishment of the Health Information and Quality Authority (HIQA) and the extension of the remit of the Irish Social Service Inspectorate will pose huge challenges to the determination of nationally agreed standards for services and monitoring compliance. Finally, national media campaigns are essential to raise awareness; inform people of their rights; reduce stigma; encourage reporting of abuse and form part of preventive strategies.

References

Adams, A., Buckingham, C., Arber, S., McKinley, J. B., Marceau, L. and Link, C. (2006) 'The influence of patient's age on clinical decision-making about coronary heart disease in the USA and UK', *Ageing and Society* 26: 303–21.
Age Concern (2002) *Black and Minority Ethnic Elders' Issues.* London: Age Concern.
Alzheimer Europe (2005) *Annual Report 2004*. Luxembourg: Alzheimer Europe.
Alzheimer Europe (2006) *Annual Report 2005*. Luxembourg: Alzheimer Europe.
Alzheimer Europe (2007) www.Alzheimers-europe.org. Luxembourg: Alzheimer Europe.
Alzheimer's Society (2004) Declaration of Interests, June 2004. London: Alzheimer's Society.
Alzheimer's Society (2005) *Review of the Year 2004–5*. London: Alzheimer's Society.
Alzheimer's Society (2006a) Press Release 23 January 2006. London: Alzheimer's Society.
Alzheimer's Society (2006b) see update on the controversy 'Nice appeal: latest news' 20 July 2006, and press release 'Counting pennies, destroying lives 26 May 2006 on www.alzheimers.org.uk/News_and_Campaigns/News/060720appeal_news.htm and www.alzheimers.org.uk/News_and_Campaigns/Press_Releases/m_060526Nice.htm. London: Alzheimer's Society.
Alzheimer's Society (2006c) Appeal submitted in June 2006. London: Alzheimer's Society: 13.
Alzheimer Society of Ireland (2006a) 'Alzheimer drug policy queried', Irishhealth.com, 24 January 2006. Dublin: Alzheimer Society of Ireland.
Alzheimer Society of Ireland (2006b) Interview with CEO of Alzheimer Society of Ireland and Chair of Alzheimer Europe, 21 November 2006. Dublin: Alzheimer Society of Ireland.
Alzheimer Society of Ireland (2006c) *What is Alzheimer's Disease?* www.alzheimer.ie/index/info_what, accessed 17.12.2006. Dublin: Alzheimer Society of Ireland.
Alzheimer Society of Ireland (2006d) from interview with Information Research Officer and Events Manager of Alzheimer Society of Ireland, 3 April 2006. Dublin: Alzheimer Society of Ireland.
Alzheimer Society of Ireland (n.d.) *Your Guide to Understanding Alzheimer's Disease and Other Dementias.* Dublin: Alzheimer Society of Ireland: 10.
Alzheimer Society of Ireland (n.d.b) from Alzheimer Society of Ireland leaflet *'The signs of Alzheimer's disease can be everyday . . .'*. Dublin: Alzheimer Society of Ireland.
Angel, R. J. and Angel, J. L. (1997) *Who Will Care For Us? Aging and Long-Term Care in Multicultural America.* New York: New York University Press.
Angell, M. (2004) *The Truth About Drug Companies: How They Deceive Us and What to do About It.* New York: Random House.
Aricept.com (2006) Aricept.com/about/index.aspx, accessed 2006.

Barnard, H. and Pettigrew, N. (2003) *Delivering Benefits and Services for Black and Minority Ethnic Older People.* Leeds: Corporate Document Services for Department for Work and Pensions.

Barrett, A. and Bergin, A. (2006) 'Assessing age-related pressures on the public finances, 2005–50', in Callan, T. and Doris, A. (eds), *Budget Perspectives 2006.* Dublin: ESRI: pp. 3–20.

Barry, M., Tilson, L., Ryan, M. (2008) 'Drug expenditure in Ireland: explaining recent trends', in O'Donovan, O. and Glavanis-Grantham, K. (eds), *Power, Politics and Pharmaceuticals.* Cork: Cork University Press: 105–16.

Beard, R. (2004a) 'Advocating voice: organisational, historical and social milieux of the Alzheimer's disease movement', *Sociology of Health and Illness* 26 (6): 797–819.

Beard, R. (2004b) 'In their voices: identity preservation and experiences of Alzheimer's disease', *Journal of Aging Studies* 18: 415–28.

Bigby C. (2004) *Ageing with a Lifelong Disability.* London: Jessica Kingsley.

Biggs, S., Phillipson, C. and Kingston, P. (1995) *Elder Abuse in Perspective.* Buckingham: Open University Press.

Binstock, R. and Cluff, L. (1999) *Home Care Advances: Essential Research and Policy Issues.* New York: Springer.

Blackman, T. (2001) 'Social care in Europe', in Blackman, T., Brodhurst, S. and Convery, J. (eds), *Social Care and Social Exclusion: A Comparative Study of Older People's Care in Europe.* Houndmills: Palgrave: 10–26.

Blaikie, A. (1999) *Ageing and Popular Culture.* Cambridge: Cambridge University Press.

Bligh, W. (2003) 'Alzheimer Society of Ireland 21 years a growing', *Alzheimer Society of Ireland Newsletter* 3: 4.

Blume, S. and Catshoek, G. (2002) *Articulating the Patient Perspective: Strategic Options for Research.* Amsterdam: PatientenPraktijk.

Boseley, S. (2007) 'NHS watchdog rules out Alzheimer's U-turn', *The Guardian,* 9 Jan. 2007.

Bowes, A. (2006) 'Mainstreaming equality: implications of the provision of support at home for majority and minority ethnic older people', *Social Policy and Administration* 40 (7): 739–57.

Bowling, A. (1999) 'Ageism in cardiology', *British Medical Journal* 319: 1,353–5.

Bradley, S. and Humphries, N. (1999) *From Bosnia to Ireland's Private Rented Sector: A Study of Bosnian Housing Needs in Ireland.* Dublin: Clann Housing Association.

Burke, H. (1987) *The People and the Poor Law in Nineteenth Century Ireland.* Littlehampton: WEB.

Burke, H. (1999) 'Foundation stones of Irish social policy, 1831–1951', in Kiely, G., O'Donnell, A., Kennedy, P. and Quin, S. (eds), *Irish Social Policy in Context.* Dublin: UCD Press: 11–32.

Burton, A. (1997) 'Dementia: a case for advocacy?' in Hunter, S. (ed.), *Dementia: Challenges and New Directions.* London: Jessica Kingsley: 194–211.

Butt, J. and O'Neil, A. (2004) *Let's Move On: Black and Ethnic Minority Older People's Views on Research Findings.* York: Joseph Rowntree Foundation.

Bytheway, B. (1995) *Ageism.* Buckingham: Open University Press.

Caritas Europa (2006) *Migration, a Journey into Poverty?* Brussels: Caritas Europa.
Carone, G., Costello, D., Diez Guardia, N., Mourre, G., Przywara, B., Salomaki A. (2005) *The Economic Impact of Ageing Populations in the EU25 Member States.* European Economy Economic Working Paper no. 236. Brussels: European Commission.
Collier, J. (1998) 'Drug and Therapeutics Bulletin defends its stance over donepezil', *British Medical Journal* 316: 1,092.
Commission of the European Communities (1999) *Towards a Europe for All Ages: Promoting Prosperity and Intergenerational Solidarity.* Com/99/0221 final. Brussels: European Commission.
Commission of the European Communities (2002) *Europe's Response to World Ageing: Promoting Economic and Social Progress in an Ageing World – A Contribution of the European Commission to the 2nd World Assembly on Ageing.* Com/02/143 final. Brussels: European Commission.
Commission of the European Communities (2004) *First Annual Report on Migration and Integration.* Com/04/508 final. Brussels: European Commission.
Commission on Financial Management and Control Systems in the Health System (2003) *Brennan Report.* Dublin: Stationery Office.
Comptroller and Auditor General (2000) *Report on Value for Money Examination: Special Housing Aid for the Elderly.* Dublin: Stationery Office.
Comptroller and Auditor General (2001) *Investigation by the Ombudsman of complaints regarding payment of nursing home subventions.* Dublin: Stationery Office.
Comptroller and Auditor General (2002) *Department of Health and Children: Nursing Home Subventions.* Dublin: Stationery Office.
Connelly, N., Forsythe, L. A., Njike, G., and Rudiger, A. (2006) *Older Refugees in the UK: A Literature Review.* London: Refugee Council.
Conroy, P. (1999) 'From the fifties to the nineties: social policy comes out of the shadows', in Kiely, G., O'Donnell, A., Kennedy, P. and Quin, S. (ed.), *Irish Social Policy in Context.* Dublin: UCD Press: 33–50.
Conroy Jackson, P. (1993) 'Managing the mothers, the case of Ireland', in Lewis, J. (ed.), *Women and Social Policies in Europe.* London: Edward Elgar: 72–91.
Convery, J. (2001a) 'Social inclusion of older people in the health and social services in Ireland', in *Towards a Society for All Ages: Conference Proceedings.* Dublin: National Council on Ageing and Older People: 27–32.
Convery, J. (2001b) 'Ireland', in Blackman, T., Brodhurst, S. and Convery, J. (eds), *Social Care and Social Exclusion: A Comparative study of Older People's Care in Europe.* Houndmills: Palgrave: 83–95.
Cousins, M. (1995) *The Irish Social Welfare System: Law and Social Policy.* Dublin: Round Hall.
Cousins, M. (2005) *Explaining the Irish Welfare State: An Historical, Comparative and Political Analysis.* Lampeter: Edwin Mellen.
Cronin, J. and O'Connor, M. (1993) *The Identification and Treatment of Women Admitted to an Accident and Emergency Department as a Result of Assault by Spouse, Partners.* Dublin: Women's Aid.

Crossley, N. (2006) 'The field of psychiatric contention in the UK, 1960–2000', *Social Science and Medicine*, 62: 552–63.
CSO (1994) *Labour Force Survey 1994*. Dublin: Central Statistics Office.
CSO (1997) *Labour Force Survey 1997*. Dublin: Central Statistics Office.
CSO (2002) *Census 2002*. Dublin: Central Statistics Office.
CSO (2003) *Principal Demographic Results*. Dublin: Central Statistics Office.
CSO (2004) *Population and Labour Force Projections 2006–36*. Dublin: Central Statistics Office.
CSO (2006) *Census 2006 Preliminary Report*. Dublin: Central Statistics Office.
Dennis, I. and Guio, A. (2003) *Poverty and Social Exclusion in the EU after Laeken*, Part 1, Statistics in Focus. Population and Social Conditions. Eurostat.
Department of the Environment (1991) *A Plan for Social Housing*. Dublin: Stationery Office.
Department of the Environment and Local Government (2000) *Action on Housing*. Dublin: Stationery Office.
Department of the Environment, Heritage and Local Government (2005) *Housing Policy Framework: Building Sustainable Communities*. Dublin: Stationery Office.
Department of the Environment, Heritage and Local Government (various years) *Annual Housing Statistics Bulletin*. Dublin: Stationery Office.
Department of Foreign Affairs (2002) Task Force on Policy Regarding Emigrants *Ireland and the Irish Abroad*. Dublin: Stationery Office.
Department of Health (1984) *The Psychiatric Services: Planning for the Future*. Dublin: Stationery Office.
Department of Health (1988) *The Years Ahead: A Policy for the Elderly*. Report of the Working Party on Services for the Elderly. Dublin: Stationery Office.
Department of Health (1994) *Shaping a Healthier Future: A Strategy for Effective Healthcare in the 1990s*. Dublin: Stationery Office.
Department of Health and Children (1998) *Working for Health and Well-Being: Strategy Statement 1998–2001*. Dublin: Stationery Office.
Department of Health and Children (2001a) *Quality and Fairness: A Health System for You*. Dublin: Stationery Office.
Department of Health and Children (2001b) *Report of the National Advisory Group on Palliative Care*. Dublin: Stationery Office.
Department of Health and Children (2001c) *National Health Promotion Strategy 2000–5*. Dublin: Stationery Office.
Department of Health and Children (2001d) *Primary Care: A New Direction*. Dublin: Stationery Office.
Department of Health and Children (2002a) *Acute Hospital Bed Capacity: A National Review*. Dublin: Stationery Office.
Department of Health and Children (2002b) Working Group on Elder Abuse *Protecting Our Future*. Dublin: Stationery Office.
Department of Health and Children (2003a) *Elder Abuse National Implementation Group (EANIG)*. Dublin: Stationery Office.

Department of Health and Children (2003b) *The Health Information and Quality Authority (HIQA)*. Dublin: Stationery Office.
Department of Health and Children (2003c) *Review of the Nursing Home Subvention Scheme*. Dublin: Stationery Office.
Department of Health and Children (2005) *Statement of Strategy 2005–7*. Dublin: Stationery Office.
Department of Health and Children (2006a) *A Vision for Change: Report of the Expert Group on Mental Health Policy*. http://www.dohc.ie/publications/vision_for_change.html. Dublin: Stationery Office.
Department of Health and Children (2006b) *Annual Statistics 2005*. Dublin: Stationery Office.
Department of Health (UK) (2000) *No Secrets*. London: HMSO.
Department of Justice, Equality and Law Reform (1996) *A Strategy for Equality: Report of the Commission on the Status of People with Disabilities*. Dublin: Stationery Office.
Department of Justice, Equality and Law Reform (1998) *Employment Equality Act 1998*. Dublin: Stationery Office.
Department of Justice, Equality and Law Reform (1999a) *National Disability Authority (NDA) Act* 1999. Dublin. Stationery Office.
Department of Justice, Equality and Law Reform (1999b) *Integration: A Two Way Process: Interdepartmental Working Group on the Integration of Refugees in Ireland*. Dublin: Stationery Office.
Department of Justice, Equality and Law Reform (2004) *Employment Equality Act 2004*. Dublin: Stationery Office.
Department of Social, Community and Family Affairs (2002) *Building an Inclusive Society: Review of the National Anti-Poverty Strategy under the Programme for Prosperity and Fairness*. Dublin: Stationery Office.
Department of the Taoiseach (2007) *Social Inclusion: Building an Inclusive Society, the National Plan for Social Inclusion*. Dublin: Stationery Office.
Deyo, R. and Patrick D. (2005) *Hope or Hype. The Obsession with Medical Advances and the High Cost of False Promises*. New York: Amacom.
Director of the National Centre for Pharmacoeconomics (2006) www.aricept.com/about/index.aspx, accessed 07.09.2006.
Disney, R. (1996) *Can We Afford To Grow Older? A Perspective on the Economics of Aging*. Harvard: MIT Press.
Downey, D. (2005) 'Access denied? The challenge of affordability for sustainable access to housing', in Norris, M. and Redmond, D. (eds), *Housing Contemporary Ireland: Policy, Society and Shelter*. Dublin: IPA: 44–68.
Doyle, M. (2006) 'Market: role in the financing and provision of home care', in Timonen, V., Doyle, M. and Prendergast, M. (eds), *No Place Like Home: Domiciliary Care Services for Older People in Ireland*. Dublin: Liffey Press: 47–79.
Dr Foster Intelligence (2006) 'Keeping people out of hospital: the challenge of reducing emergency admissions'. www.drfoster.co.uk, accessed 30.9.2006.

Drury, M. (2005) 'Ageing and mental health', in Quin, S. and Redmond, B. (eds), *Mental Health and Social Policy in Ireland*. Dublin: UCD Press: 115–29.
Eastern Health Board (1998) *10 Year Action Plan for Services for Older Persons 1999–2008*. Dublin: Eastern Health Board.
Ermisch, J. (1983) *The Political Economy of Demographic Change: Causes and Implications of Population Trends in Britain*. London: Heinemann.
ESRI (2003) *Irish National Survey of Housing Quality* (INSHQ), *2001–2*. Dublin: ESRI.
Estes, C. L. (1979) *The Ageing Enterprise: A Critical Examination of Social Policies and Services for the Aged*. London: Jossey-Bass.
Estes, C. L. and Associates (2001) *Social Policy and Aging: A Critical Perspective*. London: Sage.
Estes, C. L., Biggs, S. and Phillipson, C. (2003) *Social Theory, Social Policy and Ageing: A Critical Introduction*. Buckingham: Open University Press.
European Commission (1993) *Ageing at Work: The European Perspective*. Luxembourg: Office for Official Publications of the European Communities.
European Commission (1999a) *Towards a Europe for All Ages*. Luxembourg: Office for Official Publications of the European Communities.
European Commission (1999b) *Active Ageing: Promoting a European Society For All Ages*. Luxembourg: Office for Official Publications of the European Communities.
European Commission (2000) *Survey on the Current Status of Research into 'Ageing' in Europe*. Luxembourg: Office for Official Publications of the European Communities.
European Commission (2001) Burden of Disease in Old Age Network Project (BURDIS). Luxembourg: Office for Official Publications of the European Communities.
European Commission (2002) *Europe's Response to World Ageing: Promoting Economic and Social Progress in an Ageing World: A Contribution of the European Commission to the 2nd World Assembly on Ageing*. Luxembourg: Office for Official Publications of the European Communities.
European Commission (2004) *Increasing the Employment of Older Workers and Delaying the Exit from the Labour Market*. Luxembourg: Office for Official Publications of the European Communities.
European Social Fund Evaluation Unit (1996) *Mobility in the EU Implications for the European Social Fund. Discussion Paper*. Dublin: European Social Fund Programme Evaluation Unit and Department of Enterprise and Employment.
Eurostat (2006) *Non-National Populations in the EU Member States*. Luxembourg: Office for Official Publications of the European Communities.
Evandrou, M. (2000) 'Social inequalities in later life: the socio-economic position of older ethnic minority groups in Britain', in *Population Trends*. London: HMSO.
Evandrou, M. (2003) *Growing Old in London: Socio-Economic Inequalities*. Sage Discussion Paper no. 15. www.lse.ac.uk.depts/sage, accessed 16.11.2006.
Evandrou, M. (2005) *Health and Well-Being Amongst Older People in Britain at the Start of the 21st Century*. Sage Discussion Paper no. 22. www.lse.ac.uk.depts/sage, accessed 16.11.2006.

Evandrou, M. and Falkingham, J. (2004) *How Have Older People Fared Under New Labour?* Sage Discussion Paper no. 19. www.lse.ac.uk/depts/sage, accessed 03.11.2006.
Evenhuis, H., Henderson, C. M., Beange, H., Lennox, N. and Chicoine, B. (2000) *Healthy Ageing: Adults with Intellectual Disabilities: Physical Health Issues.* Geneva: WHO.
Fahey, T. (1995) *Health and Social Care Implications of Population Ageing in Ireland 1991–2011.* Report No. 42. Dublin: National Council for the Elderly.
Fahey, T. (1998) 'Population ageing, the elderly and health care', in Leahy, A. L. and Wiley, M. (eds), *The Irish Health System in the 21st Century.* Dublin: Oak Tree Press: 183–98.
Fahey, T. (2003) 'Is there a trade-off between pensions and home ownership? An exploration of the Irish case', *Journal of European Social Policy* 13 (2): 159–73.
Fahey, T. and Fitzgerald, J. (1997) *Welfare Implications of Demographic Trends.* Dublin: Oak Tree Press in association with Combat Poverty Agency.
Fahey, T. and Murray, P. (1994) *Health and Autonomy for the over 65s in Ireland.* Dublin: National Council on Ageing and Older People.
Fahey, T. and Nolan, B. (2005) 'Housing expenditures, housing poverty and housing wealth: Irish home owners in comparative context', in Norris, M. and Redmond, D. (eds), *Housing Contemporary Ireland: Policy, Society and Shelter.* Dublin: IPA: 69–99.
Fahey, T. and Russell, H. (2001) *Older People's Preferences for Employment and Retirement in Ireland.* Dublin: National Council of Ageing and Older People.
Fanning, B. (1999) 'The mixed economy of welfare', in Kiely, G., O'Donnell, A., Kennedy, P. and Quin, S. (eds), *Irish Social Policy in Context.* Dublin: UCD Press: 51–69.
Fanning, B. (2003) 'The construction of social policy', in Fanning, B. and McNamara, T. (eds), *Ireland Develops: Administration and Social Policy 1953–2003.* Dublin: IPA: 3–18.
FÁS (2006) *Population and Migration Estimates: Irish Labour Market Review, April 2006.* Dublin: FÁS.
Featherstone, M. and Hepworth, M. (1995) 'Images of positive ageing: a case study of *Retirement Choice* magazine', in Featherstone, M. and Wernick, A. (eds), *Images of Ageing: Cultural Representations of Later Life.* London: Routledge: 29–47.
Feldman, S. (1999) 'Please don't call me "dear": older women's narratives of health care'. *Nursing Inquiry* 6 (4): 269–76.
Fenton, E. and Mitchell, T. (2002) 'Growing old with dignity: a concept analysis', *Nursing Older People* 14 (4): 19–21.
Fine, M. D. (2007) *A Caring Society? Care and the Dilemmas of Human Services in the Twenty First Century.* Houndmills: Palgrave Macmillan.
Finnish Centre for Interdisciplinary Gerontology (2004) *Disability in Old Age: Final Report of the Burden of Disease Network (BURDIS) Project.* http://www.jyu.fi/BURDIS/FinalReport.pdf.
Fisk, M. (2001) 'Housing policy frameworks and the social exclusion of older people in Northern Ireland and the Republic'. Paper presented to the Irish Social Policy Association Conference, Dublin, 28 July, 2001.

FitzGerald, J. (2004) *Ireland: An Ageing Multicultural Economy.* ESRI Working Paper 157. Dublin: ESRI.

Forfás (2001) *Labour Force Participation Rates of Over 55s in Ireland.* Dublin: Forfás.

Foucault, M. (2001) *Madness and Civilization. A History of Insanity in the Age of Reason.* London: Routledge.

Fox, P. (1989) 'From senility to Alzheimer's disease: the rise of the Alzheimer's disease movement', *Milbank Quarterly*, 67, 1: 58–102.

Gallagher, C. (2006) 'Social policy and a good life in old age', in O'Dell, E. (ed.), *Older People in Modern Ireland: Essays on Law and Policy.* Dublin: First Law: 48–71.

Garavan, R., Winder, R. and McGee, H. (2001) *Health and Social Services for Older People (HeSSOP)*, Report no. 64. Dublin: National Council on Ageing and Older People.

Goffman, E. (1961) *Asylums: Essays on the Social Situation of Mental Patients and Other Inmates.* New York: Doubleday.

Government of Ireland: Interdepartmental Committee on the Care of the Aged (1968) *The Care of the Aged.* Dublin: Stationery Office.

Government of Ireland (1996) *Refugee Act, as amended.* Dublin: Stationery Office.

Government of Ireland (2001) *Mental Health Act 2001.* Dublin: Stationery Office.

Government of Ireland (2002) Social Inclusion: *Building an Inclusive Society*, the National Plan for Social Inclusion. Dublin: Stationery Office.

Government of Ireland (2006) *Towards 2016: Ten-Year Framework Social Partnership Agreement 2006–15.* Dublin: Stationery Office.

Grimley Evans, J. (1997) 'The rationing debate: rationing health care by age: the case against', *British Medical Journal* 314: 822.

Grundy, E. (2006) 'Ageing and vulnerable elderly people: European perspectives', *Ageing and Society* 26: 105–34.

Gubrium, J. F. (1975) *Living and Dying at Murray Manor.* London: St James Press.

Gubrium, J. F. (1993) 'Voice and context in a new gerontology' in Cole, T. R., Achenbaum, W. A., Jakobi, P. L. and Kastenbaum, R. (eds), *Voices and Visions of Aging: Towards a Critical Gerontology.* New York: Springer.

Gubrium, J. F. and Holstein, J. A. (1999) 'Constructionist perspectives on aging', in Bengston, V. L. and Schaie, K. W. (eds), *Handbook of Theories of Aging.* New York: Springer: 287–305.

Gubrium, J. F. and Holstein, J. A. (2000) 'Introduction', in Gubrium, J. F. and Holstein, J. A. (eds) *Aging and Everyday Life.* Oxford: Blackwell: 1–11.

Guio, A. (2005) *Income Poverty and Social Exclusion in the EU25. Statistics in Focus. Population and Social Conditions.* Luxembourg: Eurostat.

Haslett, D. (2003) *The Role and Future Development of Day Services for Older People in Ireland.* Dublin: National Council on Ageing and Older People.

Hazan, H. (1994) *Old Age: Constructions and Deconstructions.* Cambridge: Cambridge University Press.

Health Evidence Network (HEN) (2003) *What Are the Main Risk Factors for Disability in Old Age and How Can Disability be Prevented?* http://www.euro.who.int/document/E82970.pdf.

Health Service Executive (HSE) Employer Representative Division (2005) *Trust in Care.* Dublin: HSE.

Hepworth, M. (2003) 'Ageing bodies: aged by culture', in Coupland, J. and Gwyn, R. (eds), *Discourse, the Body and Identity.* Houndmills: Palgrave Macmillan: 89–106.

Herskovits, E. (1995) 'Struggling over subjectivity: debates about the "self" and Alzheimer's disease', *Medical Anthropology Quarterly* 9 (2): 146–64.

Hickman, M. and Walter, B. (1997) *Discrimination and the Irish Community in Britain.* London: Commission for Racial Equality.

Hockey, J. and James, A. (1993) *Growing Up and Growing Old: Ageing and Dependency in the Life Course.* London: Sage.

Howlin, N., Shariff, M. and Del Rio, A. (2006) 'The Health Bill fiasco: thirty tears of doublethink?' in O'Dell, E. (ed.), *Older People in Modern Ireland Essays on Law and Policy.* Dublin: First Law: 495–584.

Hudson, R. B. (2005) 'Contemporary challenges to age-based policy', in Hudson, R. B. (ed.), *The New Politics of Old Age Policy.* Baltimore MD: Johns Hopkins University Press: 1–19.

Hugman, Richard (1994) *Ageing and the Care of Older People in Europe.* London: Macmillan.

Igoe, D., Keogh, F. and McNamara, C. (1997) 'A survey of Irish palliative care services', *Irish Journal of Medical Science* 166 (4): 206–11.

Illich, I. (1994) 'Brave new biocracy: health care from womb to tomb', *New Perspectives Quarterly* 11 (1): 4–13.

Interdisciplinary Centre for Comparative Research in the Social Sciences (ICCR) (2005) *ACTIVAGE: Overcoming the Barriers and Seizing the Opportunities for Active Ageing Policies in Europe.* http://www.iccr-international.org/activage/en/index.html.

International Organisation for Migration (IOM) (2006) *Managing Migration in Ireland. A Social and Economic Analysis.* Dublin: NESC.

Irish Council for Social Housing (2005) *An Overlooked Option in Caring for the Elderly: A Report on Sheltered Housing and Group Housing Provided by Housing Associations in Ireland.* Dublin: Irish Council for Social Housing.

Irish Hospice Foundation (2004) *Nationwide Survey on Death and Dying.* Dublin: Irish Hospice Foundation.

Irish Hospice Foundation (2006) *A Baseline Study on the Provision of Hospice/Specialist Palliative Care Services in Ireland.* Dublin: Irish Hospice Foundation.

Irish Nurses Organisation (2006) *Pre-Budget Submission for Budget 2007: Priority Investments for our Public Health Service.* Dublin: Irish Nurses Organisation.

Joint Oireachtas Committee on Health and Children (2005) *Report on the Report on Certain Issues of Management and Administration in the Department of Health & Children associated with the Practice of Charges for Persons in Long-Stay Care in Health Board Institutions and Related Matters.* Dublin: Stationery Office.

Kaduszkiewicz, H., Zimmermann, T., Beck-Bornholdt, H., van den Bussche, H. (2005) 'Cholinesterase inhibitors for patients with Alzheimer's disease: systematic review of randomised clinical trials', *British Medial Journal* 331: 321–7.

Katz, S. (1996) *Disciplining Old Age: The Formation of Gerontological Knowledge.* London: University Press of Virginia.

Kelleher, P., Kelleher, C. and O'Connor, M. (1995) *Making the Links.* Dublin: Women's Aid.

Kennedy, P. (1999) 'Women and social policy', in Kiely, G., O'Donnell, A. Kennedy, P. and Quin, S. (eds) *Irish Social Policy in Context.* Dublin: UCD Press: 231–53.

Kent, A. (2007) 'Should patient groups accept money from drug companies? Yes', *British Medical Journal* 334: 934.

Kinsella, R. and Kinsella, M. (2006) 'The long stay care crisis: a case study in policy failure', in O'Dell, E. (ed.), *Older People in Modern Ireland Essays on Law and Policy.* Dublin: First Law: 371–92.

Klawiter, M. (1999) 'Risk, prevention, and the breast cancer continuum: The NCI, the FDA, health activism and the pharmaceutical industry', *History and Technology* 18 (4): 309–53.

Klinthäl, M. (2006) *Immigration, Integration and Return Migration. Paper to International Symposium on International Migration and Development.* International Symposium on International Migration and Development Turin, Italy, 28–30 June 2006.

Knapp, A. and Kremla, M. (2002) *Older Refugees in Europe: Survey Results and Key Approaches.* London: ECRE.

Kosberg, J. and Garcia, K. (1995) *Elder Abuse: International and Cross-Cultural Perspectives.* New York: Haworth Press.

Krug, E., Straus, M., Gelles, R., Steinmetz, S. and Gerbner, G. (2002) *World Report on Violence and Health.* Geneva: WHO.

Landzelius, K. (2006) 'Introduction: Patient organisation movements and new metamorphoses in patienthood', *Social Science and Medicine* 62 (3): 529–37.

Lanzieri, G. (2006) *Long-term Population Projections at National Level.* Luxembourg: European Communities.

Law Reform Commission (LRC, 2003) *Law and the Elderly.* Dublin: Law Reform Commission.

Law Reform Commission (LRC, 2005) *Vulnerable Adults and the Law: Capacity.* Dublin: Law Reform Commission.

Law Reform Commission (LRC, 2006) *Vulnerable Adults and the Law.* Dublin: Law Reform Commission.

Layte, R., Fahey, T. and Whelan, C. T. (1999) *Income, Deprivation and Well-Being Among Older Irish People.* Dublin: National Council on Ageing and Older People.

Lewis, G. (2000) 'Introduction: expanding the social policy imaginary', in Lewis, G., Gewirtz, S. and Clarke, J. (eds), *Rethinking Social Policy.* London: Sage: 1–21.

Little, M. (2002) *Improving Older People's Services: Policy into Practice: Inspection of Older People's Services.* London: Social Services Inspectorate, Department of Health.

Livingstone, G. and Sembhi, S. (2003) 'Mental health of the ageing immigrant population', *Advances in Psychiatric Treatment* 9: 31–7.

Lookinland, S. and Anson, K. (1995) 'Perpetuation of ageist attitudes among present and future health care personnel: implications for elder care', *Journal of Advanced Nursing* 21: 47–56.

Lupton, D. (2000) 'Food, risk and subjectivity', in Williams, S. Gabe, J. and Calnan, M. (eds), *Health, Medicine and Society. Key Theories, Future Agendas.* London: Routledge: 123–45.
Lyman, K. A. (2000) 'Bringing the social back in: a critique of the biomedicalisation of dementia', in Gubrium, J. F. and Holstein, J. A. (eds), *Aging and Everyday Life.* Oxford: Blackwell: 340–56.
Lymbery, M. (2005) *Social Work with Older People: Context, Policy and Practice.* London: Sage.
Maggini, M., Vanacore, N. and Raschetti, R. (2006) 'Cholinesterase inhibitors: drugs looking for a disease?' *PLoS Medicine* 3 (4): e140.
Maitre, B., Nolan, B. and Whelan, C. T. (2006) *Reconfiguring the Measurement of Deprivation and Consistent Poverty in Ireland.* Policy Research Series no. 58. Dublin: ESRI.
Malcolm, E. (1996) *Elderly Return Migration from Britain to Ireland: A Preliminary Study.* Dublin: National Council for the Elderly.
Malpass, P. (2005) *Housing and the Welfare State: The Development of Housing Policy in Britain.* London: Palgrave Macmillan.
Mangan, I. (2003) *Older People in Long Stay Care.* Dublin: Irish Human Rights Commission.
McCashin, A. (2004) *Social Security in Ireland.* Dublin: Gill & Macmillan.
McGee, H. M., O'Hanlon, A., Barker, M., Stout, R., O'Neill, D., Conroy, R., Hickey, A., Shelley. E. and Layte, R. (2005) *One Island – Two Systems: A Comparison of Health Status and Health and Social Service Use by Community-Dwelling Older People in the Republic of Ireland and Northern Ireland.* Dublin: Institute of Public Health in Ireland.
Minichiello, V., Browne, J. and Kendig, H. (2000) 'Perceptions and consequences of ageism: views of older people', *Ageing and Society,* 20: 253–78.
Mintzes, B. (2007) 'Should patient groups accept money from drug companies? No', *British Medical Journal* 334: 935.
Moran, J. (2003) *Housing Refugees: A Good Practice Guide.* Dublin: Housing Unit.
Moran, J. (2005) 'Mental health and new communities' in Quin, S. and Redmond, B. (eds), *Mental Health and Social Policy in Ireland.* Dublin: UCD Press.
Moreira, T. (forthcoming) 'Testing promises: truth and hope in drug development and evaluation in Alzheimer's disease', in Ballenger, J., Whitehouse, P., Lyketsos, C., Rabins, P. and Karlawish, J. (eds), *Do We Have a Pill for That? Interdisciplinary Perspectives on the Development, Use and Evaluation of Drugs in the Treatment of Dementia.* Baltimore: Johns Hopkins University Press.
Morris, J. (1991) *Pride Against Prejudice: Transforming Attitudes to Disability.* London: Women's Press.
Moynihan, R. and Henry, D. (2006) 'The fight against disease mongering: generating knowledge for action', *PLoS Medicine* 3 (4): e191.
Mullins, D., Rhodes, M. and Williamson, A. (2003) *Non-Profit Housing Organisations in Ireland, North and South: Changing Fortunes, Challenging Futures.* Belfast: Northern Ireland Housing Executive.

Murray, K. and Norris, M. (2002) *Profile of Households Accommodated by Dublin City Council: Analysis of Socio-Demographic, Income and Spatial Patterns, 2001*. Dublin: Housing Unit and Dublin City Council.

National Council for the Aged (1985) *Housing of the Elderly in Ireland.* Dublin: National Council for the Aged.

National Disability Authority (NDA) and NCAOP (2006) *Ageing and Disability: A Discussion Paper.* Dublin: NDA and NCAOP.

National Institute for Health and Clinical Excellence (NICE, 2005) *Final Appraisal Determination. Donepezil, Galantamine, Rivastigmine (Review) and Memantine for the Treatment of Alzheimer's Disease.* London: National Institute for Health and Clinical Excellence.

National Pensions Board (1993) *Developing the National Pension System: Final Report of the National Pensions Board.* Dublin: Stationery Office.

NCAOP (National Council on Ageing and Older People, 2001a) *Age and Attitudes: Ageing in Ireland Fact File no. 13*. NCAOP.

NCAOP (2001b) *Demography: Ageing in Ireland Fact File no. 1*. Dublin: NCAOP.

NCAOP (2001c) *Employment and Retirement among the Over-55s: Patterns, Preferences and Issues.* Dublin: NCAOP.

NCAOP (2001d) *Housing. Ageing in Ireland Fact File no. 5*. Dublin: NCAOP.

NCAOP (2001e) *Return Migration Ageing in Ireland Fact File no. 12*. Dublin: NCAOP.

NCAOP (2005a) *An Age Friendly Society: A Position Statement.* Dublin: NCAOP.

NCAOP (2005b) *Perceptions of Ageism in Health and Social Services in Ireland.* Dublin: NCAOP.

NESC (2005) *The Developmental Welfare State.* Dublin: NESC.

NESC (2006) *Migration Policy.* Dublin: NESC.

NESF (2003) *Labour Market Issues for Older Workers,* Forum Report no. 26. Dublin: NESF.

NESF (2005) *Care for Older People.* Report no. 32. Dublin: NESF.

Neville, G. (2004) 'Mother Courage? Irish Mothers and Emigration to North America', Kennedy, P. (ed.) (2004), *Motherhood in Ireland: Creation and Context.* Cork: Cork University Press.

Ní Laoire, C. (2004) *Coming Home: A Geography of Recent Return Migration to the Republic of Ireland,* NMR Working Paper presented to the 2nd International Population Geographies Conference, August 2004.

Nolan, B. and Wiley, M. M. (2001) *Private Practice in Irish Public Hospitals.* Dublin: Oak Tree.

Nord, E., Street, A., Richardson, J., Kuhse, H. and Singer, P. (1996) 'The significance of age and duration of effect in social evaluation of health care', *Health Care Analysis* 4 (2): 103–11.

Norris, M. (2005) 'Social housing', in Norris, M. and Redmond, D. (eds), *Housing Contemporary Ireland: Policy, Society and Shelter.* Dublin: IPA: 160–82.

Norris, M. and Winston, N. (2004) *Housing Policy Review 1990–2002*. Dublin: Stationery Office.

O'Connell, M. (2005) 'Overcoming the stigma of dementia', *Alzheimer Society of Ireland Newsletter* 22 (4): 4–5.
O'Connor, D. (1999) 'Constructing community care: (re)estorying support, in Neysmith, S. M. (ed.), *Critical Issues for Future Social Work Practice with Aging Persons*. New York: Columbia University Press: 71–96.
O'Connor, J., Ruddle, H., and O'Gallagher, M. (1989) *Sheltered Housing in Ireland: Its Role in the Care of the Elderly, Report no 20*. Dublin: National Council for the Elderly.
O'Dell, E. (2006) *Older People in Modern Ireland Essays on Law and Policy*. Dublin: First Law.
O'Donovan, O. (2007) 'Corporate colonisation of health activism? Irish health advocacy organisations' modes of engagement with pharmaceutical corporations', *International Journal of Health Services*, (37) 4: 711–733.
ODPM (2005) *Improving Services, Improving Lives: Evidence and Key Themes*. A Social Exclusion Unit Interim Report. London: Office of the Deputy Prime Minister.
ODPM (2006) *A Sure Start to Later Life: Ending Inequalities for Older People*. London: Office of the Deputy Prime Minister.
OECD (1992) *Urban Policies for Ageing Populations*. Paris: OECD.
OECD (1996) *Ageing in OECD Countries: A Critical Policy Challenge*. Paris: OECD.
OECD (1998) *Maintaining Prosperity in an Ageing Society*. Paris: OECD.
OECD (2001) *Ageing and Income: Financial Resources and Retirement in 9 OECD Countries*. Paris: OECD.
OECD (2004) *Ageing and Employment Policies*. Paris: OECD.
OECD (2006a) *Ageing and Employment Policies: Ireland*. Paris: OECD.
OECD (2006b) *Live Longer, Work Longer* (Executive Summary): http://www.oecd.org/dataoecd/32/50/36218997.pdf.
Office of the Ombudsman (2001) *Nursing Home Subventions*. Dublin: Office of the Ombudsman.
Office for Social Exclusion (2002) *Building an Inclusive Society*. Dublin: Office for Social Exclusion.
O'Flynn, J. (2004) *Building Common Purpose to Support the Irish Abroad Reflections from a 2004 Emigrant Advice Network International Conference on Irish Emigration*. Dublin: EAN.
O'Hanlon, A., McGee, H., Barker, M., Garavan, R., Hickey, A., Conroy, R. and O'Neill, D. (2005) *Health and Social Services for Older People (HeSSOP II): Changing Profiles from 2000 to 2004*. Report no. 91. Dublin: National Council on Ageing and Older People.
Oireachtas Committee on Health and Children (2007) *The Adverse Side Effects of Pharmaceuticals Eighth Report*. Dublin: Stationery Office.
O' Loughlin, A. (2002) 'The "pocket money" issue: financial exploitation of older people: an Irish case study', *Irish Social Worker* 20 (1–2): 14–15.
O'Loughlin, A. (2005) 'Social policy and older people', in Quin, S., Kennedy, P., Matthews, A. and Kiely, G. (eds.) *Contemporary Irish Social Policy*, 2nd edn. Dublin: UCD Press: 206–30.

O'Loughlin, A. and Duggan, J. (1998) *Abuse, Neglect and Mistreatment of Older People: An Exploratory Study.* Dublin: National Council on Ageing and Older People.

O'Neill, D. (2006) *A Review of the Deaths at Leas Cross Nursing Home 2002–5.* Dublin: Health Service Executive.

ORAC (Office of the Refugee Applications Commissioner, 2004) *Annual Report.* Dublin: ORAC.

ORAC (Office of the Refugee Applications Commissioner, 2005) *Annual Report.* Dublin: ORAC.

O'Shea, E. (2000) *The Cost of Caring for People with Dementia and Related Cognitive Impairments.* Dublin: National Council for Ageing and Older People.

O'Shea, E. (2002) *Review of the Nursing Home Subvention Scheme.* Dublin: Stationery Office.

O'Shea, E. and Gillespie, P. (2006) 'Health policy in Ireland' in Healy, S., Reynolds, B. and Collins, M. (eds), *Social Policy in Ireland: Principles, Practice and Problems.* Dublin: Liffey Press: 271–95.

O'Shea, E. and O'Reilly, S. (1999) *An Action Plan for Dementia, Report no. 54.* Dublin: National Council on Ageing and Older People.

O'Síoráin, L. and Ling, J. (2005) 'The future of palliative care in Ireland', in Ling, J. and O'Síoráin, L. (eds), *Palliative Care in Ireland.* Maidenhead: Open University Press: 203–11.

Patel, N. (1999) *Black and Ethnic Minority Elderly: Perspectives on Long-Term Care.* London: PRIAE.

Patel, N. and Traynor, P. (2006) *Developing Extra Care Housing for Black and Minority Ethnic Elders: an overview of the issues, examples and challenges.* London: Housing Learning and Improvement Network.

Paterniti, D. A. (2003) 'Claiming identity in a nursing home', in Gubrium, J. F. and Holstein, J. A. (eds), *Ways of Aging.* Oxford: Blackwell: 58–74.

Peace, S., Kellaher, L. and Willcock, D. (1997) *Re-evaluating Residential Care.* Buckingham: Open University Press.

Phillips, J., Ray, M., and Marshall, M. (2006) *Social Work with Older People,* 4th edn. Houndmills: Palgrave Macmillan.

Phillipson, C. (1982) *Capitalism and the Construction of Old Age.* London: Macmillan.

Phillipson, C. (1998) *Reconstructing Old Age: New Agendas in Social Theory and Practice.* London: Sage.

Phillipson, C. and Walker, A. (1986) *Ageing and Social Policy: A Critical Assessment.* Gower: Aldershot.

Player, S. and Pollock, A. M. (2001) 'Long-term care: from public responsibility to private good', *Critical Social Policy: A Journal of Theory and Practice in Social Welfare* 21 (2): 231–55.

Pollock, A. M. (2005) *NHS plc: The Privatisation of Our Health Care.* London: Verso.

Prendergast, D. (2006) in Timonen, V., Doyle, M. and Prendergast, D. (eds), *No Place Like Home: Domiciliary Care Services for Older People in Ireland.* Dublin: Liffey Press.

PRIAE (2004) *Summary Findings of the Minority Elderly Care (MEC) Project.* London: PRIAE.

Public and Corporate Economic Consultants (2001) *Labour Market Participation of the Over-55s.* Dublin: Forfás.

Quadagno, J. and Reid, J. (1999) 'The political economy perspective in aging', in Bengston, V. L. and Shaie, K. W. S. (eds), *Handbook of Theories of Ageing.* New York: Springer: 344–58.

Rait, G., Hofman, A., Rocca, W., Brayne C., Breteler, M., Clarke, M. and Cooper, B. (1996) 'Age, ethnicity, and mental illness: a triple whammy', *British Medical Journal* 313: 1,347–8.

Redmond, B. and D'Arcy, J. (2003) 'Ageing and disability', in Quin, S. and Redmond, B. (eds), *Disability and Social Policy in Ireland.* Dublin: UCD Press: 129–38.

Robb, C., Chen, H. and Haley, W. E. (2002) 'Ageism in mental health and health care: a critical review'. *Journal of Clinical Geropsychology* 8 (1): 1–12.

Robinson, W. (2003) *Transnational Conflicts: Central America, Social Change, and Globalization.* London: Verso.

Ruddle, H., Donoghue, F. and Mulvihill, R. (1997) *The Years Ahead: A Review of the Implementation of its Recommendations.* Dublin: National Council on Ageing and Older People.

Russell, H. and Fahey, T. (2004) *Ageing and Labour Market Participation.* Dublin: Equality Authority.

Safe Home Programme (2000) www.safehomeireland.com/truelives.

Sarbin, T. R. and Kitsuse, J. I. (1994) 'Prologue', in Sarbin, T. R. and Kitsuse, J. I. (eds), *Constructing the Social.* London: Sage: 1–18.

Scharf, T. (1998) *Age and Ageing Policy in Germany.* Oxford: Berg.

Shakespeare, T. (2000) 'The social relations of care', in Lewis, G., Gewirtz, S. and Clarke, J. (eds), *Rethinking Social Policy.* London: Sage: 52–65.

Sheridan, K. (2006) 'Ireland will settle 200 hundred Iraqi refugees', *The Irish Times,* 17 February 2006.

Silke, D. (1994) *Older People's Attitudes to their Accommodation.* Dublin: Trinity College and Dublin Central Mission.

SONAS (2005) *Final Report.* Dublin: SONAS.

Stevenson, O. (1989) *Age and Vulnerability: A Guide to Better Care.* London: Edward Arnold.

Stratton, D. (2004) *The Housing Needs of Older People.* Dublin: Age Action Ireland.

Stratton, D. (2006) *Promoting Choices for Older Workers..* Dublin: Age Action Ireland.

Sutton, G. C. (1997) 'Will you still need me, will you still screen me, when I'm 64?' *British Medical Journal* 315: 1,032–3.

Task Force on Security for the Elderly (1996) *Report to the Minister for Social Welfare.* Dublin: Stationery Office.

Taylor, B. and Donnelly, M. (2006) 'Professional perspectives on decision making about the long-term care of older people', *British Journal of Social Work* (36): 807–26.

't Hoen, E. (2002) 'TRIPs, pharmaceutical patents, and access to essential medicines: a long way from Seattle to Doha', *Chicago Journal of International Law* 3 (1): 27–46.

Timonen, V. (2006) 'Introduction', in Timonen, V., Doyle, M. and Prendergast, D. (eds), *No Place Like Home: Domiciliary Care Services for Older People in Ireland.* Dublin: Liffey Press: 1–13.

Timonen, V. and Doyle, M. (2006) 'The historical and systemic context', in Timonen, V., Doyle, M. and Prendergast, D. (eds), *No Place Like Home: Domiciliary Care Services for Older People in Ireland.* Dublin: Liffey Press: 31–46.

Timenon, V. and McMenamin, I. (2002) 'Future care services in Ireland: old answers to new challenges', *Social Policy and Administration* 36 (1): 20–35.

Tormey, B. (2003) *A Cure for the Crisis: Irish Healthcare in Context.* Dublin: Blackwater Press.

Towle, A. (1998) 'Changes in health care and continuing medical education for the 21st century', *British Medical Journal* 316: 7,127.

Tsuchiya, A., Dolan, P. and Shaw, R. (2003) 'Measuring people's preferences regarding ageism in health: some methodological issues and some fresh evidence', *Social Science and Medicine* 57(4): 687–96.

Tussing, A. D. and Wren, M. A. (2006) *How Ireland Cares: The Case for Health Care Reform.* Dublin: New Island.

UN (1982) The *Vienna International Plan of Action on Ageing.* New York: UN.

UN (1990) *United Nations Principles for Older Persons.* New York: UN.

UN (1992) *Standard Rules on the Equalisation of Opportunities for Persons with Disabilities.* New York: UN.

UN (2002a) *World Population Prospects, 2002 Revision.* New York: UN.

UN (2002b) *Report of the Second World Assembly on Ageing, Madrid, 8–12 April 2002.* http://www.un.org/esa/socdev/ageing/waa/a-conf-197-96.htm, accessed 16.11.2006.

UN (2006) *Ageing: International Plan of Action on Ageing.* http://www.un.org/esa.socdev/ageing/ageipaa.htm, accessed 16.11.2006.

UN Department of Economic and Social Affairs/Population Division (2002) *Living Arrangements of Older Persons around the World. (Executive Summary)* http://www.un.org/esa/population/publications/livingarrangement/es_english.pdf.

UNECE (United Nations Economic Commission for Europe, 2002a) *Madrid International Plan of Action on Ageing.* Geneva: UNECE.

UNECE (2002b) *UNECE Ministerial Conference on Ageing 2002.* Geneva: UNECE.

UNHCR (2004) *Resettlement Handbook.* Geneva: UNHCR.

UN/IAG (International Association of Gerontology, 2002) *Research Agenda on Ageing for the 21st Century.* New York: UN.

Vignon, J. (2005) 'Responses to the new demographics: present and future strategies for the European Union' in Macura, M., MacDonald, A. and Haug, W. (eds), *The New Demographic Regime: Population Challenges and Policy Responses.* New York and Geneva: UN: 45–56.

Vincent, J. (2003) *Old Age.* London: Routledge.

Walker, A. (1993) *Age and Attitudes.* Brussels: Commission of the European Communities.

Walker, A. (1999) 'Public policy and theories of aging: constructing and reconstructing old age', in Bengston, V. L. and Schaie, K. W. (eds), *Handbook of Theories of Aging*. New York: Springer: 361–78.

Walter, B., Gray, B., Dowling, L. A. and Morgan, S. (2002) *A Study of the Existing Sources of Information and Analysis about Irish Emigrants and Irish Communities Abroad. Research Study undertaken for the Task Force on Policy Regarding Emigrants.* Dublin: Department of Foreign Affairs.

Watson, D. and Williams, J. (2003) *Irish National Survey of Housing Quality, 2001–2.* Dublin: ESRI.

Whelan, C. J. and Whelan, B. J. (1988) *The Transition to Retirement, Paper no. 138.* Dublin: ESRI.

Whelan. C. T., Layte, R., Maitre, B., Gannon, B., Nolan, B., Watson, D. and Williams, J. (2003) *Monitoring Poverty Trends in Ireland: Results from the 2001 Living in Ireland Survey. Policy Research Series Paper no. 51*, Dublin: ESRI.

WHO (2000) *Ageing and Intellectual Disabilities – Improving Longevity and Promoting Healthy Ageing: Summative Report.* Geneva: WHO.

WHO (2002) *Active Ageing: A Policy Framework.* http://www.unati.uerj.br/doc_gov/destaque/Madri2.pdf.

WHO (2004) *Report in the Implementation of the International Plan of Action on Ageing.* Geneva: WHO.

WHO (2005) *International Plan of Action on Ageing: Report on Implementation.* http://www.who.int/gb/ebwha/pdf_files/EB115/B115_29–en.pdf.

WHO (2006) accessed at www.who.int/ageing/en 30.3.2006.

WHO/GIAN (Geneva International Academic Network, 2002) *Global Responses to Elder Abuse and Neglect.* Geneva: WHO.

WHO/INPEA (International Network for the Prevention of Elder Abuse, 2002) *Missing Voices.* Geneva: WHO.

WHO/INPEA (International Network for the Prevention of Elder Abuse/Ryerson University, 2004) *The Toronto Declaration on the Global Prevention of Elder Abuse Elder Abuse.* Geneva: WHO.

Wiepking, P. and Maas, I. (2005) 'Gender differences in poverty: a cross-national study', *European Sociological Review* 21 (3): 187–200.

Williams, B. O. (2000) 'Ageism helps to ration medical treatment', *Edinburgh Health Bulletin* 58 (3): 198–202.

Williams, F. (2000) 'Principles of recognition and respect in welfare', in Lewis, G., Gewirtz, S. and Clarke, J. (eds), *Rethinking Social Policy.* London: Sage: 338–52.

Wilson, G. (2000) *Understanding Old Age: Critical and Global Perspectives.* London: Sage.

Winston, N. (2002) The *Return of Older Irish Migrants, An Assessment of Needs and Issues.* Dublin: Irish Episcopal Commission for Emigrants and Department of Social, Community and Family Affairs.

World Bank (1994) *Averting the Old Age Crisis: Policies to Protect the Old and Promote Growth.* Oxford: Oxford University Press.

Wren, M. A. (2003) *Unhealthy State: Anatomy of a Sick Society.* Dublin: New Island.

Yeates, N. (2001) *Globalisation and Social Policy*. London: Sage.

Yu, W. K. (2000) *Chinese Older People: A Need for Social Inclusion in Two Communities*. Bristol: Policy Press in association with the Joseph Rowntree Foundation.

Zaidi, A. (2006) *Poverty of Elderly People in EU25*, Policy Brief, European Centre for Social Welfare Policy and Research, August 2006.

Index